The political materialities of borders

Manchester University Press

RETHINKING BORDERS

SERIES EDITORS: SARAH GREEN AND HASTINGS DONNAN

Rethinking Borders focuses on what gives borders their qualities across time and space, as well as how such borders are experienced, built, managed, imagined and changed. This involves detailed and often richly ethnographic studies of all aspects of borders: finance and money, bureaucracy, trade, law, new technologies, materiality, infrastructure, gender and sexuality, even the philosophy of what counts as being 'borderly,' as well as the more familiar topics of migration, nationalism, politics, conflicts and security.

Previously published
Migrating borders and moving times: Temporality and the crossing of
borders in Europe
Edited by Hastings Donnan, Madeleine Hurd and Carolin Leutloff-Grandits

The political materialities of borders

New theoretical directions

OLGA DEMETRIOU AND ROZITA DIMOVA

Manchester University Press

Published by Manchester University Press
Altrincham Street, Manchester M1 7JA

www.manchesteruniversitypress.co.uk

British Library Cataloguing-in-Publication Data
A catalogue record for this book is available from the British Library

ISBN 978 1 5261 2385 5 hardback

First published 2019

Typeset by
Servis Filmsetting Ltd, Stockport, Cheshire
Printed in Great Britain by
TJ International Ltd, Padstow

Contents

List of figures   vi
List of contributors   vii
Series foreword   x
Preface   xi
Acknowledgements   xviii

1 Introduction: theorizing material and non-material mediations on the
   border   1
   Olga Demetriou and Rozita Dimova

2 Materiality, imbrication, and the *longue durée* of Greco-Turkish borders   16
   Olga Demetriou

3 Memory as border work: the 2008 Italy–Libya Friendship Treaty and the
   reassembling of Fortress Europe   36
   Chiara De Cesari

4 Ontologies of borders: the difference of Deleuze and Derrida   56
   Tuija Pulkkinen

5 Lines, traces, and tidemarks: further reflections on forms of border   67
   Sarah Green

6 Materializing the border-as-line in Sarajevo   84
   Stef Jansen

7 Borders as ghosts   103
   Eleni Myrivili

8 Materialities of displacement: borders in contemporary Macedonia   116
   Rozita Dimova

Index   132

Figures

6.1 Map of the south-eastern end of the Sarajevo agglomeration. The dotted line that runs more or less vertically through the map is the Inter-Entity Boundary Line (IEBL). (© openstreetmap contributors, www.openstreetmap.org)   88

8.1 Map of the Republic of Macedonia (source: The Cartographic Section of the United Nations (CSUN) from Wikimedia commons, CC-BY-SA licence)   117

8.2 The Serbian military cemetery, Zeitnlik, Thessaloniki (photo: the author)   119

8.3 The French military cemetery, Bitola (photo: Snezana Stankovic)   119

8.4 The British military cemetery, Policastro (photo: Snezana Stankovic)   120

8.5 The British military cemetery, Dojrani (photo: Snezana Stankovic)   120

8.6 The *Warrior on a Horse* monument in central Skopje (photo: Jane Stojanoski)   125

8.7 Portal Macedonia (photo: Jane Stojanoski)   126

Contributors

Chiara De Cesari is an anthropologist and Assistant Professor in European studies and cultural studies at the University of Amsterdam. She completed her PhD in socio-cultural anthropology at Stanford University in 2009 and has been a postdoctoral researcher at Utrecht University and at the Institute for Cultural Inquiry in Berlin as well as a lecturer and coordinator of the MA in heritage and museum studies in the Department of Archaeology and Anthropology at Cambridge University. She is co-editor of the book *Transnational Memories: Circulation, Articulation, Scales* (de Gruyter, 2014, with Ann Rigney) and is currently finishing a book entitled *Heritage and the Struggle for Palestine* (forthcoming). De Cesari is the Amsterdam team leader in the Horizon 2020 'Critical Heritages' (CoHERE) project, funded by the European Union, which explores whether and how people feel 'European', and is also part of the 'CHEurope' (Critical Heritage Studies and the Future of Europe) project, funded under the Horizon 2020 Marie Skłodowska-Curie Innovative Training Networks programme. Her most recent project explores how Europe imagines itself as a cultural space, particularly through its cultural and, more specifically, heritage policies and museums – and, in turn, the image of Europe that these policies institutionalize.

Olga Demetriou is Associate Professor of Post Conflict Reconstruction and State-Building at the Durham Global Security Institute, School of Government and International Affairs at Durham University, UK. She is the author of *Capricious Borders: Minority, Population, and Counter-Conduct between Greece and Turkey* (Berghahn, 2013, 2017) and *Refugeehood and the Post-Conflict Subject: Reconsidering Minor Losses* (2018). Her work examines questions of political subjectivity, especially relating to minorities, migration, refugeehood, and gender. She works at the intersection of anthropology, conflict studies, sociology, and international relations and she has published in various journals in these fields. She has carried out fieldwork in border regions in Greece and Cyprus for the last two decades.

Rozita Dimova is Associate Professor of Slavonic and East European Studies in the Department of Languages and Cultures at Ghent University. She obtained her MPhil degree in anthropology from Cambridge University (1996) and her PhD in anthropology from Stanford University (2004), with a dissertation analysing ethno-nationalism, materiality, and aesthetics in Macedonia that won the Robert Texture Award for outstanding anthropological creativity. She is a recipient of prestigious international grants and awards, among which are a five-year doctoral fellowship from the Center for International Studies at Stanford University, a doctoral field-work grant from the National Science Foundation (USA), and the Geballe Dissertation Fellowship. After completing her doctorate at Stanford in 2004, Dimova was awarded a postdoctoral fellowship at the Max Planck Institute for Social Anthropology in Halle, Germany (2003–06), where she worked on a project on refugees from Former Yugoslavia living in Berlin. The subsequent years in Berlin opened the doors for area studies as she joined the Institute for East European Studies at Free University, Berlin, with a grant from the Volkswagen Foundation (2006–09), and the Department of Slavonic and South-East European Studies at Humboldt University in Berlin (2010–15) with a five-year grant from the German Research Council (DFG).

Sarah Green is Professor of Social and Cultural Anthropology at the University of Helsinki. She specializes in the anthropology of location, which in her research involves border relations, the EU, the Balkans, and the Aegean region. She is the author of many publications, including *Notes from the Balkans: Locating Marginality and Ambiguity on the Greek–Albanian Border* (Princeton University Press, 2015). She is currently the principal investigator of a European Research Council Advanced Grant project called 'Crosslocations in the Mediterranean: Rethinking the Sociocultural Dynamics of Relative Positioning', which grew out of the work that she discusses in this volume. For that project, she is developing new research on border regimes that regulate the movement of animals, and is also further developing the 'lines, tidemarks, and traces' idea into a wider interest in what could be called geometrical anthropology.

Stef Jansen is Professor of Social Anthropology at the University of Manchester (UK). On the basis of long-term ethnographic research in the post-Yugoslav states of Bosnia and Herzegovina, Serbia, and Croatia, he has published widely on questions of hope, the state, borders, political subjectivity, home-making, and post-cold war transformations. His recent publications include the single-authored book *Yearnings in the Meantime: 'Normal Lives' and the State in a Sarajevo Apartment Complex* (2015, Berghahn) and the volume *Negotiating Social Relations in Bosnia and Herzegovina: Semiperipheral Entanglements*, co-edited with Čarna Brković and Vanja Čelebičić (2016, Routledge).

Eleni Myrivili earned her PhD in social anthropology from Columbia University and is Assistant Professor at the University of the Aegean, Greece. She has a long-standing commitment to projects that go beyond the walls of the academy: designing multimedia museum exhibitions, curating events and festivals, and participating in civil society organizations. Between 2007 and 2012 she became active in politics as part of the leadership team of the Greek Green Party. She has also hosted thirteen one-hour episodes of a public television documentary series on various approaches to sustainable living, and an international documentary film festival focusing on socio-political and historical documentaries. Since 2014, she has been an elected council member in the City of Athens, and in 2016 she was appointed Chief Resilience Officer for Athens (as part of '100 ResilientCities', pioneered by the Rockefeller Foundation). In January 2018 she was appointed Vice Mayor for Urban Nature, Resilience, and Adaptation to Climate Change for the City of Athens.

Tuija Pulkkinen is Professor of Gender Studies at the University of Helsinki. Her research is in the area of feminist theory and philosophy, political theory, and history of concepts. She is the author of *The Postmodern and Political Agency* (SoPhi Academic Press, 1996, 2000) and co-editor of *The Politics and History of Democratization in Europe* (Ashgate, 2008), *Hegel's Philosophy and Feminist Thought: Beyond Antigone?* (Palgrave Macmillan, 2010), and *Siveellisyys: poliittisen käsitteen historia* [Decency: History of a Political Concept] (SKS, 2011). She is also a co-editor-in-chief of the journal *Redescriptions: Political Theory, Conceptual History and Feminist Theory*.

Series foreword

Rethinking Borders

Crossing to the other side has many meanings, depending on what is crossing, where, when and why. Yet it always involves borders: there can be no other side without a dividing line, something that gives the sense of a difference between here and that other place. Equally, refusing to cross, or refusing to accept the crossers, requires such a marker.

Rethinking Borders focuses on what gives borders their qualities across time and space, as well as on how such borders are experienced, built, managed, imagined and changed. This involves detailed and often richly ethnographic studies of all aspects of borders: finance and money, bureaucracy, trade, law, new technologies, materiality, infrastructure, gender and sexuality, even the philosophy of what counts as being 'borderly,' as well as the more familiar topics of migration, nationalism, politics, conflicts and security.

While there has been much discussion about globalisation, transnationalism, networks and digital technologies, and how these have radically changed relations between people and places, the world is still full of efforts to cut through the flow, to create stops somewhere. This is both so as to control movement (not only of people, but also of goods, animals, plants, money, ideas, diseases) and so as to define somewhere as being different from somewhere else. The *Rethinking Borders* series is dedicated to scholarship which provides fresh ways to think about these continuing efforts to mark differences spatially, and to understand both the major and more localised ways in which that has been changing.

The series originated with the work of a COST research network, EastBordNet (www.eastbordnet.org). EastBordNet was dedicated to rethinking the concept of border in the eastern peripheries of Europe. In the first decade of the twenty-first century, it was clear that something radical was happening with borders in that region, but more collaborative work across multiple borders was needed to understand and rethink the process. The first few volumes of *Rethinking Borders* reflect the regional origins of the series, but we welcome manuscripts from any part of the world.

Preface

Rozita Dimova and Olga Demetriou

This volume is based on a series of workshops and conference panels organized as part of the EastBordNet, a scholarly network initiated at a meeting in Manchester in May 2006 connecting researchers working in the north-east regions of Europe (Baltics and surrounding regions) with researchers working in the south-east regions (Balkans and environs). The objective of the network was to form a scholarly community that would examine borders and their meaningfulness across space and time.

COST IS0803, the research network that became the EastBordNet project, was officially launched with a management committee meeting in Brussels in February 2009. Researchers from Austria, Bulgaria, Croatia, Cyprus, the Czech Republic, Denmark, Finland, Germany, Greece, Hungary, Israel, Italy, Latvia, the Netherlands, Norway, Russia, Slovenia, Sweden, and the UK signed up to the project. The first Work Groups were held in Nicosia and Rome in April 2009, and the idea for this volume sprouted from that very first workshop in Nicosia held on 14–15 April 2009. Under the terms of EastBordNet, Work Group 1, which began in Nicosia, became a forum over the life of the network, in which researchers exchanged ideas about the theory and ontology of borders. The Work Group started with the question 'what are borders?' It focused on the concept of borders and drew on empirical and conceptual material to map out the state of research on border ontology. The Work Group ultimately sought to outline what the concept of 'remaking borders' might mean from a wide range of perspectives, and how that might be used to address questions that other meetings in EastBordNet asked: the relation of borders to technology, difference, and translation, and the role of money, gender, and concepts of time and the 'east' to the constitution of borders. All of these are topics covered in the current series.

Entitled 'Productive Borders: Perspectives on the Critique of Duality', the Nicosia meeting was conceptualized and organized by Olga Demetriou. It sought to examine borders first and foremost as markers of division that signify a duality. This duality, the meeting recognized, was critiqued by many philosophical strands, including post-colonialism, phenomenology, and post-structuralism. The work of the delegates focused on this theorization and on the multiplicities or singularity that a dual understanding of the world obscures. Yet at the end of the meeting the general conclusion was that both of these perspectives were limited by their own excess: endless multiplicity as well as the singularity of identity and difference seem to lead to a vanishing point that escapes description. The Nicosia Work Group meeting therefore addressed different ways in which singularity and multiplicity have been related to each other across theoretical strands, and enquired into how these might be brought to bear in understanding how borders produce difference and/or its disappearance.

Several of the current contributions were initially conceived at this 2009 Nicosia Work Group 1 meeting. The chapter written by Sarah Green addressed the issue that would soon become one of the main cornerstones of the EastBordNet theoretical approach. The paper 'Lines, Traces and Tidemarks: Reflections on Forms of Borderli-ness' examined the notion of difference dominating border literature, and introduced the concepts of traces and tidemarks. If borders mark differences, Green insisted, they do not all do so in the same way. And while this has been studied from a range of angles, border literature has rarely focused on the forms that borders take, in both material and conceptual terms. Most often borders are thought of as lines, or entities related to lines: walls, barriers, fences, perimeters, edges. Green's paper maintained that lines always evoke a sense of two sides, and of course, that has been critiqued by scholars who prefer to think in terms of rhizomes, webs, fractals, or networks. Borders are often experienced as a series of points rather than lines as such: points at which people, things, animals cross; or fail to cross. Lines only really appear on images of borders – maps, GIS images, aerial photographs. Traces, in contrast, evoke a sense of time in a way that lines do not: traces are not always visible, or if they are, then they are only a small fragment of the whole entity. For Green, traces are porous, leave much room for doubt and speculation, and change over time, perhaps disappearing altogether. Using the ideas of lines, traces, and tidemarks, Green's contribution began an important conversation on 'border-ness'; and as this volume reveals, the concept of tidemarks introduced by Green at that first Work Group meeting in Nicosia in 2009 has enabled many of the contributors to apply it to their own research (Demetriou, Dimova, and Jansen represent this in the current volume).

Another paper presented during the first Nicosia meeting was Tuija Pulkkinen's 'Ontologies of Productive Borders', where she also examined borders as productive of difference and identity. Responding directly to the workshop's call for a reconsideration of theoretical frames on duality and against it, Pulkkinen offered two alternative ontologies for thinking the productiveness of borders. On the one hand, she focused on the tradition of thought based on certain Hegelian reflections in Jacques Derrida's work, and on the other, on the Spinozian tradition taken up in the work of Gilles Deleuze. The 2009 paper and the chapter in this volume take as their point of reference two very different concrete historical cases of the activity of drawing borders, one being a drawing of a political border on the map of Europe in 1809 between Sweden and Russia, and the other being an epistemic border drawn in the discourses on sexualities in the late nineteenth century, both with multiple subsequent effects in terms of identities and differences. Inspired by previous work on these two cases and seeing them as examples of the productivity of borders, the paper related them to the two intellectual approaches taken by Derrida and Deleuze. Pulkkinen showed how these processes could be interpreted under these terms and what the consequences for such thinking would be in terms of activity or passivity and positivity or negativity, among other aspects. By considering Deleuze's classic work *Difference and Repetition*, together with Derrida's idea of *différance*, thinking about them and against one another, the paper became part of ongoing work on the philosophical topic of contemporary ontological approaches and their effects. These are questions which Pulkkinen uses to re-examine issues addressed in previous work on the political history of Finland and on theorizing sexual identity.

The first meeting in Nicosia was also the place where Rozita Dimova initially formulated her ideas about this volume's contribution. The paper presented there was entitled 'Neoliberalism, Nationalism and Border Arrangements in the Southern Balkans', and there Dimova explained the contemporary contradiction between political dispute and economic exchange between Greece and the Republic of Macedonia. In doing so, she traced how neoliberal political-economic regimes are reconfiguring relationships between two countries entangled in a name dispute. Importance was placed on the reconfiguration of contemporary states and the growing range of privatizing domains and private authorities involved in larger transnational economic investments – an aspect that is overshadowed by the political dispute over the name.

One year later, in April 2010, Dimova hosted the second meeting of Work Group 1 in Berlin in a workshop entitled 'Borders, Materiality, Signification'. This workshop directly posed the question of borders' visibility. What defines their materiality and how do borders cope with multiple significations attached to them during and after radical regime change? This meeting continued to assess conceptual questions related to borders, but now by focusing on issues of materiality and multiple significations. Just as they had used the space of the city of Nicosia at the meeting a year earlier, the organizers used the specificity of the meeting's location – the city of Berlin – to launch the discussion by addressing the cold war legacy and the twentieth anniversary of the fall of the Berlin wall, as well as the multiple sediments left by intersecting borders across different temporal and spatial axes in and beyond this city (e.g. East–West).

Two papers presented at this workshop are in the current volume: Stef Jansen's and Eleni Myrivili's. Jansen's presentation focused on the materiality of a border without the visible shape of a border (such as a barrier, a fence, a checkpoint, a customs office, uniformed border officers, etc.) that nevertheless structures the lives of those living around it in deeply material ways. The so-called Boundary Line between the two entities of Bosnia-Herzegovina is a recently established border that only briefly drew its efficacy from visible, 'built' dimensions – first as a frontline through the anti-building of destruction and abandonment, and then as an armistice line through built checkpoints policed by soldiers under a UN mandate. Now 'unbuilt', it nevertheless continues as the material axis of practical geography and of a struggle for sovereignty. Taking into account these shifts in border craft, Jansen explored how the (in)visible and (im)material modalities of this border are differentially embedded in everyday practices of (non-)crossing and in competing projects of state-formation. Stef Jansen re-addressed this theme in a later panel, at the network's conference in Catania, using the prism of a 'tidemark'. As his chapter now does, that paper traced the formation of the Inter-Entity Boundary Line in Dobrinja, in the suburban outskirts of the capital Sarajevo. Based on ethnographic research, his paper proposed an integrated three-dimensional interpretation of the sedimentation of the line-ness of this border, which is constitutive of the largely nationally homogenized entities Republika Srpska and the Federation of Bosnia-Herzegovina, and which, in the Dayton Agreement, consolidated the crystallization of difference onto territory. His chapter in this volume argues, as that presentation did, that this tidemark, in its brutal arbitrariness, came into being and is consolidated through social practices on the intersection of geopolitical processes and the affective patterns through which people engage with them. It thus proposes to push an understanding of this border as a 'tidemark' as far as possible, while keeping human practice resolutely at the centre of the argument through a materialist focus on the social-practices-over-time that constitute it from Dobrinja to Dayton and back again.

In her Berlin presentation, Eleni Myrivili asked how the border manifests itself when it is liquid. Carrying on the concern to theorize 'what borders are', Myrivili related her ethnographic findings to the work of Foucault and Bataille. For these two thinkers, the limit/border assumes its fullness of being, its 'density', its 'materiality', at the moment of its negation, the moment of its transgression. At the Prespa border region, three limits, those of Albania, Greece, and Macedonia, cut and partition the waters of a large mountain lake with their formless power. They are invisible and ghostly, only to become spectacularly tangible in violence that ensues following their transgression. In the 1980s, electric fences came all the way down to the lake. In the 1990s, the national guards shot warning shots before aiming directly at the border violators. In November 2009, the prime ministers of the three countries met in the Prespa region and talked about the transnational environmental park of Prespa and the green local economy, and set the year 2014 (a hundred years after the beginning of the First World War) as the target year for a new beginning, a new era that would see the Western Balkans as part of the EU. In the paper and this volume's contribution, Myrivili posed the question of what kind of subjects are formed around these borders, around these strange presences of power and violence. How did the people of these borders experience them then, and what kind of experiences form their subject positions now?

Several new papers were solicited and modifications of the earlier papers were made at the first and second EastBordNet conferences in Catania (January 2011) and Berlin (January 2013). These conferences consolidated the work of the Work Groups across the EastBordNet network. In this context, the first EastBordNet conference that took place in Catania in 2011, featured a panel co-organized by Olga Demetriou and Rozita Dimova entitled 'The Visible through the Sensible: (Im) materialities of Borders' that brought together the conversations initiated during the Nicosia and Berlin meetings in 2009 and 2010 by exploring different ways of talking about visibility (ocularity) of borders beyond the material/immaterial or tangible/intangible dualisms. We asked if borders have to be material in order to become visible. What constitutes a border's materiality, or when do (could) borders become immaterial? How can we speak convincingly about the relation between material and conceptual borders in ways that go beyond 'bridging the gap' between the two? The panel addressed the following themes through the notions of (in)tangibility, (non)materiality, and (in)visibility by contrasting them to comparative approaches to the theorization of borders and by drawing on the literary and philosophical techniques used to conceptualize borders to address issues such as interaction between time, space, and politics as elements constituting the border's appearance and disappearance.

One of the papers given at the Catania panel was Chiara De Cesari's 'Memory Voids and the Making of Europe's Borders', which presented ideas on which her chapter in the current volume draws. Focusing on the relationship between collective memory and the making of geopolitical boundaries, De Cesari placed the main focus on the ongoing institutional project of creating a heritage for Europe, that is, the recent flurry of initiatives by policy-makers and intellectuals to promote a common European memory so as to 'thicken' European Union (EU) citizens' weak European identity. In particular, she discussed the opening exhibition of the Museum of Europe in Brussels by pointing at the memory voids at the heart of such projects, particularly the Arab Islamic heritage of Europe and Europe's entangled, transnational, trans-European history. De Cesari's paper pointed out the oblivious making of boundaries out of transitory, porous, and unstable geographies. For this volume, the paper was further developed and focused explicitly on the oblivion written into the Italy–Libya friendship treaty.

Olga Demetriou's paper at the Catania conference similarly set forth ideas out of which her current contribution developed. The paper, entitled 'The Militarisation of Opulence on the Cypriot Border', concentrated on the materiality of a specific site on the Cypriot UN Buffer Zone, Ledra Palace Hotel, and used it to address the conceptual ways in which the 'Cyprus conflict' is produced. Demetriou proposed a multi-faceted analytic approach that drew on political economy, heritage literature, and gender studies to investigate what hegemonic conceptualizations of 'the conflict' have obfuscated. Her chapter in this volume continues this investigation, treating borders as devices for knowing and questioning the world. The material-conceptual structures through which borders are produced, Demetriou argues here, have diachronic relevance but may nevertheless appear at specific instances and specific locations. Taking account of the *longue durée* of borders requires that we consider ways of knowing the border alongside its material manifestations.

These previous meetings and presentations all came together at the final EastBordNet conference in Berlin in January 2013, when the conference marked the completion of the investigative work for the EastBordNet research network. This network enabled us to put together this volume, which now is the second volume in the Rethinking Borders series. The key to developing the new approach to borders was the refusal to take borders for granted: rather than assume their existence and go on from there to analyse their effects, we began from the position of questioning what 'border' and 'borderliness' actually mean, and looked into how that was diversely expressed across time and space.

That first 2009 Nicosia workshop seems a long time ago now. But as the papers from the various meetings were reworked, debated, and employed in multiple conversations within the Work Group and across the network, our understanding of the ontology and epistemology of borders opened new directions of enquiry and new ways of thinking about borders. This volume represents the epitome of this rethinking, which has spawned, almost a decade later, new theoretical directions in considering the political materialities of borders.

Reconsideration is of course an endless process. We were keenly reminded of this at the final stages of preparing the volume, as the refugee reception crisis of 2015 unfolded on the Greco-Turkish border, and continued to reverberate, through the arduous foot journeys of refugees across the Balkans: regions that a number of contributors to this volume know well. Our individual empirical research, as well as our conceptual toolbox, seemed in need of further revision. Ethical questions were keenly felt as we revised chapters for the final manuscript. Should political standpoints be addressed in clearer terms, in the face of disappointing responses from political elites? Was academic 'rethinking' an indulgent task, ultimately? If ontologies and epistemologies of borders had sat at the heart of the volume's concerns, another, more urgent concept now appeared in need of ontological and epistemological understanding: 'crisis'. The terms in which border crossings were now spoken of seemed to describe differing regimes of power and indeed, political materialities. Was this a 'refugee crisis', a 'migration crisis', a 'border crisis', or indeed a crisis of 'reception'? And what indeed, does the term 'crisis' do politically in each of these contexts? Whatever we chose to call it, the 'crisis' inevitably impinged on our individual projects, and revealed unprecedented entanglements of care, surveillance, control, humanitarian aid, militarization of borders, and myriads of affects. Although we were cognizant of these questions as we finalized the chapters, it has been impossible to reflect new knowledge, data, and the theorization that may have ensued from their collection here. We can only hope that as we engage in conversations across geographical and disciplinary boundaries on the global effects of this 'crisis', our thinking about what borders are or are not, and how we come to know and speak of them, may be of use to understanding the expected and unexpected events and practices that unfold through them and that unmake and remake them on multiple levels.

Acknowledgements

This book began life in the EastBorderNet network project, where we both served as country representatives, for Cyprus and Germany respectively. We are thankful to the project for bringing us together and serving as the springboard for many collaborations we have undertaken since. Of course, the inspiration and principal investigator of the project, Sarah Green, deserves our deepest gratitude for her foresight in exploring what still remained ontologically fascinating about borders, and her care in nurturing the work of many dozens of young academics across Europe, who like us, back in 2008, were full of ideas but less invested in their material translations.

Through the journey of this COST-funded research project, we have found invaluable colleagues to whom we have turned at points for support, intellectual stimulation, and insights. The authors of the chapters herein are owed a special acknowledgement for their perseverance and patience in what turned out to be a long road. Other colleagues and friends in COST who engaged with our project and its specific pursuits include Jane Cowan, Hastings Donnan, Elissa Helms, Yael Navaro, Sissy Theodosiou, Christian Voss, and Effi Voutira.

At Manchester University Press, we would like to thank Tom Dark for a flawless process and Fiona Little for her meticulous editing work.

And for their support at home, with smaller and bigger tasks, which ultimately allowed us the time to reflect on the issues in the following pages, we thank our families.

Introduction:
theorizing material and non-material
mediations on the border

Olga Demetriou and Rozita Dimova

The border as process: tracing theoretical genealogies

Social analysis has always recognized that politics is invested in the material. Capitalism and nationalism are projects shown to be rooted in the materialities of production, consumption, commodification, and the reconfiguration of definitions of 'the human' in relation to the material world. We may trace a trajectory in the materiality-politics nexus from the Hegelian roots of historical materialism to the Marxist separation between infrastructure and superstructure, through the post-war work of the Frankfurt School on consumerism (Adorno and Horkheimer 1972; Benjamin 1999a; Benjamin 1999b; Marcuse 1991), French neo-Marxist takes on subjectivity (Althusser 1971), and critical theory strands on human-thing assemblages (Deleuze and Guattari 1987; Latour 2005). In this theoretical trajectory materiality is the result of power dynamics obfuscated by the seemingly non-material, which, however, also has material underpinnings. Analytical attention to these blurs the distinction between materiality and non-materiality but makes politics more visible in the process.

Space, architecture, and visual art have offered particularly strong examples of how the material and ideological consolidation of the modern capitalist state takes place (Harvey 2009; Gupta and Ferguson 1997; Thrift 2005). These fields of production have been scrutinized for their role as conduits between materiality and ideology, most notably since Benjamin's studies of Parisian arcades (1999a). In this volume, we draw on insights from these strands of thinking to examine the implications of the material and non-material constitution of borders. For borders, being perhaps more immediately metonymic of 'the state', seem to have received an altogether different treatment from space, architecture, and visual art in the theorization of their materiality until very recently.

Borders have been widely conceptualized as symbolic of the 'nation' and/or 'state' since the pioneering work of Wilson and Donnan (1998). More recently, advances in technology and shifts in the definition of 'security' have prompted an interest in the ways in which borders change (see Rumford 2006 for an overview).

An object-like materiality may not be the most appropriate way to conceptualize borders, it has been argued; borders should instead be seen as processes (Newman 2006). And yet their materiality, as lines on the ground or on maps, continues to be taken for granted. That is to say, discussion has all too often proceeded from the assumption of a smooth line of separation to questioning of the manifestations of governing difference and connection within the state. Thus, border studies often seem to take borders as de facto material manifestations of state apparatuses even though emerging literature has sought to question this. Paasi, for example, argues that new spatialities of networks that extend above and below the state are reconfiguring borders in globalization as ideological apparatuses for territorial power (Passi 2009). Agnew proposes a new conceptualization of borders stemming from a redefinition of political community 'as not being co-extensive with nation-state' (Agnew 2008: 186). Going further, Van Houtum suggests that we see the border as a lie, promising the desire for (comm)unity while masking the fear of incompleteness (Van Houtum 2010: 126). These studies effectively question the view of the border as the limit where the capitalist nation-state, contested and re-created at its centre, becomes fixed (see also Balibar 2009).

The fact that the state apparatuses congealing around a border actually hover between materiality and ideology in the forms of nation-state ideologies, territorial claims, or discourses of community alerts us to the need for closer scrutiny of borders as key structures in this mediation between materiality and abstraction. In this volume, we focus on exactly this mediation. Our emphasis is neither on the ontology of borders (what they are, or what they are not) nor on their function (what they do), but rather on the question of how the relationship between materiality and abstraction is established. We explore the *relationship* between what borders are and what they do and the ways in which function affects their perceptions and vice versa. We see, in other words, the processual aspect of borders as a question of this mediation.

In contrast to buildings, documents, films, statues, markets, bodies, or arcades, political philosophy has only recently turned to borders as a field within which to think materiality and politics. The scrutiny of capitalism, liberalism, and sovereignty, this volume shows, needs to take the border into account, most obviously because it is a node between the levels such scrutiny tries to connect: state, inter-state, local, supra-national, global, and so on. In pointing this out we also want to also address the persistence in border studies to dwell primarily on the connections between state, territory, sovereignty, and space but less on the more mediated ideologies they call forth (i.e. beyond the statist 'us' and 'them'). In this volume we want to highlight the intrinsic question of materiality that underlies that of borders. Hence, our question here is how these connections produce frames of governance anew: how, in other words, the border comes to be a process.

Thinking borders through metaphors

In each of the cases that make up the present volume the materialities of the border are deeply implicated in the reproduction of political ideology, its shifts and changes. The borders in Greece, Turkey, and Cyprus, Olga Demetriou shows, which were erected on the premises of particular configurations in the Greco-Turkish dispute, are now being reconfigured in the frame of migration-control priorities. Yet this grand shift of frame is still grounded in both infrastructural and ideological premises. Rather than overhauling them, it appears to have been subsumed by them. Looking more closely at the intricate connections, analysed through the idiom of imbrication, between these infrastructures and ideologies we begin to see the contours of exclusion that provide the continuities between older and new frames and priorities: militarism, an ethnicity-citizenship dyad, a peripheral role within the West. In other case studies, we see continuities of colonialism and cascading hierarchies of state power. Chiara de Cesari exemplifies that in an Italy–Libya treaty that comes to silently index EU–sub-Saharan migrant relations. The materiality of the document makes a difference to what is stated and what remains unstated, and it is through another materiality, that of the Libyan desert, erased prison camps, and current migrant detention centres, that the silence gains its force. We are thus prompted to ask, as Tuija Pulkkinen does, what political materialities exist prior to the border and how they change after its establishment. Her examples of state and sexuality borders demonstrate clearly the problems involved in imagining 'Finns' or 'homosexuals' before the demarcations, political in different ways, established what is and what is not. These demarcations have been attended, as political projects, by materialities that drew lines on the ground and in law, and it was through those materialities that 'Finns' and 'homosexuals' came into being as specific kinds of people. The line then, as designation of the border, is in question. Sarah Green explores this central proposition by considering linear vis-à-vis other images of borders. Traces, she argues, are of particular relevance to the thinking of borders as process. But they need not replace the concept of line; rather, they can be read alongside it. Green posits that the critique of linear border thinking has shown precisely the salience of that linear image, especially as state-centred. In therefore exploring other venues, such as trace, we always need to open up the question of why lines persist. And in looking at the two simultaneously, Green offers the concept of 'tidemark' as a productive way for rethinking the line-ness and trace-producing processes that attend borders. Stef Jansen illustrates the implications of this as he examines bus routes and property purchases in Sarajevo that reinstate and solidify an otherwise absent border. The Inter-Entity Boundary Line (IEBL), he argues, is exemplary of how borders may be much more than just lines, but in the case of polity borders they are lines nevertheless. It is thus the salience of that line-ness that we must pay close attention to. On the Greek side of the Prespa Lake, Eleni Myrivili argues, the seeming lack of border policing infrastructures is deceptive: policemen and rifles emerge in fishermen's imaginations as soon as steering a boat across an unseen but thoroughly internalized border is suggested. That line-ness of the border is for Myrivili replete with traces. And these traces are ghostly. Urging us to see the border as ghost, Myrivili is able to examine the processes of statecraft that are predicated on secrecy and the foreclosure of knowledge. And while these processes arise through specific materialities on the border, they point to the heart of state politics. They do this through a ripple effect, Rozita Dimova suggests in her chapter. She shows how the Greek–Macedonian dispute ripples to the centre of the city in the form of statues and monuments. Juxtaposing this monumentality to the lack of conflict symbols on the border, Dimova shows how the mediation between materialities and immaterialities takes on different modalities in the centre and at the borders of the state, which are nevertheless connected and reinforce each other. The economics of connection at the border, we might posit, amplify the economics of conflictual nationalism in the centre of Skopje.

In each of these cases, metaphors are the vehicles through which questions of materiality come to bear specifically on the study of borders: how do borders have presence if they are not seen, as in the Prespa Lake or Sarajevo? How different is this presence from that of the border which is seen, even feared, celebrated, or enjoyed, as in Nicosia, Skopje, or the Aegean? At those instants when a particular space is imagined as a border, it is a political imagination that is at work. Imbrications, lines, traces, ghosts, and ripples reference this political work. They each show in different ways that it is not only border guards, passport scanners, or stamps that enact the state at those points. It is also bodies, thoughts, gestures, comportment. The relation between one and the other is one of dependence, and it is this dependence that often falls by the wayside when we preference one viewpoint over another. Moreover, this dependence creates 'publics', both at the border and in the heartlands of states and communities. These publics may be xenophobic, or anti-racist if the dependence is rooted in the securitization of migration. Or they may be tourist or consumerist if the dependence is centred on the enjoyment of the border. They may be tax-paying or utility-dependent if the border is invested with infrastructure or delimits the extension of power and water grids. Scrutinizing how the materialities of soil, water, buildings, grids, paper, and so on are shaped by borders, but also how they reproduce them, sheds new light on the proposition that borders extend everywhere.

We thus want to examine borders as a political condition. For if the proliferation of borders is a sign of our age, then 'borders' cannot be taken as simply a 'case' for study, an example, a localized phenomenon. They should evidence an underlying arrangement. This arrangement, we propose, can be shown in the processes of mediation between materialities and immaterialities that take shape around borders. Through ethnographic and philosophical explorations of this mediation, the volume seeks to throw light on the interaction between the materiality of state borders and the non-material aspects of state-making. This enables, it is shown, a new understanding of borders as productive of the politics of materiality, on which the state project rests, including its multifarious forms in the post-nation-state era. We therefore explore materiality as a political site. This means inserting the analysis of borders and bordering into the question about what constitutes materiality, what escapes it, and whether the material can ever be seen in disjunction from the non-material. As we will show, materiality is enmeshed with immateriality. Consequently, borders exist on both material and non-material registers and produce material configurations, actions, and abstractions that straddle the material and non-material worlds. The notions of 'difference', 'division', and 'connection', which emanate from the border, wherever it may be located, are understood within this frame.

Symbolic (b)orders and the material

A binary opposition between materiality and immateriality (or non-materiality) is obviously a problematic position to start with. Can something be outside the material, and should we consider concepts, thoughts, or ideas as non-material? An important move beyond the Cartesian dichotomy is Lacan's symbolic order, which he would claim is material. Lacan's concept of the symbolic order – the order of language, signification and meaning – is a domain of materiality. Everything that is symbolized and signified (marked), either consciously or unconsciously, is material. And yet the symbolic order is predicated on an un-symbolizable element that resists being caught up in the symbolic web of signification (an excess). This immaterial, un-symbolizable element is actually the Lacanian Real, which becomes a leftover or a surplus generated by the symbolic order, and yet is not absorbed by it. What are the conditions that allow the possibility for resistance of this element(s) to being caught up in a web of material significations? In Lacanian thought, rather than making a distinction between material and non-material, we should see these two registers as mutually constitutive with the one depending on the other (or being operationalized through the other). This take on the negotiation between materiality and immateriality points to the moment at which critical theory comes to connect production to the politics of ideology. This insight hovers at the background of the theoretical discussions that many of the chapters of this volume engage in. It is certainly relevant to the Derridean take on 'trace', on which Pulkkinen, Green, and Myrivili dwell extensively. It is also relevant to the dynamics between the visible and the unsaid, explored by De Cesari and Demetriou. But it is also relevant to the philosophical and anthropological concerns of the volume as a whole, as it has implications for disciplinary borders too. The ethnographic examination offered by many of the contributions seeks to identify what happens when different regimes generate new materialities or webs of signification, and what kind of leftovers (surpluses) unintentionally emerge out of the processes of materialization and signification. Neither the cultural nor the psychoanalytic aspects of this question are 'neutral'. There is a political assumption in Lacan when he frames the 'surplus' as formed out of 'resistance' to symbolization or failure to be symbolized. What is the energy of these 'kernels of resistance', we then ask, that are generated by these materialities, and yet are the sites of subversion, agency, and disruption? How do we locate sites of subversion, agency, and disruption in these materialities?

An unexpected theoretical site, perhaps, for a discussion of borders and materiality is Badiou's political philosophy, which exemplifies how the concept of border influences and structures otherwise abstract thinking on politics, even when the word is not invoked. Badiou's work, notably influenced by Lacan, locates exactly such disruptions and subversions. What Badiou calls an 'Event' is a form of such a disruption. An Event is of primary significance and distinguishable from any other happening because it disrupts the constitution of subjectivity, it inaugurates a new subject. Post-Event, we are completely changed, as are the conditions that constitute our subjectivity. In those conditions lie forms of materialities that give rise and determine the Event. Materiality in Badiou is thus contained within a given universe, a set. Yet the precondition of the Event, is located 'on the edge of the void' (Badiou 2006: 175). In other words, it is ultimately the border that provides the basis for agency. This proposition is nowhere more immediate than in the image of the person who 'is not registered and remains clandestine', which Badiou uses as the most concrete example of an 'evental site' (2006: 174). The border determines both the materialities of the situation (absence of papers), as well as the non-material forms by which these materialities are exceeded (the Event). The connection between the two is intrinsic and political. An 'inconsistent or rioting crowd', Badiou elsewhere suggests, is 'an emblem of [the government's] void' and what it squarely refuses to tolerate (2006: 109). Badiou's theory, although not often read as border theory, exemplifies that view of transgression, as Jansen puts it, 'in which authors often locate emancipatory potential [but in doing so actually] reinforce rather than weaken conceptions of borders-as-lines' (Jansen, Chapter 6 below). In ethnographically querying this view, the contributors here find much less emancipation than the position at the edge of the void would suggest. This philosophy of potentiality, it would seem, needs to be rethought exactly, we argue, on these premises of political materiality.

To view borders in terms of the political mediation between materiality and ideology also requires that we think of the connection between borders and history in Benjamin's terms. In his 'Arcades project' Benjamin claimed to be a historical detective who could unveil historical knowledge, the only antidote that could oppose the dream-like state of consciousness at this time – a time of industrial modernity and conspicuous consumption (Benjamin 1999a; Buck-Morss 1989). As Benjamin strips history of its legitimizing and ideological function, 'history is abandoned as a conceptual structure that deceptively transfigures the present, its cultural contents are redeemed as the source of critical knowledge that alone can place the present into question' (Buck-Morss 1989: x). Our attempt to bridge the material and the abstract in this volume is animated by these perspectives, as they apply to the questions of what historical debris in today's borders means politically and what kind of Events it may anticipate or foreclose. Benjamin's work reminds us that the materiality of borders must pay attention not only to Events but also to 'evental sites' and 'Events' that have never sprung forth. A historical materialism of borders evaluates absences, agencies, and ruptures on the limits of material structures and the (unthinkable) void. What if other wars or other conflicts, or indeed other collaborations, had taken place here? What if the clandestine agencies encountered brought about other Events than those we have come to know as history? How might these agencies have been otherwise on Prespa and in Thrace, Sarajevo, Skopje, Libya, or Finland?

Rethinking binary logics in the governmentality of borders

The chapters in this volume explore shifts of meaning and shifts in border processes together. The history of Greco-Turkish relations is visible in Nicosia's Green Line and the idiosyncratic path of the border in western Thrace. That history today allows and bars specific individuals from moving across it in different ways. The dispute over the name of the state of Macedonia (Republic of Macedonia, Former Yugoslav Republic of Macedonia or FYROM, Skopje) is marked on the squares of the capital of Skopje today and impacts the perceptions and uses of space. Colonial camps and detention centres haunt the realm of Libyan–European relations today even though they are very differently configured. Battle lines from the siege of Sarajevo also haunt residents' property and accommodation decisions decades after the end of the war. Traces of past wars are arguably still embodied in corporeal shifts that mark the Prespa border, so that the violence of the Hoxha regime is remembered in a body that shirks from venturing just a little too far in a speed boat.

Attention to these shifts destabilizes out intuitive understanding of the political. For according to that understanding, the political is undoubtedly about bordering: at its core lies the separation between similarity and difference. It might thus seem that despite attempts to criticize the intuitive perspective that what borders do is to divide (into two parts), the political work of borders remains this because the political itself is by definition a project of di-vision (in the sense of 'seeing in twos'). This central position that 'border' occupies in the thinking about the political is also the very platform on which the materiality of borders is established: a space where material and conceptual merge, where 'political' can no longer be exclusively equated to 'ideological' without infrastructural underpinnings, and power cannot be divided between mental and physical forms. 'Border' thus becomes productive exactly of this knot of materiality and politics.

From this perspective, we ask what results from this production. Border-making in its various manifestations is not only symptomatic of but also informs the political, which itself is also manifested as multiple dualities. By disentangling these political formations at each instance we might better understand the disjunctions and continuities that inform what Foucault called 'governmentality' (2007): the logic of organizing people and things in particular ways so as to make populations more manageable. Colonialism, migration, bilateral disputes, financial cooperation, and so on are all frames of (dual) thinking that stem from the assumption of 'border' (as divisive) and reproduce ways of being that straddle, mediate, and struggle against divisions.

This question brings into view the reconsideration of subjectivity as a form in which the mediation also between materiality and immateriality is achieved in the context of power relations. This reconsideration brings into perspective the interaction of people and place. What kinds of subjects do borders produce (crossers, citizens, or aliens, consumers, policy-makers) and to what extent is the materiality of borders sustained or undermined by these forms of subjectivity? What are the diachronic connections and disconnections between material borders and the identities they give rise to, circumscribe, exclude, and govern? What kinds of structures (material and conceptual) sustain and undermine borders? In critically exploring the mediation between material and immaterial we ask what the interaction with, contemplation of, and experience of borders enables. When does agency (as corollary to power) begin to be reconstituted as more complex but also a clearer instance of state–subject relations?

New materialities in the government of borders, from biometric technology and satellite-assisted patrolling to humanitarian practice, have brought the Foucauldian notions of governmentality and biopolitics to the forefront of border studies (Epstein 2007; Muller 2008; Salter 2008; Walters 2011; Rygiel 2010; Andersson 2014; Tazzioli 2015). A point of convergence in this literature is the need to look at border infrastructures as constitutive of the populations that states and their assemblages (be it supra-state entities or 'non-state' agencies) govern. The materialities that constitute such populations are not only the fences, the cameras, the guards, the controls, or the physical landscape of a border. They are also the passports, the documents that substitute them, the spaces and people involved in the production of such documents (legal as well as 'fake'), the laws and policies guiding the use and abuse of such documents, the tools for implementing those laws, and the bodily effects of such implementation. These are all different levels on which these materialities may be intuitively tied to the border. They are modalities of materiality, as Althusser (1971) proposed.

They are also the discourses (in verbal, written, or acted forms, communicated *en masse* or inter-subjectively) that give meaning to concepts of 'security', 'desire', 'freedom', and so on. While some of these materialities may be intuitively tied to the border, a thoroughly politicized mediation takes shape the moment each of them comes into being. The law paints the continuum between citizenship and deportation. A passport references the poles of security and its absence. These mediations are not located on the border; they proliferate within states, in the high seas, and in the black holes of sovereign exceptions. Borders are the mechanisms (*dispositifs*), in a Foucauldian reading, of a governmentality that structures the field of the political well beyond them (see also Demetriou 2013).

And while the structures of borders and the structures of the political are mutually constitutive, they are also in a constant shift in their interrelations. Texture and fluidity have provided strong metaphors to articulate these connections. The political significance of state borders may wax and wane through changing visa regimes and border controls, but traces are nevertheless left of the border that used to be or the border that was absent (Green, Chapter 5 below). From another perspective, the political may take on specific material forms at power centres away from the border which are eventually transported at different intensities, like tidal waves, to the border periphery (Dimova 2013). These shifts take on potent materialities as they impact the register of 'subject'. Who is or is not a citizen, a visa national, an illegal, is a product not only of the law or the border regime at a given time, but also of concepts that preceded it – for instance of the nation-state, of morality, or of kin and economic alliances. It is just as important to study those shifts and the violences that attended them as 'critical events' (Das 1995) in the formation of both the border and the political as it is to explore their pasts and their legacies (Demetriou, Chapter 2 below). Studying the border from the point of view of political subjectivity affords this perspective into the temporal aspect of the material–(im)material mediation.

Subjects, objects, and the modalities of political materiality

At the same time, the focus on shifts, critical events, and the agency that attends them opens up the question of the 'subject' and the centrality of the 'human' in that conceptual construct vis-à-vis the agency of materiality and objects. In the materiality analysis of actor-network theory the distinction between humans and non-humans is erased along the lines of network-like ontology, where non-human beings are part of the social fabric. In *Reassembling the Social*, Latour (2005) extends the qualiy of the subject on non-human beings and objects (Latour 2005: 50–2), and thus his actor-network theory, introduces the role of the actor (*actant*), where he divorces agency from human beings and insists that anything that is a source of action, and anything that is able to propose their own understanding of action, has a capacity to act (Latour 2005: 57).

Along similar lines, archaeologists have made major contributions to theorizing the power of objects. Hodder's work in the Baringo area in Tanzania, for instance, rejected the view that material culture only reflects, mirrors, or expresses behaviour (Hodder 1982: 38). He argued that artefacts do not have only a passive role: while material culture does reflect and express groups' identities and their competition, it is evident that 'material culture can actively justify the actions and intentions of human groups and that symbols are actively involved in social strategies' (Hodder 1982: 38). The power of symbols and signs and the ensuing (layered) contexts of meaning (such as rooms, sites, pits, or burials) 'seize the muteness of objects' (Hodder 1982: 5).

Similarly, drawing on her research on object worlds in ancient Egypt, Meskell argues that 'the Egyptian project of materiality was so complex and central within the lifeworld that its potency could promise to secure the future, and similarly threaten to manifest eternal annihilation' (Meskell 2004: 10). The agency of the material world thus reveals that the Egyptian construction of the subjects and objects was a complex process where the two were 'porous, overlapping, sometimes indistinguishable entities' (Meskell 2004:10), with the possibility of objects to assume 'new taxonomic roles as beings, deities, oracles, agents, mediators and so on' (Meskell 2004:6). This new move in archaeology, away from environment, economics, motivations, or meanings, engages in the dialectics of people and things, where subjects and objects are collapsible in particular contexts (Meskell and Pels 2005: 4).

These dialectics are present in the chapters that follow as they analyse the power shifts and dynamics of separations and connections. The materiality of borders that we examine here unfolds on a multiplicity of levels, on each of which the material is enmeshed into the abstract. This enmeshment complicates the dyads not only of subject and object, but also those of material/immaterial, concrete/abstract, and visibility/invisibility.

In the first instance, there is the landscape of the border, visualized chiefly in the form of the state border, complete with signs, surveillance posts and devices, crossings, checks, guards, and so on. This landscape of the border may be abstracted through the notion of 'environment': a sea border is different from a river border, as the cases of eastern Greece, Cyprus, and Italy show (Demetriou, De Cesari), and different from a lake or land border, as the cases of northern and western Greece do (Myrivili, Dimova). But that difference is not exhausted in the materiality of that 'environment' *per se*. The form of liquidity (sea, river, lake) determines the kind of controls established, in other words the forms of governing that border. In turn, the arrangement of people and objects that this governmentality organizes also produces the political subjectivities coming into being on those borders: the 'trespasser' is differentiated as rescued boatperson, smuggler, Albanian, fisherman, and so on. This has implications for the practices that may or may not take place in the moment of crossing, in anticipation of it, and after it (arrest, surveillance, shooting, destruction of documents, payments, forgery, overfishing). So the abstraction of the border materiality yields not only the concept of 'environment' but also that of 'control'. These in turn are not non-material concepts: they are thoroughly materializable as actions, effects on bodies and objects, and transformative moments. The material and non-material become thoroughly enmeshed into each other so that 'landscape', 'environment', and 'control' are no longer forms of materiality propelled onto the plane of ideology, action, and affect. They are the planes upon which materiality and non-materiality are mediated.

This mediation imbricates all levels where the material and non-material are enmeshed. As a second such level, we identify that of documentation. Treaties that decide where the border should be set, passports that identify people as citizens, and visas that facilitate their crossing are all forms of materialities that mediate the abstract notion of 'law'. The practices associated with crossing and/or failing to cross a border as exemplified above are linked back to these materialities, as they are invoked to legitimize or delegitimize entry, exit, and their interruptions. As a political device, the border accentuates the stakes in this mediation, rendering, for example, the difference a passport makes, a difference that touches on the boundary between life and death (by drowning, shooting, or causing a mine explosion, for example), rather than 'simply' (to the extent that incarceration can ever be a simple matter) a difference between freedom and its lack (through arrest, but also equally forced labour endured for sake of escaping arrest, as in trafficking). So material and non-material are enmeshed, imbricated rather, and concrete and abstract are interactive, practice and ideology co-productive. The metaphor of imbrication is taken by Demetriou in her chapter as a way of connecting these different levels and thinking about their complex relations in tandem. The mediation between all these is where we see the political as emerging. The political is a process, in other words: a process, we might further add, that is circular or spiral, where subjects and objects co-emerge. Differences (friend–enemy, self–other) are recurring poles perhaps, but always shifting in content and expanding or contracting in the breadth of their representation.

Size and grandeur can also have agency in shaping people's perceptions and reactions to material appearances (Dimova 2013). The material presence of conspicuously decorated houses in Macedonia, for instance, has had an effect on residents that could be viewed as part of the 'baroque mechanism' (Lambert 2004), with its main feature being to move the spectator and to unleash feelings of wonder, amazement, or disorientation (Lambert 2004: 28). This sublime effect of the Baroque mechanism could, in effect, be at work in other situations where the size and outlook of materiality may suddenly affect the observer and thus shape how people view each other. Dimova's chapter in this volume reveals how the 'displaced borders' at the centre of the capital of Macedonia, Skopje, are materialized through grand buildings and monuments referring to a classical past and antiquity. This trend, which started in 2008 and is part of the 'Skopje 2014' project, is conditioned by the political dispute with Greece about the right to use the name 'Macedonia'. While on the Greek–Macedonian border itself there is an absence of any markers referring to this conflict, the centre of the capital Skopje has become the primary battleground of the symbolic and aesthetic borders built not only between the Republic of Macedonia and Greece, but also between Macedonia, Europe, and the rest of the world, which has been seen as complicit with the Greek denial of the right of the governing structures in Macedonia to use the constitutional name 'Macedonia'.

At each of these levels of mediation we thus see a predominance of shift and change. Shifts in materiality prompt changes in political subjectivity, even if those changes take place for the sake of stabilizing those very subjectivities. As Navaro-Yashin shows of Turkish-Cypriots, for example, the uncanny ways in which things emit affect in Northern Cyprus are conceptually worked upon to rehabilitate discomfort and integrate it into the political everyday (2012). We return here to the notion of 'community' as the primary abstraction of what the border creates. In the impossibility of its foundation we see the very shift that gives rise to political subjectivity: 'community' always needs an immutability which is unattainable (nation-state homogeneity, stereotype of 'our people', etc.). In this dialectic between immutability and unattainability the subjects of 'minority', 'dissent', 'margins', and 'the periphery' emerge. And as they proliferate, 'normalcy', 'majority', and 'typicality' lose their ground as normative structures and begin to disappear.

We recall here that Barth (1969) rooted the enquiry about borders into the mutability of 'change': description and ascription changes, and as it does so, the border may shift as well between 'inside' and 'outside'. If we are then to insist on this shift as fundamental to the political materiality of borders, we must also ask about the limit: how much shift is tolerable before 'community' morphs into something else? Is it a matter of gradual change? As Green (2005) put it, how much difference makes a difference? Jean-Luc Nancy (1991) has forcefully argued the point that 'community' is always a question of co-emergence. It does not exist the before individual, nor is it separate from individuals. It is always a challenge to individuality because it happens at the point of interaction, when part of that 'individuality' is already being lost (see also Demetriou 2013). A border then wedges itself into the welding together of individual and community, disappearing as it does so but nevertheless being conceptually instrumental (see also Pulkkinen, Chapter 4 below). Materiality and immateriality can no longer be distinguished or extracted from each other.

It is at this limit that 'evental sites' (Badiou 2006) may be located. 'Community' begins to be rethought when the self is repositioned vis-à-vis a radical 'other'. It would thus seem that the outside, what is unaccounted for or outside the 'set', is what drives the materiality of the border arrangement. But even after such 'events', after such ruptures of subjectivity, traces remain of what has been. Borders leave their marks, both as they recede and as they are reaffirmed. Population shifts, for example in Greece and Cyprus, have both destabilized the notions 'Greek' and 'Turk' and reaffirmed the efficacy of their opposition in the face of its material undermining (e.g. through the presence of minorities and refugees considered 'other'). Those shifts have left their mark on the understandings of current migration dynamics, where 'others' may no longer be 'Turks' but the efficacy of the border as a Greco-Turkish one remains.

As the volume explores these shifts and connections, the authors of the chapters offer different propositions about reconceptualizing borders and political materialities. In the following three chapters, different premises for examining border materialities are addressed. Conceptually, Olga Demetriou uses the idiom of imbrication as a conceptual tool for enriching the analyses of the connections at the heart of the volume: politics, materiality, and borders. Chiara De Cesari sets out a temporal and juridical premise providing an ethnography of this border time, paying close attention to the relations between Italy and Libya in the last years of the Qadhafi era and the historical memories and forgettings that they embody. Philosophically, Tuija Pulkkinen takes further the theoretical lines we have sketched in this introduction to compare Derrida's and Deleuze's offerings on the conceptualization of borders and materiality.

Following that, Sarah Green's chapter inaugurates the second half of the volume, which engages in a conversation on particular aspects of border materialities: lines, traces, and tidemarks. This second part distils beautifully the numerous discussions out of which the volume and the present series emerged, in the context of the COST-funded network EastBordNet, which Green chaired. Placed right at the centre of the volume, then, her chapter on lines, traces, and tidemarks reflects the centrality of these theoretical takes. In direct response to this, Stef Jansen's chapter takes up the question of line, while Eleni Myrivili's chapter reconfigures the concept of trace into 'ghost'. Finally, Dimova's chapter appropriately closes the volume by revisiting temporality and space together under the metaphor of waves rippling inwards from the border, and echoing many of the themes and images that populate the volume.

Conclusion: four positions on the political materiality of borders

In concluding, we would like to recapitulate some of the points that have guided our thinking in putting this volume together. Firstly, we see borders as marking the points at which materiality and immateriality become indistinguishable. They do this because they emerge exactly out of the limitation in which structural binaries fail. In this sense, borders may be said to be symptoms of post-structuralism, in the manner outlined in the theoretical literature surveyed here.

Secondly, we posit that even though borders have so far been studied as political devices par excellence, it is in the enmeshment of materiality and immateriality that emerges through 'border' that we want to locate the political. The reading of a piece of paper as 'law' is invested with powers of state, knowledge, policing, and so on. However, it is not that 'paper' and 'law' stand on either side of the material–nonmaterial divide. They are both constituted in the folding of materialities and immaterialities into each other (state, courts, police, etc.). Our aim is to explore such forms of the political without reducing the analysis to that binary of 'materiality' that would take 'law', 'police', 'courts', 'treaties', and so on as given.

Thirdly, we have identified a number of modalities on which this enmeshment comes into being: landscape, text, and architecture. Others can also be cited: corporeality, aesthetics, infrastructure. By looking at how borders mediate the enmeshment of materiality and immateriality on each of these modalities, we reveal specific techniques of how the political aspect of borders comes into being.

Fourthly, we call for attention to temporal aspects of border practices and to shifts in the mediations that we are examining. Attention to these shifts therefore allows us to conceptualize anew questions of subjectivity, agency, community, change. The challenge of this volume is in bringing these aspects together to forge new perspectives in border research.

References

Adorno, Theodor, and M. Horkheimer (1972). *Dialectic of Enlightenment*. New York: Seabury Press.

Agnew, J. (2008). 'Borders on the Mind: Re-Framing Border Thinking'. *Ethics & Global Politics*, 1(4): 175–91.

Althusser, L. (1971). *Lenin and Philosophy*, trans. Ben Brewster. New York: Monthly Review Press.

Andersson, R. (2014). *Illegality, Inc.: Clandestine Migration and the Business of Bordering Europe*. Oakland, CA: University of California Press.

Badiou, A. (2006). *Being and Event*. London: Bloomsbury.

Balibar, É. (2009). *We, the People of Europe? Reflections on Transnational Citizenship*. Princeton, NJ: Princeton University Press.

Barth, F. (1969). *Ethnic Groups and Boundaries. The Social Organization of Culture Difference*. Oslo: Universitetsforlaget.

Benjamin, Walter (1999a). *The Arcades Project*. Cambridge, MA: Belknap Press.

Benjamin, Walter (1999b). 'Critique of Violence'. In *Walter Benjamin: Selected Writings*, vol. 1: *1913–1926*, ed. M. Bullock and M. W. Jennings, 227–300. Cambridge, MA: Belknap Press and Harvard University Press.

Buck-Morss, Susan (1989). *The Dialectics of Seeing: Walter Benjamin and the Arcades Project*. Cambridge, MA: Harvard University Press.

Das, V. (1995). *Critical Events*. Delhi: Oxford University Press.

Deleuze, Gilles, and Felix Guattari (1987). *A Thousand Plateaus: Capitalism and Schizophrenia*. Minneapolis: University of Minnesota Press.

Demetriou, O. (2013). *Capricious Borders: Minority, Population, and Counter-Conduct between Greece and Turkey*. Oxford: Berghahn Books.

Dimova, R. (2013). *Ethno-Baroque: Materiality, Aesthetics and Conflict in Modern-Day Macedonia*. Oxford: Berghahn Books.

Epstein, C. (2007). 'Guilty Bodies, Productive Bodies, Destructive Bodies: Crossing the Biometric Borders'. *International Political Sociology*, 1(2), 149–64.

Foucault, M. (2007). *Security, Territory, Population: Lectures at the Collège de France 1977–1978*, trans. G. Burchell. New York: Picador.

Green, Sarah F. (2005). *Notes from the Balkans: Locating Marginality and Ambiguity on the Greek–Albanian Border*. Princeton, NJ: Princeton University Press.

Gupta, A., and J. Ferguson (1997). *Culture, Power, Place: Explorations in Critical Anthropology*. Durham, NC: Duke University Press.

Harvey, D. (2009). 'The Art of Rent: Globalisation, Monopoly and the Commodification of Culture'. *Socialist Register*, 38: 93–110.

Hodder, I. (1982). *Symbols in Action: Ethnoarchaeological Studies of Material Culture.* Cambridge: Cambridge University Press.

Lambert, G. (2004). *The Return of the Baroque in Modern Culture.* London: A&C Black.

Latour, Bruno (2005). *Reassembling the Social: An Introduction to Actor-Network-Theory.* Oxford and New York: Oxford University Press.

Marcuse, Herbert (1991). *One-Dimensional Man: Studies in the Ideology of Advanced Industrial Society.* Boston: Beacon Press.

Meskell, L. (2004). *Object Worlds in Ancient Egypt.* Princeton, NJ: Berg

Meskell, L., and P. Pels (2005). *Embedding Ethics.* Oxford: Berg.

Muller, B. J. (2008). 'Securing the Political Imagination: Popular Culture, the Security *Dispositif* and the Biometric State'. *Security Dialogue*, 39(2–3): 199–220.

Nancy, J.-L. (1991). *The Inoperative Community.* Minneapolis: University of Minnesota Press.

Navaro-Yashin, Y. (2012). *The Make-Believe Space: Affective Geography in a Postwar Polity.* Durham, NC: Duke University Press.

Newman, D. (2006). 'Borders and Bordering: Towards an Interdisciplinary Dialogue'. *European Journal of Social Theory*, 9(2): 171–86.

Paasi, A. (2009). 'Bounded Spaces in a "Borderless World": Border Studies, Power and the Anatomy of Territory'. *Journal of Power*, 2(2), 213–34.

Rumford, C. (2006). 'Theorizing Borders'. *European Journal of Social Theory*, 9(2): 155–69.

Rygiel, K. (2011). *Globalizing Citizenship.* Vancouver: University of British Columbia Press.

Salter, M. B. (2008). 'When the Exception Becomes the Rule: Borders, Sovereignty, and Citizenship'. *Citizenship Studies*, 12(4): 365–80.

Tazzioli, M. (2014). *Spaces of Governmentality.* Lanham: Rowman & Littlefield International.

Thrift, N. (2005). *Knowing Capitalism.* Thousand Oaks: Sage.

Van Houtum, H. (2010). 'The Janus-Face: On the Ontology of Borders and B/ordering'. *Simulacrum: Kwartaalblad van het Kunsthistorisch Instituut van de Universiteit van Amsterdam*, 2/3(18): 124–7.

Walters, W. (2011). 'Foucault and Frontiers: Notes on the Birth of the Humanitarian Border'. In Ulrich Bröckling, Susanne Krasmann, and Thomas Lemke (eds), *Governmentality: Current Issues and Future Challenges*, 138–64. London: Routledge.

Wilson, T. M., and H. Donnan (1998). *Border Identities: Nation and State at International Frontiers.* Cambridge: Cambridge University Press.

Materiality, imbrication, and the *longue durée* of Greco-Turkish borders

Olga Demetriou

Borders are irreducibly material structures. Even when they refer to non-material categories (e.g. difference, mental borders, disciplinary boundaries) the image conjured up to conceptualize these is that of a state border, drawn as a line on a map and policed with people and infrastructure on the ground. And yet attempts to understand these precise borders in their materiality have shown time and again in border studies that this 'line' is a ruse, that the more we take this materiality as something obvious the more it begins to disappear, either through change or through complexity (e.g. Agnew 2008; Wilson and Donnan 1998; Newman 2006; Paasi 2009; Rumford 2006; Van Houtum 2010).[1] Time and space become factors in the changing of the border, and the border begins to expand into social, legal, and political categories, into ways in which people conceptualize themselves and others as belonging or not. These are by now well-established themes in thinking about borders, and they inform the contributions of this volume.

In this chapter, I want to take up two specific aspects of the tension between materiality and non-materiality in the ethnography of borders. One is the time–space relation, and the other is the conceptual metaphors we use to analyse it. I have in mind some of the theoretical approaches elaborated by later contributions in this volume, especially on the philosophical analytics of duality and difference (Pulkkinen) and on the corporeal aspects of border-induced subjectivities (Myrivili, Jansen). I consider these approaches alongside my long-standing interest in minoritization as a process through which 'other' populations are produced, populations that are not the ones whom the governmentality of the 'normal' (the majority) targets.[2] Recently, Martina Tazzioli (2014) has proposed seeing this as a 'techno-politics of cross-over', whereby policies with a specific target are employed to deal with a different situation – as for example in the case of Italian authorities' use of surveillance technologies that previously targeted the Libyan regime and now target boat migrants. This to me indicates a growing interest in, and indeed a need to analyse, such shifts in the technologies of governmentality. But I would claim that what takes place in the shift goes beyond expedience. It is not only a shift in technologies and *dispositifs*, but a shift in governmentality also, one that neverthe-less does not abandon previous structures. And thus, we need to theorize this shift 'in part' and the ways it builds on previous logics and instruments to become not a blunt or faulty instrument, but one indeed that moulds new subject populations in the frame of otherness.

I therefore ask here how we might think these theoretical operations in ways that allows more expansion into this otherness. In contrast to previous work (Demetriou 2013), I speak here not of ethnic otherness, but of an otherness that was not tar-geted in the first place, or not targeted initially, in the exclusions that the border was meant to effect. These 'surprising' aspects of the border – the unexpected conse-quences of the connections between the materialities and non-materialities that are induced by it – require us, I want to argue, to employ similarly expansive metaphors. I thus propose that the conceptualization of the border as process, which we suggest in the introduction, also requires a geometric metaphor that goes beyond the shift from line to area and two-dimensional area patterns (lattice, nodes, mesh, etc.). I suggest that imbrication, and the expansive pattern of layering it points to(as in fish scales or roof tiles), is one such productive metaphor.

A small digression here: as argued in the introduction, I am conceptualizing materiality and immateriality as connected and not as a dichotomy. At the same time, I speak of connections between the two in recognition of the existence of both in the process of the border. To take just one instance of materiality as an aspect of making a border: consider the case of the Greco-Turkish border, set by the Treaty of Lausanne (1923), which takes 'the course of the Maritza' river (also known as Evros in Greek and Meriç in Turkish) as its key definition (Article 2). At the point where the river passes just outside the city of Edirne, the border diverges from its watery course and proceeds on land, in 'a roughly straight line leaving in Turkish territory the village of Bosna-Keuy' (Article 2), and meets the tripartite border point between Turkey, Bulgaria, and Greece at the confluence of the Arda and Maritza rivers. This course over soil, and presumably cultivated fields, gave pause to the treaty's drafters, who called on a boundary commission to determine which state another village in the area (now the border point of Kastanies) should belong to.[3] Today, this 8 km land strip that materializes as the border is the most secu-ritized section of the 200 km borderline along the Maritza (Evros) river. A concrete fence with thermal cameras has been built to keep migrants out, and Frontex has deployed forces through various programmes since 2010.

Just as the terrain of border needs to afford an acknowledgement of the dif-ference made by a river as opposed to cultivated fields, so does 'law' need to be recognized as both words on paper and interpretation in the mind of an enforce-ment officer and boundary commission expert. If water and soil here stand for arch-signs of 'materiality', the words of the Treaty cannot be taken as any less mate-rial. They are not only ink on paper (or bytes in cyberspace); they have moulded the water and the soil into a specific 'thing' – a border – that differentiates it, from the soil and the water beyond the border. Those connections of materiality inhere in interpretations that stretch across space and time, rendering a border of ethnic differentiation (as the terms of reference of the boundary commission suggest) one that now concretizes Fortress Europe. But even in 'interpretation', the lack of materiality cannot be claimed. Not considering the various materialities that aid that interpretation and make it practice, its very moment of conceptual thinking is signalled by the materiality of brainwaves. And just as concepts are material, and everything else is thus ultimately material, everything also has a non-material aspect: those words on paper might ultimately remain 'immaterial', unheeded, untranslatable into 'practice'.

These connections between materiality and immateriality produce effects on the border that are unintended and unforeseen. It is those effects that interest me here. In looking at aspects of border experience in Greece and Cyprus, I am particularly concerned with what I have elsewhere called 'the afterlife' of the border (Demetriou 2013: 193–7). Considering that both of the borders I examine, the border between Greece and Turkey in Thrace and the Green Line separating politically contested entities in northern and southern Cyprus, were products of Greco-Turkish conflict, I am interested in what other separations, connections, differences, and transgressions, beyond the specific inter-ethnic one, they are producing. Many of these other effects speak to the lapse of time between establishment of these borders (a time marked primarily by nation-state antagonism) and post-cold-war global migration structures. How terrain, law, and socio-political processes intersect in the shift of priorities in border management from ethnic conflict to global migration is therefore my main question in analysing the *longue durée* of the borders. Here, the term *longue durée* refers to a shorter time than the centuries that Braudel used in employing it (1960): the last century in the case of Greece and half that time in the case of Cyprus. In answering this question I employ the visual metaphor of imbrication to communicate an aspect of expansiveness that I argue is necessary to understand the 'unexpected' qualities of the border.

Displacements

It is summer 2003, a short time after the Turkish-Cypriot authorities announced that they would no longer prevent people from crossing in and out of a self-declared state in northern Cyprus, and after the first mass crossings took place over the Green Line boundary since the bloody period of the 1960s and the war of 1974. A restaurant in the old commercial centre of northern Nicosia is preparing for the evening's clientele; friends I recognize are passing by, and one joins our table for drinks. There is excitement over the 'opening of the border',[4] and we reminisce about how last time we met some months ago we had to drive for an hour to the only crossable point outside a village in the east of the island, partly under United Kingdom sovereignty. There is also a mood of playfulness as we criticize societal structures that still need to change: migration is one of them, and the South Asian waiter serving us is probably exemplary of the problems of discrimination and integration still to be combated. We ask about his living conditions, and unsurprisingly hear that they are not great. But he also expresses a different concern, having himself crossed from the south after his visa expired to escape arrest and continue making a living in the north: 'Every day I wake up and look across to the other side and remember the house where I used to live, and the place where I worked. It's so near and yet I can't go …'

His words sounded strangely familiar to me then, and their echo continues to inform my understanding of 'the border' in Cyprus.[5] They were strangely familiar in multiple senses. On the one hand, they condensed the hegemonic Greek-Cypriot discourse of displacement in Cyprus: that 'our' lands are just over there, so near and yet so far, waiting for us to liberate them, having been snatched unjustly by Turkey after its invasion in 1974.[6] The motif of the Greek-Cypriot refugee 'seeing' their house but not being able to 'touch' it appears in all kinds of literature, from elementary school books, where children in short stories send kites across the Green Line, to poems, fiction, and film, where crossing animals are envied. Before the opening of the central crossing point in Nicosia, binoculars were handed to tourists by Greek-Cypriot soldiers on guard so that they could see across the other side, and in the easternmost border point in the village of Deryneia visitors to a privately owned mini zoo are invited to a coin-operated viewing machine that is turned on the abandoned beach resort of Varosha, outside the Turkish-controlled town of Famagusta: they peruse 'the border' just as they peruse caged animals and embalmed snakes.

There is a dwelling on division in Cyprus that renders it, as I have argued elsewhere (Demetriou 2006), a Lacanian knot. The tragedy of Greek-Cypriot refugees, the rhetoric goes, is that they are 'refugees in their own country'.[7] The impossibility of crossing the border 'to go home' was for many years packaged as a corporeal experience for tourists, who were especially bussed to these look-out posts and encouraged to become ambassadors for the cause of 'return'. For the Greek-Cypriot-schooled public, the effect was to cultivate a sense of 'generalized refugeehood', which made the definition of 'refugee' seem obvious and the sentiments of loss that were expected to attend it a structure of feeling that the whole population should share.

So to hear this discourse articulated on the opposite side of the divide seemed strange. Firstly, the unreachable 'other side' was now the south, not the north. This was only partly strange. Turkish-Cypriots have often articulated longing for homes left in the south since 1963, and this has been well researched. Yet this articulation is often cognizant of and opposed to the official rhetoric that has emphasized forgetting and looking forward to a brighter future in new homes in the north after the war of 1974. Even when not so, it is positioned against this background so that the longing for return and lament for not reaching the unreachable are complexly ambivalent.[8] What seemed strange, in this sense, was a kind of geographic dislocation of affect: not that homes in the south are not pined for, but that they are pined for in this (Greek-Cypriot) way.

Secondly, the time of this affective expression seemed strange. The inability to 'go home' that produced this longing was not marked by the solidity of the border. It took shape precisely at the moment when the border 'opened up', and when it seemed that in fact it was about to be dissolved altogether.[9] 'Going home' was one of the primary activities Greek-Cypriots with ties to the north had been engaging in, *en masse* and on a daily basis throughout the previous months. Middle-aged men and women visited homes they remembered from childhood, elderly parents were driven to meet neighbours and friends, and collect movable possessions, agricultural produce from fields was saved and collected by those now living in their 'old' homes, and youngsters were guided through houses that suddenly seemed much smaller and landscapes perhaps less grand than they had remembered or imagined. There was ambivalence here too in the encounters between different 'owners' and in the performance of 'return'. But there was a definite sense that the main barrier to whatever 'return' might ensue was slowly being lifted.

So on that evening, the emblematic articulation of Greek-Cypriot refugee-hood seemed misplaced, in both place and time. And ultimately the cause of that misplacement was the strangeness of a specific subjectivity. It seemed strange, in this sense, to hear what I had come to recognize as a Greek-Cypriot discourse on loss articulated by a 'foreigner' – an immigrant with no apparent familial ties to Cyprus, a stranger (a notion that needs expanding for the essentialisms of self – other that it articulates).

So what did its strangeness mean? Is there an affect that the Green Line exudes when it is un-crossable that goes beyond the ethnic conflict? Has the ethnic divide that materializes on the Green Line come to envelop everyone in Cyprus, and not just Greek-Cypriots and Turkish-Cypriots? Is the 'so near yet so far' discourse actually the articulation of something obvious, perhaps not the epitome of Greek-Cypriot politics at all but something banally self-evident? And does this banality point to something universally applicable rather than a feature of political culture? At the time, the waiter's comment seemed a spontaneous attempt to relate the excitement of meeting someone coming from the side that had become inaccessible. I have since wondered whether it might have also been mediated by the experience of having lived in the south and among the Greek-Cypriot refugee discourse. But it is these questions about the border *per se* that I have repeatedly returned to, and which I want to highlight as inroads into the political materialities of borders in Cyprus and beyond.

Imbrication, infrastructures, and the *longue durée*

The questions I am interested in exploring here are to a large extent about situating relations: how do discourses of division and about the border relate to each other in different contexts (Greek-Cypriot to Turkish-Cypriot, local to migrant, north to south, south to north, before and after mass crossings, pre- and post-referendum)? Taking each of these apart and examining it separately can indeed help us untangle the complexity of the political at each instant. I would like to attempt a different analytic strategy instead. I want to examine these relations not as 'knots' that need to be 'untangled' in order to get to clarity, but as entities inextricably bound together in ways that make the picture clearer when we in fact take these relations together. We have spoken of this in the previous chapter in terms of modalities that can be imagined as a layering – cascading, imbricating, enmeshing. It is the metaphor of imbrication that I would like to build on here.

References to imbrication have been made in recent discussions related to materiality, particularly when describing how planes are entangled in one another (e.g. the political in the social, the local in the global; see Brenner 2000: 368 and Surin and Hasty 1994: 22, among others). The metaphor of imbrication seems to be taken for granted, without much discussion of what it might help us to conceptualize. An imbricated arrangement, the definition goes, is one 'composed of parts (leaves, scales, or the like) which overlap like tiles' (*New Oxford Shorter English Dictionary* 1993: 1313). Roof tiling is given in most dictionaries as the key image for this definition, and the Latin origin of the word points to a gutter tile (*imbrex*) that carries away the rainwater (*imber*). Valpy's *Etymological Dictionary of the Latin Language* of 1828 relates this to the Greek word for rain ὄμβρος (Valpy 1828: 197), where, in classic etymological fashion, the tracing stops. This etymology can in fact be taken as exemplary of my point about imbrication: I do not see etymology as holding some truth in itself, so that one can follow a route (e.g. down the gutter tiles) and arrive at some beginning of time located in Greek antiquity, but as offering interesting overlaps that can help us expand a conceptual tool, in this case a metaphor, which inevitably will hit upon its own limitations too.

Imagined as the effect of tiling a roof, therefore (and not the 'original' gutter tiling), imbrication speaks of an expansive layering and patterning that is different from three close alternatives: (i) stacking, where layers overlap completely, (ii) alignment (as in gutter tiles), where there is no layer but a singular route, and (iii) enmeshing, where layers are dissolved into one. Imbrication, furthermore, retains something of substantive differentiation (with regard to individual tiles) but in an arrangement that is neither fixed (as in that much-problematized metaphor of co-existence, the mosaic) nor completely arbitrary. The unexpected arises in imbrication as the interaction of matter with process (tiles, water, soil and animal droppings, rain, wind, or nesting). Imbrication is expansive in that it goes beyond a single-layer mesh, beyond a single type of interaction, as in the mosaic that is looked at and makes sense only in being looked at.

In the examples I use in this chapter, imbrication concerns the material and non-material aspects of bordering that give rise to these interactions. Alongside the different ways in which authors in this volume compel us to think about borders as constantly in process, and never as either material or immaterial, I want to propose that we may approach this much-critiqued dichotomy from an angle that both recognizes a difference and rejects the opposition. I say this starting from the recognition that it would be futile to insist on the primacy of either matter or non-matter, which would take us back to a Cartesian opposition between existence and perception. Just as Descartes can declare that it is perception that makes the material matter (thought over being), we could also claim that perception is also matter, whether it is seen brainwaves on a machine, charged leaps between synapses, or a glint in the eye. This is another take on the over-stated 'thing-ism' that Jansen (Chapter 6 below) problematizes in actor-network theory (Latour 2005).

If the border in Nicosia exudes an aspect of trauma and loss for a migrant, a tourist, or a refugee, this cannot happen without the politicization in which it is thoroughly embedded. While differently configured in each case, this politicization is neither anterior nor posterior to the ontology of the border; it is, as Myrivili (Chapter 7 below) says in the case of Prespa, the effect of conflict, violence, and war, as well as of policing and the continuous re-enactment of forms of violence that policing entails. By seeing this relation between the border and politicization in terms of an imbrication of material and non-material, we no longer oppose one to the other, nor prioritize one over another: both materiality and non-materiality belong to and infuse the border and its politicization.

But at the same time, there is also something more specific that can now be said. The relation between border and politicization, materiality and non-materiality, is not an amorphous 'embedding' or 'enmeshment'. It consists of specific processes unfolding in time and space and influencing one another through their materialities and in ways that go beyond the material. This is how I approach the *longue durée* of borders. In this approach, the *longue durée* is considered in its political manifestations; it is not merely the millennial process of nature shifting the earth's crust to form mountains and seas that Braudel separates out from the historical process of human activity in order to examine its effects on that activity – effects that are largely conceptualized on a positive plane of interaction, cultures in sync with nature. The *longue durée* of the political materialities that I am interested in is a bi-directional interaction of terrain and culture that is fraught with violence, and which institutes that violence as a norm that is repeatable. Crossers who in former periods were stripped of their citizenship for crossing (as was the case for Turkish minority members in Greece) are now incarcerated and stripped of rights for the very same crossing (as is the case today for migrants detained or pushed back at Evros). At the same time, the attention to the material contexts of this politicized *longue durée* also resists a conspiratorial approach that would have an invisible hand of the state taking a calculated approach to the meting out of that violence. A border may throw up unexpected practices, surprising crossings, like that from southern to northern Nicosia, which are spurred by the interaction of current practices and historical legacies and ways of thinking (about the Cyprus conflict, for example). This view of the *longue durée* then requires that we look at that imbrications of politics, materiality, culture, practice, and policy as structured but also unpredictable connections.

In Cyprus, access to rights relating to migrant and refugee protection, as well as its limitation, is mediated through the structure of the conflict. The quotation of the waiter above is indicative of how work and residence, denied by migration law on one side of the divide, can materialize on the other, while this denial can produce discourses that emulate political subjectivities of unlikely populations. This is a similar situation to that of the Evros river and the Greco-Turkish border, which transformed from a heavily militarized border between two arch-enemies (Greece and Turkey) and between the 'West' and the 'beyond' of the Iron Curtain (Greece and Turkey vis-à-vis Bulgaria), into a migrant gateway into the European Union (from Turkey to Greece) and an internal European border controlled by Schengen visa rules (between Greece and Bulgaria). The policing practices around this border, although radically different from those a few decades ago, draw on infrastructures and discourses oriented towards Turkey as an enemy state.

There is a confluence in this geography between ethnic conflict and migration, when, for example, Turkey is presented in Greek discourse as a malicious actor sending illegals to Greece. The historical depth expressed in this discourse is an aspect of imbrication. A history of conflict is not alluded to in a simply incidental way. As I show in the next section, it is carefully layered over a discourse of anti-immigration and its connected discourse of Islamophobia to present Turkey as a location from which evils, old and new, come to Greece. The political force of this layering is considerable. It is not a confused conflation of populist discourse that fails to hold up to scrutiny. It is a considered, racist rhetoric that has been embraced by the mainstream and extreme right in Greece, being vocalized at times by state officials, and which today sustains much of the vote share of the far right Golden Dawn party (see also Ellinas and Lamprianou, 2017). The links between ethnic enemies and migrants are an important part of this layering.

And as these links engulf the materialities around them, they form an imbricated frame that sustains the infrastructures that shape lives and subjectivity. These are not the Marxist infrastructures that are the material underpinnings of ideological (and thus purportedly immaterial) superstructures. They merge the two to form the bedrock on which new structures (policing, political campaigning, refugee and immigration procedures) are deposited. Imbrication is manifest here in its geological sense, as the formation arising from sediments deposited in an alluvial or other channel. Time is crucial to this layering, whereby governmentalities oriented towards one kind of population at a particular point in time (Turks as ethnic enemies) come to subjectivize others (migrants) as the border develops into something else. These connections are worth exploring in detail.

Discourse and terrain

Effie Voutira argued some time ago that the conceptualization of 'refugee' identity in Greece, tightly connected to the 1923 forced exchange of populations between Greece and Turkey, had a great impact on Greece's later refugee policy. One aspect of this was that 'the collective perception of the 1923 rural refugee settlement as a success case has shaped Greek state policy towards new immigrants' (Voutira 2003b: 146). Speaking specifically of Greek 'repatriates' from the Former Soviet Union, she found that

> because the Greek host-state of 1989 was not that of 1923 and because the sub-stance of state policy did not match its rhetoric, the policies intending to duplicate the success of the 1923 case, or at least the policies moulded in its image, led to false expectations on the part of both the hosts and the newcomers, which have led, in turn, to mutual disillusionment. (Voutira 2003b: 146)

Worse still has been the record regarding non-Greek refugees, foreign asylum seekers, the reception of whom is guided by the

> cultural assumption concerning the genuineness of the 'refugee' label, which pre-sumes that the only **true** refugees must be of Greek origin … [and hence] is biased because of these cultural assumptions, which imply that Sudanese, Palestinian, Ethiopian, Iraqi or Afghani asylum seekers are seen as 'foreign refugees' and thus as essentially 'others', whose treatment is to be guided exclusively by a rigid application of the 1951 Refugee Convention, which is not 'common knowledge'. (Voutira 2003a: 74, emphasis in original)

Note that the latter point is made in reference to statements by a Greek-Cypriot politician (commenting on Greece), which is exemplary of how the same discursive structure also applies in Cyprus, where 'real' refugees are the internally displaced Greek-Cypriots of 1974. Migration in the two countries is already historically framed within the legacy of wars with Turkey.

Consider the application of this at the very moment of crossing and the level of the border terrain: apart from being the location where the recognized minority group of Turkish-speakers exempted from the population exchange resides, Thrace is also one of the main entry points of migrants into the EU, who cross the Evros river from Turkey to Greece throughout the year. Apart from this point, the sea borders in the Aegean and especially the stretches between Greek islands just off the Turkish coast (Lesvos, Chios, Samos, Kos) are by far the most frequently crossed irregularly – a fact that was brought starkly to international public attention in the summer of 2015, when Lesvos alone allegedly saw close to a million refugees pass through the island on the way to Athens. Practices that flagrantly flout international law in policing these crossings have been well documented for years, and long before these locations came under international scrutiny as hotspots of reception for fleeing Syrian refugees in that summer of 2015. Reports by Amnesty

International (2005; 2010a; 2010b; 2013; 2014a; 2014b), Pro Asyl (2007; 2012; 2013), and Human Rights Watch (2008a; 2008b; 2009; 2011) have diachronically spoken of informal re-admission where dinghies are slashed and towed off the Turkish coast, migrants beaten and tortured, bodies found ashore by islanders and buried in unmarked graves, and unaccompanied minors left to fend for themselves.

The authorities' response to such 'allegations' had, prior to 2015, ranged from indifference to empty investigation pledges and to inter-state policy formulation, often not in the interest of migrants' rights. In 2007 a large-capacity holding facility was built in the village of Fylakio, where the three state borders (Greek, Turkish, Bulgarian) meet each other, with the aim of providing detention conditions that adhere to human rights standards. By 2010, riots in the 2,000-capacity facility, which had been converted from a disused factory, had revealed the same problems that human rights organizations had been identifying for years elsewhere: overcrowding, poor sanitation, long-term detention, lack of medical and other facilities. In 2012 the same tri-partite border area was closed off on the eastern side by a state-of-the-art fence 13 km long, erected by Greek authorities to 'stem migration flows'. The area had been identified as a weak point because it is there that the Greek-Turkish state border veers away from the river, allowing it to flow into the outskirts of the major city of Edirne in Turkey, as explained earlier. Crossing migrants had for years used this land entry point as one alternative to the dangerous river crossing. The Fylakio centre was largely financed by the EU before the financial crisis hit Greece, while the fence was erected using public money amid the crisis and in spite of the European Commission's opposition to the project.

Both the fence and the detention centre share an ideological infrastructure other than the ambivalent frame of EU norms with its dual discourse of human rights and outsourcing of border security. This link is the orientation of security policy vis-à-vis Turkey. In 2007, the then Greek Minister of Foreign Affairs, Dora Bakoyianni, said that 'Greece cannot shoulder any more illegal immigrants', and that 'we look forward to closer cooperation [with the Turkish authorities] in order to face together the problem, which comes from the Turkish coast'.[10] In pointing the finger of blame at Turkey primarily, the problem of human rights abuses (the topic on which she was being asked to comment) was eschewed and downgraded. The framing of migration issues within Greco-Turkish politics disperses accountability for the degradation of human rights and buries the rights of 'others' under the fold of friend–enemy politics. A Greek coastguard commander on Lesvos is presented in the 2007 Pro Asyl report as claiming that illegal immigrants crossing from Turkey constitute a military threat ('an Islamic invasion') not only to Greece but to Europe as a whole because they are 'all men between 15 and 35 years of age … very well trained, they swim very well! … They are all warriors!' (Pro Asyl 2007: 13). This builds on a discourse that criminalizes the fact that 'illegal migrants' come from Turkey.

The Pro Asyl report of 2007 drew direct links between the treatment of irregular migrants and Greco-Turkish relations: it commented on the detention of migrants

in military zones on the Evros border that are difficult to access; it featured quota-
tions from police officers involved in migrant 'rescue' operations that relate the
difficulties to the 'cold war' environment existing on the Greco-Turkish sea border;
and it pointed to the thin line between covert and non-covert operations of the
coastguard on the border. These are all points of imbrication between discourses of
migration and the Greco-Turkish dispute and between material and non-material
aspects of the border. The practices that result from them are documented in the
reports cited above, as well as in statements and public communication documents issued by the Council of Europe and UN High Commissioner for Refugees.
Over the years, research by such organizations has rendered such practices more
transparent by securing greater amounts of data. The ideological fault-lines that
perpetuate them, however, have not always been as clear.

The financial crisis that has devastated the Greek economy since 2008 has added
an extra layer to this structure, whereby policies to stem migration now appear as
a response to a mounting violent agenda of the far right. Its key representative, the
Golden Dawn party, has been targeting immigrants for years, especially through
attacks against them in urban centres before and after a surge in voting strength in
the early 2010s – it elected its first municipal councilor in Athens in 2010 and entered
parliament in 2012 (see Ellinas, 2013; Ellinas and Lamprianou, 2017). Since the initi-
ation of criminal proceedings against the party in 2013 connected to the investigation
into the murder of the anti-fascist activist Pavlos Fyssas, its links to the Greek police,
suspected and reported on for years, have come under scrutiny. Golden Dawn's
rhetoric is firmly based on drawing links between the double threat of migration and
Turkish aggression. This rhetoric can be seen as the vocal underside of ideological
infrastructures that underlay Greek nationalist discourse and policy for several years
(Frangoudaki, 2013), and which the upheaval of the financial crisis has 'turned over'
and made visible. The coastguard commander quoted above was making precisely
these infrastructures audible back in 2007. It is arguably no coincidence that in the
most recent elections of September 2015, while disillusionment with political alternatives and the hope for change that the left-wing Syriza failed to deliver registered
record rates of abstention, Golden Dawn saw not only its percentages rise, but also
saw a rise in absolute numbers in those regions that are on the migration trail and
on the Greco-Turkish border (Dodecanese, Lesvos, Samos, Evros).[11] At the same
time, the fact that a government hailing from the alternative left (the Syriza party)
was in power in 2015 has been catalytic in putting in place policies that shifted the
discourse from 'illegal migration' to 'solidarity' with refugees and European states
(Papataxiarchis 2016). This shift, alongside the ongoing proceedings against Golden
Dawn, helped to stem anti-immigrant violence and allow passage into Europe, at
least until the signing of the EU–Turkey statement on re-admission in April 2016.

During a field visit with a human rights lawyer to migrant detention centres in
the Evros border area back in 2005, I met a number of such potential 'warriors' sent
from Turkey. Some came from conflict zones in Iraq and Afghanistan and were

visibly traumatized. Some originated from Turkey and spoke of persecution as Kurds. We also met women from these areas who were held in separate locations, sometimes apart from their families. We heard stories of multiple attempts to cross and of police capturing people mid-river and 'returning' them over the boundary line. During a transfer from one centre to the other in an army jeep, a soldier offered to show us the riverbank while we silently wondered about what might be taking place at other times in that spot: had arrested migrants been driven in that same jeep and also 'shown' the riverbank? In some of the detainees' stories we heard that 'returns' had also taken place after apprehension on land on the Greek side of the river and that crossers were put on army jeeps, taken to the riverbank, and told to swim back. Nothing of this could be proven, a local journalist who had heard these stories before lamented, because this was a military zone. 'You cannot just go to the river, climb a tree, and wait for the dark until they come and you video tape – there is no access.' After 2015, when the refugee reception regime on the Aegean islands became to an unprecedented degree transparent through the mass arrival of humanitarian initiatives, the Evros area remains difficult to access and secure data about. The legal governmentality that combats abuse through international human rights treaties stumbles here on the border and on the material and non-material imbrications of terrain, access, evidence, and the enemy-state threat that guides zone designations.

Terrain and the law

Compare this situation with that in Cyprus, where the Green Line separating north from south has been heavily militarized for the last four decades (and even longer in the case of Nicosia), even despite the fact that it is not officially an inter-state border. In 2004, when Cyprus joined the European Union (EU), a special caveat was added to the Treaty of Accession intended to regulate this abnormality. Protocol 10 clarifies that '[t]he application of the acquis shall be suspended in those areas of the Republic of Cyprus in which the Government of the Republic of Cyprus does not exercise effective control' (article 1). This in effect leaves the north in a state of legal suspension, within the EU but without EU laws, bordered by a boundary that without being a border is the EU's easternmost limit, controlled by Turkish military authorities that do not form government structures but are internationally recognized and held accountable as 'occupation troops' as well as by indigenous (Turkish-Cypriot) authorities that do have a governmental structure but are not internationally recognized and therefore not monitored by international bodies. The pervasiveness of this abnormality is clear in all political discourse on the island and imbricates migration-related discourse too.

In parallel with the Greek discourse I have outlined, the Cypriot Ministry of Foreign Affairs has on occasion presented the problem of illegal immigration as Ankara's ploy to flood the Republic of Cyprus with migrants and jam the entire state mechanism. Presenting the situation on a milder tone, the President of the Republic stated on 19 June 2009, having just returned from an EU summit:

> I have said that Turkey, which illegally occupies 37% of Cypriot soil, controls 54%–58% of the north-eastern coast of the Republic of Cyprus, which the legal Government cannot control. This coast of course, and as long as Turkey is not taking the necessary steps, is a place of embarkation of illegal immigrants. I also said that in some cases this happens in an organised fashion as well, that is to say, that so-called 'cruises' take place, or in any case [sea] lines operate, which carry people, who at the end of the day pass through the ceasefire line to the free areas and are illegal immigrants. (Cyprus News Agency 2009)

Indeed, for some time after it was initially opened in 2007, a sea route from Latakia in Syria to the port of Famagusta in northern Cyprus was a priority in the Republic's foreign policy, which sought and ultimately secured its closure. In this statement, this political concern appears to be effectively translated into a border security concern at EU level. Thus the dispute regarding keeping or closing the sea route is a prime example of how migration policy in Cyprus is tightly linked to the political problem, which the Republic defines as one of 'invasion and occupation of a third of the island by Turkey'.

The particular problem of the sea route is in fact one extension of the more general problem of policing of the Green Line, since this takes place in the absence of substantive cooperation between the authorities in charge of it on either side. During a meeting with the EU parliamentary Committee on Civil Liberties, Justice, and Home Affairs (LIBE) on the occasion of the latter's fact-finding mission on the island, the Minister of the Interior 'explained, to the members of the committee, that the problem in Cyprus concerning illegal migration is the occupied territories, since the largest percentage of asylum seekers come from the occupied areas' (Press and Information Office 2008). This explanation is reflected in the committee's report, which has been praised by the Republic's authorities on a number of occasions:

> The Green Line has evolved into a very serious problem regarding illegal immigra-tion. This problem should be addressed by Council and Commission in the ongoing negotiations with regard to Turkey's accession to the EU. Turkey should take up its responsibility as the impact on the government-controlled parts of Cyprus will soon lead to a situation that is unmanageable, from a demographic, political as well as financial point of view.
>
> In addition to the above-mentioned, and more in general, it should be noted that over the past 18 months no developments have been made on the bilateral working agreement between Turkey and Frontex. This is simply unacceptable. It is high time for Turkey and the EU to reach a common understanding on the importance of urgent and close cooperation in this field. (EU Parliament 2008)

In this line of argument, the concern is not whether Turkey (or Turkish-Cypriot authorities) should be held accountable for respecting migrants' rights in northern Cyprus so that there is less incentive to cross to the south (although this would also partake of a securitizing xenophobic discourse). It is rather the fact that in the process of arguing this, the policing of the Green Line is projected as the major issue of concern (not the treatment of migrants, some of whom may be refugees) and that this affects the definitions used to categorize migrants, which in turn affects the rights afforded to them. In the statements of government representatives, there is a consistent labelling of irregular crossers from the north as 'illegal migrants' (*lathrometanástes*), who then become 'asylum-seekers'. This appears to imply that there are two strands of asylum seekers, those who come from the north with relative ease and those who come directly to the south and face more barriers in the process.

Building on this categorization, there is the further implication that those who come via the Green Line are less genuine as claimants of refugee protection; they are, in a sense, more 'illegal'. The police annual report for 2007 states that the Aliens and Immigration Unit arrested 666 'illegal migrants' during the year and deported 2,892 persons (Republic of Cyprus Police 2008, Appendix J). The same report quotes a figure of 7,770 'illegal migrants' which came to the unit's attention, but this number, it is noted, also includes 'asylum seekers from the occupied territories' – *etités asílu apó ta katehómena* (Republic of Cyprus Police 2008, appendix J). This categorization is repeated in the reports of 2008 (Appendix H), 2009 (appendix E), 2010 (appendix E), and 2011 (appendix F). This raises a question as to whether some asylum seekers are automatically classified as illegal migrants and thus not granted the same access to the asylum process as other asylum seekers. It is as if crossing the Green Line becomes a prima facie reason for rejecting refugee or other protection. In the reports of 2009 (p. 51) and 2010 (p. 30), special sections are devoted to comparative statistics of asylum seekers from the free and occupied areas, noting the drop in the latter as an achievement. The criminalization of crossing is underscored further in the 2011 report, which includes general crossing statistics, and not just those related to 'illegal migration', under the columns 'Greek Cypriots to the occupied areas', 'Turkish Cypriots to the free areas' 'entry not allowed', and ' arrested' (appendix B). This was the situation before the Syrian crisis and the mass displacements of 2015. Interestingly, until the time of writing in late 2016, refugee arrivals in Cyprus were very limited in comparison to those in Greece. And while Cyprus's sheer geography as an island not conducive to onward travel renders it an unattractive transit point, these past practices and policies have done nothing to arouse confidence that Syrian refugees might find a hospitable shelter there. Indeed, activists and organizations have noted serious problems with reception conditions for the few hundred Syrian refugees who have arrived since 2015.

Apart from reports, this gradation of legitimacy among refugee and migrant groups bifurcates in many other ways. Kurds, for example, may be seen as more legitimate asylum claimants than other Turks, rendering their illegal crossing of the Green Line somehow less so than the 'absolutely' illegal crossing of Turks from the north, whom the Republic considers settlers. At the same time, the mediation of this framing structure by EU law also creates paradoxical situations that put the rigidity of local positions into question. The free movement of Bulgarian Turks, some of whom may be considered to have been 'settlers' in the north, is one such example. Consider the equivocal position expressed by the Special Advisor to the President of the Republic of Cyprus in 2007 when queried by journalists on the matter:

> As Bulgarian citizens, they are considered, as from 1 January 2007, to be EU citizens, with the rights and responsibilities this entails. Their right as European citizens, to move freely to the areas controlled by the State, does not, of course, annul the enforcement and application of the relevant laws of the Republic of Cyprus, as long as these laws are harmonized with the acquis communautaire. On the basis of these laws, the persons in question have committed the offence of illegal entry and stay in the Republic and may have possibly violated the property rights of displaced Greek-Cypriots. Bulgarian Turks [*Turkovúlghari*] who live in the occupied areas, can rightfully pass to the areas controlled by the Government of the Republic of Cyprus. But they cannot be absolutely certain that they will not be criminally prosecuted for their illegal entry and stay in the Republic of Cyprus. (Press and Information Office 2007)

I would read this statement as a sovereignty claim against the EU's exceptionalization of this particular group of 'settlers' (who were allowed free entry to the 'areas controlled by the Republic's authorities' under EU law and its specific application to Cyprus via Protocol 10). But it appears to be a claim of questionable applicability, a claim that targets individual persons, persons who are informed that they are at risk of prosecution on a case-by-case basis. If the opposite of refugee determination could be legally formulated (i.e. where the state extends not protection but persecution based on individual circumstance), this might be a starting point.

Consider the experience of Emin, whose family migrated to Turkey from Bulgaria to escape the pressures of the Zhivkov regime shortly before its collapse in 1989.[12] Emin barely remembers this move, or the one to northern Cyprus which followed, incentivized by Turkish policy to increase the population there. He grew up in northern Nicosia, attended school there, and got a job as a manual labourer. When arrested for a minor offence, he was given a deportation order because he was not a citizen of the Turkish Republic of Northern Cyprus. His family had not gone through the naturalization paperwork, and even though they now could, since he was an adult they discovered that they had lost the right to extend citizenship to him. Emin 'returned' to stay with extended family in Bulgaria but became depressed. He realized he could return to Cyprus via the south, where Bulgarians, as EU citizens since 2007, had residence and work rights. The evening Emin arrived in Larnaca airport he was picked up by his Turkish-Cypriot childhood friends and partied to celebrate his return to the island. He began searching for work in the south, made contact with his family who could cross to visit him, and rented a room in a house with other migrants. Speaking no Greek or English, he failed to secure jobs, and soon discovered that his Turkish was frowned upon in the south. He found it difficult to adjust to the filth in the house where he lived: the mattress had bugs, he told me, the sink was piled with unwashed dishes for days, cockroaches roamed, and the bathroom and toilet were hardly usable. Emin was never arrested in the Republic for having lived in the north and possibly having violated Greek-Cypriot property rights, and nor were his visiting family when they crossed to see him. But within two months of his arrival, and without any prospects for work or better living standards, he left for Bulgaria again, returning to the unwelcoming family the freedom from whom he had celebrated.

Emin had found himself in southern Nicosia pining for the loss of access to his house and family. His words resemble closely those of the South Asian waiter mentioned earlier. Of interest to me is that this resemblance occurs in a geography aligned with the discourse on loss of the bulk of Greek-Cypriot refugees, which those words, 'misaligned' as they are, echo. Emin had used EU law to circumvent the penalties imposed by law in northern Cyprus, just as the waiter had used the same law to move to the north and circumvent restrictions imposed by laws in the south.[13] Like the waiter, Emin had little investment in the Cyprus conflict up to that point, and had never before hit upon the border. But he became engulfed in the conflict the moment he was forced to become mobile. 'Forced migration' may be the wrong term here in a technical sense, but it is nevertheless a term that speaks, in the very misrepresentation of ideas about origins and stability that it implies, to the situation of becoming lodged in the crevices of legal, social, and political structures that under other conditions one might simply glide over, like rainwater. Imbrication may entail traps as well as leakages.

The ways in which the terrains of policy discourse as presented through government statements and law intersect are instructive. But they need to be seen as more than 'nodes' along a line-like structure. People's experience points to an expansive way of conceptualizing these overlaps. Laws need not reflect policy, and policy need not translate into action. But their confluence, on a material–non-material continuum, throws up the unexpected of experience: it makes words sound the same but communicate different life-worlds; it makes borders police movements, behaviours, and affects that they were not intended to police; it extends the life of the border far beyond the nation-state in the materialities of multi-state unities and in the bodies of non-citizen residents. People are caught in the folds of this but also create pathways of escape, like rainwater over a roof. And this reminds us that the state is not the only actor with tile-laying capacities: tiles may be broken, go amiss, create holes, harbour their own ecosystem, or cause collapse. The politics that drive these processes inhere neither in the tiles nor in the extra-material forces around them solely. They are the imbrications that make, sustain, and destroy a roof.

Conclusion

In structuring the present chapter around the metaphor of imbrication, I have sought to provide a different angle for approaching the political materialities of borders.

As much as borders entail some irreducible materiality, so do they entail a politics through and through. Yet neither that materiality nor those politics can be taken as a given: they are part of the process of the border. But however surprising they may be, their layering along the contours of time and space may often be patterned in ideological infrastructures that inform and emplace, or displace as the case may be, current material and non-material arrangements. As I have shown through the examples of terrain, discourse, and law here, imbrication is both a metaphor and a method for connecting the material and the non-material without losing sight of the political.

Notes

1   The specifics of these approaches are outlined in Demetriou and Dimova (Chapter 1 above).
2   I am following a Foucauldian approach here in conceptualizing 'population' as a process of governmentality (Foucault 2007).
3   Article 2 of the Treaty of Lausanne thus states that the 'village of Tchorek-Keuy [presumably today's Kastanies] shall be assigned to Greece or to Turkey according as the majority of the population shall be found to be Greek or Turkish by the Commission for which provision is made in Article 5, the population which has migrated into this village after the 11th October, 1922, not being taken into account.'
4   I elaborate on this in Demetriou (2007).
5   I develop this in Demetriou (2018).
6   I explore this discourse in detail in Demetriou (2014a).
7   Elsewhere (Demetriou 2014b; Demetriou 2018), I compare this phrase to the legal term 'displaced', which appears much less frequently in public discourse and carries references to the international legal terminology on 'internal displacement'. On the basis of this, I have argued that the phrase is best understood as a specific strategy of hegemonizing an exclusive form of refugeehood by instituting an exception (of Cypriot refugees) which normatively does not exist (refugees as people who have not crossed an international boundary).
8   Navaro-Yashin (2012) has insightfully documented this nuanced affective positioning.
9   Turkish-Cypriot authorities decided to allow crossings across the Green Line in April 2003, during a period (2002–04) of intense political negotiations to reach a settlement on the 'Cyprus problem', which yielded a plan for reunification, put to referendum in April 2004. The 'Annan Plan' was rejected by Greek-Cypriots and thus the dissolution of the border was deferred.
10   30 October 2007: http://www.in.gr/2007/10/30/greece/i-ellada-den-antexei-alloys-paranomoys-metanastes-dilwse-i-ntora-mpakogianni/ (last accessed 28 April 2018).
11   In those elections, losses in urban centres resulted in an overall drop of Golden Dawn's share. For a detailed breakdown see http://ekloges.ypes.gr/current/v/public/index.html?lang=el&fullsite=1#{"cls":"main","params":{}} (last accessed 10 December 2015).
12   On Turkish policy regarding these immigrants under the then Prime Minister Ozal, see Parla (2003).

13 These laws on immigration were reformed in the context of harmonization of the Republic of Cyprus's law with the EU directive on the status of third-country nationals who are long-term residents (European Council 2003). The directive sets out a limit of five years of continuous residency as the criterion for eligibility for permanent residence status. At the point of harmonization, the authorities of the Republic, who had a much longer limit for eligibility for permanent residence, instituted a policy of reviewing work permits of foreign nationals who had exceeded or were close to reaching the five-year limit and refusing to renew them, expelling a large number of people. This left the waiter in question, who might otherwise have continued to 'enjoy' a life of marginalization in the south (guaranteed, had the directive not been incorporated into national law, by legal stay but without any real prospect of permanency), with the choice of being expelled if discovered in irregularity, or escaping the authorities in some other way.

References

Agnew, J. (2008). 'Borders on the Mind: Re-Framing Border Thinking'. *Ethics & Global Politics*, 1(4) 175–91.

Amnesty International (2005). *Greece: Out of the Spotlight: The Rights of Foreigners and Minorities are Still a Grey Area.* 4 October 2005, index no. EUR 25/016/2005.

Amnesty International (2010a). *Greece: Irregular Migrants and Asylum-Seekers Routinely Detained in Substandard Conditions.* 27 July 2010, index no. EUR 25/002/2010.

Amnesty International (2010b). *Greece: The Dublin II Trap: Transfers of Asylum-Seekers to Greece.* 22 March 2010, index no. EUR 25/001/2010.

Amnesty International (2013). *Greece: Frontier Europe: Human Rights Abuses on Greece's Border with Turkey.* 9 July 2013, index no. EUR 25/008/2013.

Amnesty International (2014a). *Greece: A Law unto Themselves: A Culture of Abuse and Impunity in the Greek Police.* 3 April 2014, index no. EUR 25/005/2014.

Amnesty International (2014b). *Greece: Frontier of Hope and Fear: Migrants and Refugees Pushed Back at Europe's Border.* 29 April 2014, index no. EUR 25/004/2014.

Brenner, N. (2000). 'The Urban Question: Reflections on Henri Lefebvre, Urban Theory and the Politics of Scale'. *International Journal of Urban and Regional Research*, 24(2): 361–78.

Cyprus News Agency (2009). Press release from the Presidential Office, President's press conference in Brussels, 19 June.

Demetriou, O. (2006). 'Streets Not Named: Discursive Dead Ends and the Politics of Orientation in Intercommunal Spatial Relations in Northern Greece'. *Cultural Anthropology*, 21(2): 295–321.

Demetriou, O. (2007). 'To Cross or Not to Cross? Subjectivization and the Absent State in Cyprus'. *Journal of the Royal Anthropological Institute*, 13(4): 987–1006.

Demetriou, O. (2013). *Capricious Borders: Minority, Population, and Counter-Conduct between Greece and Turkey.* Oxford: Berghahn Books.

Demetriou, O. (2014a). 'Situating Loss in the Greek-Turkish Encounter in Cyprus'. In V. Lytra (ed.), *When Greeks and Turks Meet: Interdisciplinary Perspectives on the Relationship since 1923*, 45–64. London: Routledge.

Demetriou, O. (2014b). '"Struck by the Turks": Reflections on Armenian refugeehood in Cyprus'. *Patterns of Prejudice*, 48(2): 167–81.

Demetriou, O. (2018). *Refugeehood and the Post-Conflict Subject: Reconsidering Minor Losses.* State University of New York Press.

Ellinas, A. (2013). 'The Rise of Golden Dawn: The New Face of the Far Right in Greece'. *South European Society and Politics*, 18(4) 543-65.

Ellinas, A. A., and Lamprianou, I. (2017). 'How Far Right Local Party Organizations Develop: The Organizational Buildup of the Greek Golden Dawn'. *Party Politics*, 23(6), 804-20.

European Council (2003). Council Directive 2003/109/EC, concerning the status of third-country nationals who are long-term residents, 25 November, https://eur-lex.europa.eu/legal-content/EN/TXT/PDF/?uri=CELEX:32003L0109&from=en (last accessed 29 April 2018).

European Parliament (2008). Report from the LIBE Committee delegation on the visit to Cyprus, 25–7 May 2008. Rapporteur: Jeanine Hennis-Plasschaert, Brussels, 11 July 2008, document no. DV\736332EN, www.europarl.europa.eu/document/activities/cont/200902/20090226ATT50476/20090226ATT50476EN.pdf (last accessed 28 April 2018).

Foucault, M. (2007). *Security, Territory, Population: Lectures at the Collège de France, 1977–1978.* London: Palgrave Macmillan.

Frangoudaki, A. (2013). Ο εθνικισμός και η άνοδος της ακροδεξιάς [*Nationalism and the Rise of the Far Right*]. Athens: Alexandria.

Human Rights Watch (2008a). *Left to Survive: Systematic Failure to Protect Unaccompanied Migrant Children in Greece.* Report, 22 December 2008, https://www.hrw.org/report/2008/12/22/left-survive/systematic-failure-protect-unaccompanied-migrant-children-greece (last accessed 29 April 2018).

Human Rights Watch (2008b). *Stuck in a Revolving Door: Iraqis and Other Asylum Seekers and Migrants at the Greece/Turkey Entrance to the European Union.* Report, 26 November 2008, https://www.hrw.org/report/2008/11/26/stuck-revolving-door/iraqis-and-other-asylum-seekers-and-migrants-greece/turkey (last accessed 29 April 2018).

Human Rights Watch (2009). *No Refuge: Migrants in Greece* Report, 1 November 2009, https://www.hrw.org/report/2009/11/01/no-refuge/migrants-greece (last accessed 29 April 2018).

Human Rights Watch (2011). *The EU's Dirty Hands: Frontex Involvement in Ill-Treatment of Migrant Detainees in Greece.* Report, 21 September 2011, https://www.hrw.org/report/2011/09/21/eus-dirty-hands/frontex-involvement-ill-treatment-migrant-detainees-greece (last accessed 29 April 2018).

Latour, B. (2005). *Reassembling the Social: An Introduction to Actor-Network-Theory.* Oxford: Oxford University Press.

Navaro-Yashin, Y. (2012). *The Make-Believe Space: Affective Geography in a Postwar Polity.* Durham, NC: Duke University Press.

Newman, D. (2006). 'Borders and Bordering: Towards an Interdisciplinary Dialogue'. *European Journal of Social Theory*, 9(2): 171–86.

The New Oxford Shorter English Dictionary (1993). Oxford: Clarendon Press.

Paasi, A. (2009). 'The Resurgence of the "Region" and "Regional Identity": Theoretical Perspectives and Empirical Observations on Regional Dynamics in Europe'. *Review of International Studies*, 35(S1): 121–46.

Parla, A. (2003). 'Marking Time along the Bulgarian–Turkish Border'. *Ethnography*, 4(4): 561–75.

Papataxiarchis, E. (2016). 'Being "There": At the Front Line of the "European Refugee Crisis", Part 1'. *Anthropology Today*, 32(2): 5–9.

Press and Information Office, Republic of Cyprus (2007). Statement, 5 January.

Press and Information Office, Republic of Cyprus (2008). Statement, 27 May.

Pro-Asyl (2007). 'The Truth May be Bitter, but it Must be Told: The Situation of Refugees in the Aegean and the Practices of the Greek Coast Guard', www.statewatch.org/news/2008/mar/greece-pro-asyl.pdf (last accessed 28 April 2018).

Pro-Asyl (2012). *Walls of Shame: Accounts from the Inside. The Detention Centres of Evros*. PRO ASYL Foundation and Friends of PRO ASYL in cooperation with the Greek Council for Refugees and Infomobile/Welcome to Europe, https.www. proasyl.de/wp-content/uploads/2015/12/PRO_ASYL_Report_Walls_of_Shame_Accounts_From_The_Inside_Detention_Centers_of_Evros_April_2012-1.pdf (last accessed 28 April 2018).

Pro-Asyl (2013). 'Pushed Back: Systematic Human Rights Violations against Refugees in the Aegean Sea and at the Greek–Turkish Land Border', November 2013, https://www.proasyl.de/wp-content/uploads/2015/12/PRO_ASYL_Report_Pushed_Back_english_November_2013.pdf (last accessed 28 April 2018).

Republic of Cyprus (1960). Constitution of the Republic of Cyprus, http://www.presidency.gov.cy/presidency/presidency.nsf/all/1003AEDD83EED9C7C225756F0023C6AD/$file/CY_Constitution.pdf (last accessed 28 April 2018).

Republic of Cyprus Police (2008–11). Ετήσια Έκθεση [Annual Report], http://www.police.gov.cy/police/police.nsf/dmlreport_gr/dmlreport_gr?OpenDocument (last accessed 28 April 2018).

Rumford, C. (2006). Theorizing Borders'. *European Journal of Social Theory*, 9(2): 155–69.

Surin, K., and J. Hasty (1994). '"Reinventing a Physiology of Collective Liberation": Going "beyond Marx" in the Marxism(s) of Negri, Guattari, and Deleuze'. *Rethinking Marxism*, 7(2): 9–27.

Tazzioli, M. (2014). *Spaces of Governmentality*. London: Rowman & Littlefield International.

Treaty of Peace with Turkey Signed at Lausanne, 24 July 1923. In *The Treaties of Peace 1919–1923*, vol. 2. New York: Carnegie Endowment for International Peace, 1924.

Valpy, F. E. J. (1828). *An Etymological Dictionary of the Latin Language*. London: Printed by A. J. Valpy, sold by Baldwin and Co.

Van Houtum, H. (2010). 'Human Blacklisting: The Global Apartheid of the EU's External Border Regime'. *Environment and Planning D*, 28(6): 957–76.

Voutira, E. (2003a). 'Refugees: Whose Term is it Anyway? Emic and Etic Constructions of "Refugees" in Modern Greek'. In J. Van Selm (ed.), *The Refugee Convention at Fifty: A View from Forced Migration Studies*, 65–80. Lanham: Lexington.

Voutira, E. (2003b). 'When Greeks Meet Other Greeks: Settlement Policy Issues in the Contemporary Greek Context'. In R. Hirschon (ed.), *Crossing the Aegean*, 145–59. New York and Oxford: Berghahn.

Wilson, T. M., and H. Donnan (1998). *Border Identities: Nation and State at International Frontiers*. Cambridge: Cambridge University Press.

3

Memory as border work: the 2008 Italy–Libya Friendship Treaty and the reassembling of Fortress Europe

Chiara De Cesari

A border is made real through imagination. (Van Houtum 2012: 412)

In this chapter, I examine one peculiar border zone, namely the Mediterranean Sea – and more precisely that stretch of sea extending between Italy and Libya – in order to explore how memory-making contributes to its re-bordering. The cemetery of an astonishing and growing number of migrants and asylum seekers, this stretch of sea has become a symbol of Fortress Europe and of the deadly toll of the securitization of bordering practices or 'integrated border management', as it is called in the technical jargon of the European Union (EU) and its agency for coordinating external border control, Frontex (Bigo and Guild 2005; Van Houtum and Boedeltje 2009). According to the United Nations High Commissioner for Refugees, in 2014, out of an estimated 350,000 boat people, 4,272 have reportedly died while making the crossing, the vast majority (3,419) in the Mediterranean. According to activists and research networks, over 27,000 people have lost their lives on European borders since 2000 (Jansen, Celikates, and de Bloois 2015a), many in accidents on what has been called 'la Mer Mortelle'.[1] The thickening of Europe's borders is a multi-layered process, marked by ontological multi-dimensionality (Van Houtum 2012: 405); it involves material and immaterial dimensions that illustrate well the nature of borders as complex assemblages crossing scales and exceeding their most immediate material manifestations. Much recent work in critical border studies, especially concerning Europe, has emphasized how globalization has produced a world with more and not fewer walls (Brown 2010). These 'walls', however, are quite different from the traditional Westphalian understanding of borders. Processes of re-bordering are marked not only by the proliferation but also by the 'heterogeneization' and 'immaterialization' of borders that go along the heightened 'illegalization' or 'irregularization' of migration (Bialasiewicz 2011; Bigo 2015; Jansen, Celikates, and de Bloois 2015b; Mezzadra and Neilsen 2013). Italy's and Europe's border with Libya is indeed made up of multiple materialities and non-materialities: patrol boats and migrant detention centres, asylum regimes and international treaties, memories and socio-spatial imaginaries of Europe, as well as the very bodies and lives of those who make or police the crossing. In this chapter, I will focus on one non-material element of border work, namely, the production of memory and forgetting that goes along the heightened 'illegalization' of geopolitical boundaries. While largely non-material, such memories have very real, material effects, by feeding back into, reproducing, and strengthening physical borders, both solid (the traditional lines or walls demarcating Westphalian sovereignties) and liquid (new forms of smart, digitalized borders through various technologies of surveillance). In particular, I will discuss the Italy–Libya Friendship Treaty of 2008 and the way it simultaneously worked as (non-)site of memory and bordering device. I am interested in the kinds of forgetting, which I see as border work, that make possible the making of the hard walls of Fortress Europe out of porous and unstable geographies. In Sarah Green's words (Chapter 5), the treaty functions as a 'trace' in the border-making process of memory.

On a much-publicized visit to celebrate the signing of the Italy–Libya Friendship Treaty, Muammar Al-Qadhafi landed on Italian soil in June 2009 with an old photograph pinned to his breast. The photograph was of Umar Al-Muktar, the hero of the Libyan struggle against Italian colonialism. Some of Al-Muktar's family, as well as descendants of the over 100,000 victims of colonialism in Libya, accompanied Qadhafi's large delegation. Yet despite such pronounced symbolism, Qadhafi's injunction to remember colonialism was an ambiguous one. The Treaty included an aid package of US$5 bn in compensation for colonial atrocities, in exchange for Libya's collaboration with Italy and the EU on migration control and strengthening European external borders – in other words, for assuming the role of Europe's gatekeeper. But the gist of the Treaty was also economic and strategic, with the promise of long-term Italian investment in oil-rich Libya. 'Fewer illegal immigrants, more gas and more oil' is how Italian Prime Minister Silvio Berlusconi, the then head of a right-wing bloc with a strong anti-immigrant platform, described the purpose of the Treaty (Gramaglia and Garofalo 2011: 54).

Shortly before the visit, Italy's interior ministry had also – in open defiance of international humanitarian law – ordered the rejection of several boats carrying hundreds of African refugees and migrants about to reach the Sicilian coast. Sent back to Libya, the migrants were interned in prisons where human rights violations are known to be a regular occurrence (Human Rights Watch 2009). These prisons closely resemble the old colonial detention camps, where the Libyan hero Umar al-Muktar was hanged in 1931. Some have been built with Italian funding (European Commission 2005; Klepp 2010: 80). Notwithstanding Qadhafi's rhetoric, the carceral heritage of Italian colonialism in Libya still, years after the Treaty, represents a strong and under-investigated case of social forgetting; its official purpose notwithstanding, the Treaty did not either aid a broader awareness of this heritage of suffering or support human rights.

Critical European border studies have examined how, in stark opposition to its normative image of an open society, of a borderland, Europe has increasingly reproduced a nation-state model of territoriality writ large by 'drawing fixed borders around it[self]' (Agnew 2005: 578, quoted in Boedeltje and Van Houtum 2008: 363). This bordering process essentially consists in 'hardening the external boundaries while consolidating political community within the EU' (Scott and Van Houtum 2009: 271), which also means othering the non-EU by means of a renewed, rather essentialist identity politics grounded in the fundamental assumption of a distinctive European heritage and civilization (Boedeltje and Van Houtum 2008; Van Houtum 2012; see also Shore 2000, 2006). Symbolic geopolitics – the flag and the anthem but also the creation of Europe-wide remembrance days as well as the promotion of recognisable heritage icons and memories – is also part of this border work. For Boedeltje and Van Houtum the invention of Europe as a bounded cultural and political entity is a betrayal of the original project and goes against the necessary openness and multiplicity of Europe. The effects of such border work are deadly ones indeed (Van Houtum and Boedeltje 2009).

What does this have to do with the Italy–Libya Treaty? It is my main argument here that by activating materialities of border enforcement like patrol boats and security fences but also memory-making, the Treaty activates an assemblage of material and non-material elements that go into such border work. It also reshapes or rather displaces – by the very means of international law – the contours of EU legality itself (Andrijasevic 2010). Luiza Bialasiewicz (2012) has built on Didier Bigo's argument on securitization and the ways in which liberal states mobilize illiberal means to achieve their goals, exposing the complexity and specificity of EU bordering practices. For her, EU bordering works through a 'fluid assemblage of functions, mechanisms, and actors', for example by relying on bilateral agreements between EU member states and third countries that often do not have migration control as their explicit focus. In this context, European policies' rhetoric of democratization and collaboration with 'neighbours' barely conceals an increasing focus on security and securing 'border management', which now get the lion's share of funding. When border management is outsourced and off-shored, however,

> What we see ... is the full-scale suspension of presumed European norms and standards. Here, we are faced with what Nick-Vaughan Williams in his work on the 'generalized biopolitical border' identifies as the production of 'a global archipelago of zones of juridicopolitical indistinction' – 'off-shore' black holes where European norms, standards and regulations simply do not apply, legitimised through bi-lateral agreements declaredly aimed at combating readily recognisable 'evils' such as criminal networks and international terrorism. (Bialasiewicz 2012: 861)

The Italy–Libya Treaty constitutes precisely one such site where the complex border work of the EU is being enacted, a site that mediates materialities and non-materialities, legalities and illegalities, by informalizing and thickening the Mediterranean border.

The 2008 Italy–Libya Friendship Treaty

Signed by Qadhafi and Berlusconi in Benghazi, Libya, on 30 August 2008, the Treaty on Friendship, Partnership and Cooperation inhabits a paradoxical position between remembrance and silence. Most often, and not only by the Libyans, it has been officially presented as reparation for the abuses inflicted upon Libyans during Italian colonial rule. This was certainly how Qadhafi wanted the Treaty to be publicly represented, as his sporting of Al-Muktar's photograph shows. But Berlusconi too participated in this performance of reparation with a number of highly symbolic gestures: for example, he repatriated the Roman statue of the Venus of Cyrene, taken by Italian archaeologists in 1913, and is said, on the day of the agreement, to have bowed before Al-Muktar's son, expressing 'in the name of the Italian people, ... apologies for the deep wounds' caused to the Libyans (Di Caro 2008).

Yet the Treaty stipulates reparations for abuses that are never explicitly mentioned. Several commentators, including the most important historian of Italian colonialism, were quick to emphasize this aspect, namely the lack of history and memory (Del Boca, 2009). Following the preamble, the text of the Treaty consists of three parts: first, the general principles regulating the bilateral relationship; second, a part entitled 'Closure of the Chapter of the Past and of the Disputes', containing its most important provision (i.e. the modalities of the disbursement of the US$5 bn); and third, guidelines for future partnership, among which those concerning migration control are central.[2] The Treaty repeatedly alludes to Italian regret for past colonial abuses, and to settlement of colonial-era disputes, but only to declare them now settled and resolved. The words 'close' and 'closure' recur every time mention is made of the colonial past. The colonial past is always defined as 'the chapter of the past' or the 'painful chapter of the past', but there is no clue as to exactly what those 'sufferings' involved: they are cited only to declare that the Treaty will put an end to their legacy. Very similar language was used by both Berlusconi and Qadhafi to discuss the Treaty's relationship to the past, indeed its very 'creation of pastness' (see Trouillot 2000: 175). This suggests that those drafting the text chose the unusual phrase 'chapter of the past' (instead of, for example, 'crimes' or 'human rights violations of the past') specifically to imply its closure and to keep its meaning vague. While it is possible to end a chapter, it is more difficult to shut off a memory, particularly the legacy of colonial crimes.

While Italian school books barely mention this murderous past, historical research has revealed that at least one eighth of the Libyan population died as a direct result of the Italian occupation between 1911 and 1943 (Del Boca 2003). One policy had a particularly devastating effect on local life when the Fascist regime in the early 1930s sought to crush Umar Al-Muktar's grassroots rebellion by separating his troops from the supportive local population. Under this policy, almost all of Cyrenaica's inhabitants were interned in sixteen detention camps located in the coastal regions (Labanca 2005; Salerno 2005). Estimates vary, but it is believed that close to half of the 100,000 Bedouins imprisoned in the camps were killed or died of starvation. Today these camps are non-sites of memory, fields of unnamed graves and fenced areas covered by the desert dust, and have never been documented. Of the main Italian colonies in Africa, Eritrea, Somalia, and Ethiopia, it is rather the latter that is the object of academic study and that is remembered more widely, perhaps because of its centrality within Mussolini's imperial ideology and of the Italian brutality and the sheer quantity of Ethiopian human losses during what remained a short-lived invasion and occupation (Ethiopia was never compensated for such losses).

Paradoxically, the Italy–Libya Treaty announces the closure of a period of confrontation with this past that in fact never began. Italian colonial crimes in Libya have never been publicly narrated; they have never been the object of mainstream debate, let alone of national institutional projects such as historical commissions, museums, or memorials, or the revision of school textbooks. Apart from a handful of academics and journalists, most Italians are ignorant of this history. Even highly educated people believe that Italians were not bad colonialists, if indeed they were colonialists at all; they were and are *brava gente*, goodhearted people, to use a common Italian phrase (see Del Boca 2005; von Henneberg 2004). Most Italians ignore the existence of colonial prisons and know very little about Italian colonial crimes in general, in spite of the genocidal dimension of Italian colonial rule. In this context, the Treaty did not aim to stimulate any debate, nor did it produce any kind of knowledge about this past. At the time of Qadhafi's visit, the mainstream media commented on his extravagance, the realpolitik behind the accord, and, of course, the question of migration control. The paradox is that, in spite of their spectacular visibility – attached, as it were, to the public body of Qadhafi – history and memory slipped from the radar of global public opinion. The very indistinct and misleading language of the Treaty (referring to chapter or suffering as opposed to crime) de-materialized or, better, evacuated the utter materiality of dead Libyan bodies.

Reparations as international legal practice

The Treaty consists of two key elements of reparation politics: a formal apology and substantial material compensations. Yet as commentators have shown (Gazzini 2009), it represents a very peculiar form of reparation.

Reparations belong to a new subset of socio-legal practices through which contemporary politics deals publicly with the legacies of murderous pasts, and thereby promotes democracy and more peaceful international relations (Barkan 2007; Torpey 2006). They are part of the 'politics of regret' (Olick 2007) that has recently emerged as a new principle of political legitimation and identification in the wake of the Holocaust and the growth of the human rights discourse. Among the various practices of regret, reparations *strictu sensu* imply material, usually monetary compensation for past wrongs; often, however, the term stands for what John Torpey (2006: 49) calls 'reparation politics', which includes the promotion of a broad historical consciousness of past crimes so that they will never happen again. Thus, two crucial objectives of reparation politics are to shape public memory and guarantee non-repetition, encapsulated in the phrase 'learning the lessons of history'.

While there have been numerous critiques of the politics of regret, including many that see it as largely tokenistic, most scholars would agree with Melissa Nobles that these policies do at least stimulate public debate about difficult histories and 'play an important if underappreciated part in bringing certain views about history and moral obligation to bear in public life' (Nobles 2008: xi). In the case of the Italy–Libya Treaty, however, one finds very little public debate about colonial history. How can we make sense of the fact that, in spite of the spectacle of memory, history has actually been blocked, obscured, and rendered unintelligible rather than being brought into full view?

Scholars have suggested that some apologies represent cynical attempts to 'close the memory of an event' (Howard-Hassmann 2008: 5) and that their symbolic politics works in some cases as a 'diversion' to facilitate realpolitik (Nobles 2008: 151). Nevertheless, little attention has been paid to such 'cynical' apologies, which tend to be viewed as unfortunate exceptions. I contend, however, that looking at these can yield interesting insights into fundamental flaws in the politics of regret.

The Italy–Libya Treaty cannot be easily dismissed as 'just' a case of cynical apology since it represents the only successful instance of colonial reparations.[3] It is often said that modern politicians tend to be quick to apologize, yet this is rarely the case in the context of colonial reparations. To date, nearly all cases of compensations being paid between international actors have been related to the Second World War. Before the Italy–Libya Treaty, no formal apology or compensation had been offered by the government of a former colonial power.[4] While scholars attribute different weights to the legal difficulties of claiming colonial reparations (see Howard-Hassmann 2008; Sarkin 2009; Tan 2007),[5] there is a sense that the movement for African reparations is relatively weak and enjoys only partial backing from the governments in question (Howard-Hassmann 2008: 42ff.). The movement peaked with the 2001 UN World Conference against Racism, held in Durban, South Africa. The latter was overshadowed by the 11 September attacks and was further affected by a Western boycott following allegations of anti-Semitism, which also haunted the 2009 Durban Review Conference and the Durban anniversary in 2011.[6] However, according to Naomi Klein and the United Nations Human Rights Commissioner Navanethem Pillay, the problem was that the story told at Durban about the ongoing legacy of slavery and colonialism was a 'story with which Western governments have never been comfortable'

(Klein 2009: 56). The Durban NGO Forum claimed then that the failure to acknowledge and compensate for colonialism was both a symptom of racism and a trigger of further discrimination.

What is striking about the discourse justifying the refusal to offer colonial reparation is a temporal structure of excuse, which is reflected in the paradoxical way in which the Italy–Libya Treaty foreclosed a serious engagement with the past, before the latter had even begun. In 2005, Gordon Brown, then (Labour) Chancellor of the Exchequer of the UK, emphasized on a tour of Africa that 'we should move forward ... the days of Britain having to apologize for its colonial history are over' (Brogan 2005). But when were these days of obligatory apologies? Brown's rhetorical use of the past tense – suffusing colonial apologies with the temporality of the already done – obscures the fact that the British government has never really apologized for its colonial crimes. What is also striking is that Brown's remarks about the history of the British Empire resonate with the French conservative Nicolas Sarkozy's key African speech of 2007, in spite of the two men's differing political ideologies.[7] The latter emphasized the 'pastness' of the colonial era, drawing on a strain of right-wing nationalist discourse that despises repentance and so-called 'black armband views of history'. Again, the suggestion is that 'we' have already repented more than enough, yet no-one except for Italy has actually made atonement. The value of declaring the colonial past as buried forever, of course, conceals its deep connections to and enduring legacy in the present, allowing Europeans to forget about their responsibilities towards the plight of Europe's former colonies: that the migrants whom the Treaty is designed to shield off often come from Eritrea and Somalia, Italy's ex-colonies, is telling in this regard: it is the border's *longue durée* as Demetriou would have it (see Chapter 2).

The Treaty as border device

If not remembrance, then what is the Italy–Libya Treaty really about? Gazzini (2009) has suggested that 'the financial package that Italy and Libya agreed upon would ... be better understood as the expression of a nexus of interlocking interests: on the Libyan side, Qadhafi's historical commitment to reparation politics and his quest for moral victory over the country's former colonizers, and on the Italian side, strategic and economic gains.' More than a nexus of interlocking interests, I argue that the Treaty functions as a border device, regulating and filtering population and capital flows across the Mediterranean (see also De Cesari 2012). Critical border scholars such as Nicholas De Genova and Sandro Mezzadra and Brett Neilson have examined how new walls constitute regimes of exclusion and inclusion, or rather produce forms of 'differential inclusion' (Mezzadra and Neilson 2012; see also e.g. De Genova 2010, 2012) regulating people's mobilities conceptualized as differentiated 'flows'. While promoting Italian investment and economic involvement in Libya, and thus opening up the country to the 'flow' of transnational capital, the Treaty envisages a strong cooperation in a number of security areas, especially migration control.

The main provision of the Treaty concerns the disbursement of US$5 bn over twenty years for infrastructural projects, particularly the building of a highway along the Mediterranean coast.[8] These projects, however, are to be carried out by Italian companies, which will be tax-exempt, and funds will be managed by Italy. There are also a number of special initiatives intended to settle past disputes, including the construction of 200 housing units by Italian firms, scholarships for Libyan students, a rehabilitation programme for landmine victims, and the restitution of archaeological treasures stolen under colonialism. Concerning the specifics of the partnership between the two parties, the Treaty envisions collaborations in various areas (e.g. science, culture, energy, the economy, defence, and anti-terrorism). But the most important area is migration control, as evidenced by the fact that here the cooperation activities are clearly specified, and funding is already provided (Ronzitti 2009: 129). Article 19 of the Treaty provides for the implementation of a 2007 protocol establishing joint sea patrols, and in fact the transfer of three patrol boats to Libya was the first tangible outcome of the Treaty. Most importantly, this article mandates the creation of a control system for Libyan land borders (50 per cent funded by Italy and 50 per cent by the EU) to be run by Italian companies. This was envisioned as an electronic security barrier, including a 'remote "operations and monitoring centre" (presumably in Italy), on-the-ground mobile detection devices (such as truck-mounted radar and infrared scanners) but also blimp-like patrol drones' (Bialasiewicz 2012: 859).

The Treaty was suspended following the NATO campaign against Qadhafi; in spite of several attempts by the Italian government to talk to the new Libyan rulers and reactivate the Treaty, this had not yet happened at the time of writing, owing to the ongoing civil strife in the North African country. The Italian government is especially keen on reinstating the Treaty, and this not only so as to contain the flow of migrants and refugees fleeing a Middle East under fire. Even in its short lifespan, the Treaty proved indeed a blessing for Italian and Libyan capital, consolidating Italy's position as Libya's major trading partner. The US$5 bn promised in the Treaty will be taken from taxes paid by Italian oil companies operating in Libya, the largest of which is ENI. But although ENI will contribute the lion's share of the costs, the company also greatly profits from the Treaty; in 2008 it signed new gas and oil contracts to secure its already very strong position in Libya until 2047 (Gazzini 2009). If fully implemented, the Treaty will also bring huge benefits to Italian construction companies involved in the infrastructural projects, as well as to the many smaller Italian companies operating in Libya. Libyan capital does well out of this too, for the Treaty pushed Libyan investments in Italian companies, such as Italy's largest bank Unicredit and its oil and gas group giant ENI, but also other key state-controlled firms and iconic Italian brands, like the soccer club Juventus (Picardi 2011). For example, Libya became Unicredit's biggest shareholder in 2010, with an 8 per cent stake that was then reduced to below 5 per cent (and temporarily frozen) in 2012 in the aftermath of the Libyan revolution.

To sum up, the Treaty greatly facilitated capital flows while stemming the flow of migrants and refugees through the institutionalization of a multi-layered frontier dotted with zones of informality and exception to international law. Human Rights Watch's 2009 report on Italy's unlawful forced returns of boat migrants to Libya, which also involved Frontex, strongly criticizes the EU's outsourcing of its migration and asylum policy to a country with no asylum procedures (Libya is not a party to the 1951 UN Refugee Convention and allows the UN High Commissioner for Refugees only limited action) and a proven record of human rights violations. Concerning the Libyan detention centres, testimonies from several migrants in the Human Rights Watch report emphasize how the distinction between government-run and private prisons, between police and smugglers, is blurred, and in fact many of them consider smugglers and policemen to be working together. In February 2012, the European Court of Human Rights condemned Italy for violating the principle of non-refoulement under the Treaty and for the rendition of migrants to Libya without assessment of their needs for and entitlement to international protection. Border-control policies such as the push-backs are clearly not compatible with international law and the international protection of refugees. The European Court's sentence thus exposes how the Treaty, instead of preventing abuse and unlawful behaviour, in fact nurtured them under the guise of reconciliation (see also Amnesty International 2010). Reparation, a chief instrument of a new moral international law, was used here to produce exceptions to this very framework. By externalizing and thus informalizing border control – asylum procedures being externalized to a country without an asylum system in place – the Treaty helped to produce 'zones of juridico-political indistinction' (Vaughan-Williams in Bialasiewicz 2012: 861) where certain materialities are made possible, such as denying victims their accorded protection under international law (see also Andrijasevic 2010).

Evacuating the heritage of colonialism

What is the place of memory in bordering processes? The Treaty did not trigger any awareness-raising initiatives like memorials or the institution of remembrance days and truth commissions, as is usually the case with reparations; nor did it resonate in loud calls for other colonial reparations. The silence triggered by the Treaty was so deafening that not a single piece in the mainstream Italian and international press addressed its historical dimensions (e.g. facts and figures about colonial atrocities in Libya) beyond mere descriptive reporting, both at the time of the signing and during Qadhafi's attention-grabbing first visit to Italy. More progressive Italian newspapers, such as the authoritative centre-left *La Repubblica*, did write about the concentration camps and mentioned estimated numbers of victims, but no article attempted an in-depth discussion of what happened in colonial Libya.

At the time, coverage of the Treaty in *Il Giornale,* the main Italian newspaper owned by the supposedly repentant Berlusconi, provided telling evidence of the lack of memory. Barely concealing their racism towards the 'Bedouin' Qadhafi, articles and readers' letters displayed a general discontent with Berlusconi's action, which was seen as being in the Italian interest but probably at too high a cost (Cervi 2009). There was no sign of repentance whatsoever (with references to Umar Al-Muktar as 'our enemy'), and one could clearly detect the return of colonial and Fascist language, with descriptions of Libya as a 'box of sand' ('scatolone di sabbia') and Italy's 'fourth shore' ('quarta sponda'). The repetition is not only lexical but also discursive; *Giornale* articles actually reproduced both the colonial idea of the civilizing mission (Italy modernizing Libya) and the old adage that Italian colonialism, like Italian Fascism, was ultimately rather benign (Guerri 2008).[9] Such statements may come as no surprise to those acquainted with the ideology of Italian conservatism, but it is striking that similar ideas about colonialism and the Treaty have cropped up across the Italian political spectrum, including in prominent articles in the most prestigious and widely read Italian newspaper, *Il Corriere della Sera* (see e.g. Romano 2009).

In contrast to their silence regarding Libyan victims of colonialism, the Italian press devoted significant attention to the 20,000 Italian-Libyans expropriated and exiled by Qadhafi in the 1970s, who were mostly critical of the Treaty.[10] The number of these victims was actually cited much more often than the (uncertain but much larger) number of Libyans who died. Moreover, the fate of the thousands of Libyans deported to Italian penal colonies in 1911–12 was barely mentioned in the press (Labanca 2005: 30). Indeed, it is generally other victims' bodies that grab the public attention, being made material, for example, through the Lockerbie photographs provocatively pinned to the jackets of some Italian opposition MPs during Qadhafi's visit to parliament. While other bodies with their stories of suffering materialize in the public space produced by the Treaty, Libyan corpses are invisible except in the excessive corporeality of their leader.

Most opinion pieces in Italy and abroad emphasized how both leaders' 'excessive love for show' and vaudeville mixed 'history ... with farce' (e.g. Lerner 2009). Few in the international press took this parody of international relations seriously. Yet it did have serious implications, for it occluded the memorial dimension of this political process. It made memory fade under the weight of an eccentric dictator and a murky business transaction. It is telling in this regard that most opinion pieces that discussed the colonial past appeared immediately after the first signing of the Treaty, in August 2008, and not in June 2009 during Qadhafi's visit, even though it was the spectacle of the latter that received more media interest overall. A good example of this is provided in the *New York Times* article significantly entitled

'Qadhafi Pays a Business Call on Berlusconi', which discusses the 2009 visit. The introduction is straightforward:

> Italy came to terms with its colonial past on Wednesday in a somewhat surreal news conference with two of the world's most colorful politicians, Prime Minister Silvio Berlusconi and the Libyan leader, Col. Muammar el-Qaddafi. (Donadio, 2009)

Historical memory is belittled by the spectacle of the two leaders, whose 'colourfulness' dominates the scene. The Treaty is said to be 'nominally' about the past, being described as 'one of the least notable colonial histories in Europe'; again, no mention is made of the concentration camps, nor of the number of deaths recorded during the Italian occupation. The farce evacuates and once more de-materializes not only the painfulness but also the very reality of colonial crimes; it turns them into something 'somewhat surreal'.

No articles in the mainstream international press discussed possible repercussions in terms of initiating other reparation claims. An opinion piece in the *Süddeutsche Zeitung*, the largest German liberal paper, considers the Italian treaty a potential model for colonial reparation precisely because it is convenient to ex-colonial powers, making reparation not only morally but also financially expedient (Ulrich 2008). Even so, the article is talking about colonial reparations in general; it makes no mention of Germany's own situation vis-à-vis the Herero. This kind of reparation produces silence, but no closure. Yet was the Treaty just a lamentable exception to an overall positive norm of reparation and an opportunistic parody of reparation proper by two leaders not known for their inclination towards democracy and its aesthetics?

Border work revisited

So far, I have shown that the Italy–Libya Treaty and its spectacular *mise-en-scène* failed to engender any social memory of the colonial past, at least among the former colonizers, and instead led to systematic violations of human rights in the treatment of migrants. The Treaty facilitated the occurrence of abuses by legally mandating spaces of exception to international humanitarian law. Moreover, it arguably does the opposite of preventing the repetition of the repented crimes, particularly if we read the Treaty as a neo-colonial contract promoting the interests of transnational capital in alliance with corrupt national elites. The major objective of the politics of regret being precisely to deter outbreaks of inhumanity, the Treaty can thus be seen as the reverse of reparation. What we observe in this case is different from the democratization and moralization of international relations that Barkan (2002: ix) considers as the potential long-term effect of restitution. At the same time, the Treaty points to some basic tensions that characterize reparation at large. The first is that between the full recognition of the legacy of present pasts and the creation of 'pastness' underlying the politics of regret: in other words, the simultaneity of the imperative of closure and its very impossibility. The second concerns silences and erasures of the politics of regret.

Elsewhere (De Cesari 2012) I have argued that the Italy–Libya Treaty points at the ways in which the politics of regret and reparations tend to 'forget' and obscure colonialism while denying the victims of colonial violence their rightful recognition, just as international law and international morality create their own exceptions. The Treaty indeed inhabits an ambiguous temporal dimension, marked by the simultaneous presence and absence of the colonial past, or rather by what Ann Stoler (2011: 145) has defined as 'a presence and the misrecognition of it'. Stoler (2011) has recently argued for a rethinking of taken-for-granted ideas about social forgetting through the notion of 'colonial aphasia'. Discussing the role of the colonial past in contemporary France, she argues that we cannot describe France's relationship to colonialism simply in dualistic terms of ignorance vs. knowledge. Like Italy, and to an even greater extent, France now produces a great deal of scholarship on its colonial past, and intellectual debate abounds, yet colonialism is still largely absent from French school curricula. For Stoler, France's relationship to colonialism parallels the way in which aphasics relate to the world: colonialism cannot be articulated, nor properly spoken of. 'Aphasics are often "agrammatic", displaying difficulty comprehending "structural relationships"' (Stoler 2011: 145). Aphasia means that knowledge of the colonial past is not simply present or absent in the public sphere, but rather occluded, blocked, 'disabled and deadened to reflective life, shorn of the capacity to make connections' (Stoler 2011: 122) through a variety of different practices. The Italy–Libya Treaty is a good example of aphasia, and we can trace the disabling of knowledge identified by Stoler in both its deployment and its effects. It allows for disposable pasts to be inhabited half-heartedly, even cynically, and, most importantly, in a way that does obscure their potential to speak to the present: these are memories voided of their potential to provoke critical reflection.

I take Stoler's argument to speak to the politics of regret, specifically to regret's inability and unwillingness to fully engage the colonial past and to address the latter's relationship to contemporary migrations. The Treaty's ambiguous (dis) engagement with colonialism, coupled with its simultaneous creation of 'pastness', suggests that we have already dealt with the colonial past. In so doing, it resonates with the discourse invoked by Brown and Sarkozy, which holds that it is time to stop vilifying the West and apologizing for something – the post-colonial malaise – now fully in the hands of the formerly colonized. Indeed, the European political and intellectual mainstream seems to be able to speak of colonialism only in the remote past tense. Colonial aphasia convinces us that the past has been and gone, that it has finally been mastered. It also suggests, as Stoler emphasizes, that there is no connection between what happened back then and its contemporary legacies, be they transnational migration or the often-predatory alliances between post-colonial national elites.

Here, I would like to build on this argument to reflect on the relation between colonial aphasia and the kind of securitized 'border management' that the EU and member states such as Italy have come to perform. The fact that the Treaty enacts both forms of border work, both imaginative and material, is a case in point, directing our attention to the close entanglement between colonial past and migrant present. For Scott, 'the process of bordering can be defined as the everyday construction of borders, for example through political discourses and institutions, media representations, school textbooks, stereotypes and everyday forms of transnationalism' (2012: 84). Europe's borders are made and remade through multiple representations and practices of the imagination, including the making and unmaking of memory in unlikely sites like the Treaty. By creating 'pastness' (Trouillot 2000), the Treaty discursively consigned Italian colonialism – now officially repaired – to the bygone past; it did away with colonialism's responsibilities and present legacies. Its spectacle, moreover, did not only obscure a history of deep connections and ties stretching across the Mediterranean but also reinforced the very idea of a civilizational divide running through this 'solid sea'.[11] The media represented the event by telescoping on Qadhafi's body and his obscene non-Europeanness in his attire and demeanour, by focusing their attention on his disregard for democratic values, his mockery of gender equality, or his flamboyant clothing. The paradox is that the image of Europe as beacon and defender of human rights was being reproduced and reinforced just as one of its members was violating them by means of international law. It is largely through such discursive sites – through such non-sites of memory – that European borders materialize in the apparent solidity of a homogeneous, closed Europeanness which certainly does not include 'neighbours' and 'friends'. The fact that such an imagined Europeanness clashes against normative ideals of post-national and open, border-transcending identities has been noted by critical border scholars and especially by the many NGOs and migrant organizations working to protect the rights and lives of those attempting to cross the Mediterranean in search precisely of such a European dream or attracted to the promise of welfare and democracy. Such imagined Europeanness possesses its own deadly materiality. For Didier Bigo (2015: 86),

> paradoxically, the EU becomes an entity not at the borders of its member states but at the moment it is identified with the 'common' southern liquid border of the Mediterranean Sea. It works as a limes, as an orientalist narrative differentiating 'us' from 'others', either because the Mediterranean Sea is constructed as 'dividing' civilizations or because the Mediterranean Sea is a link between the two sides, a link between rich and poor, a way for Europe to be more than Europe and to have a specific role to play in Africa and North Africa.

It is such imagined Europeanness that must be considered as one element of a heterogeneous border assemblage made up of memories as well as border patrols and detention camps, material and immaterial at the same time, stretching across multiple frontiers.

Ongoing

'The Mediterranean is not Italy's sea but the border to Europe, or rather the heart of Europe ... It is not possible in 2014 to allow a boat full of children to sink.'[12]

These are some of the arguments used by Italy's prime minister Matteo Renzi's in July 2014 when asking for EU and international collaboration in facing the humanitarian catastrophe and huge number of refugees escaping civil wars in Libya, Syria, and Iraq – in a week during which 125 refugees had died attempting to cross the Mediterranean. Renzi's apparent slip of the tongue – the Mediterranean being the border rather than the heart of Europe – is significant in several respects. Italy had indeed changed course, at least apparently, after Qadhafi's fall and the ensuing panic over 'migration tsunamis' and 'invasions' provoked by crisis of the externalized mode of border management that I have described in the previous pages.

On 3 October 2013 a boat had sunk a few miles off the coast of Lampedusa, resulting in the death of 366 persons, with 20 more missing; a few days later in another similar tragedy 34 people died, including 10 children. The single largest Mediterranean maritime tragedy in recent years was widely mediatized, and caused an apparent shift in Italian policy: authorities launched Mare Nostrum, a search-and-rescue operation carried out by the Italian military in 2013–14. The irony is that Mussolini and the Fascist propaganda used this concept of 'Mare Nostrum' – 'our sea', or a Latin name for the Mediterranean – to signify the necessity of the creation of an Italian colonial empire across the Mediterranean in the guise of a renewed Roman empire. In spite of this Fascist resonance, Mare Nostrum had managed to save at least some lives in a year, 2014, that saw an unprecedented number of people making the Mediterranean crossing: according to the United Nations High Commissioner for Refugees, more than 207,000 people had attempted the crossing as of early December, a number against which the previous known high of approximately 70,000 people in 2011, at the beginning of the Arab Uprisings, pales; still a hecatomb of over 3,400 people had died up to then that year.[13] Now almost 50 per cent of those who cross are refugees, largely from Syria and Eritrea (for the blurring of the distinction between economic migrant and asylum seeker, see e.g. Mezzadra 2015). No reception plan has been prepared by the EU.

Italy had asked the EU for help to face such emergency, so that the EU could take over some of its function; the response of the EU, however, was Triton, a border security operation coordinated by Frontex, which replaced Mare Nostrum in November 2014. Triton has a different, non-humanitarian mandate, a limited budget, much lower than that of Mare Nostrum (€2.9 m instead of €9 m per month), and a limited scope in terms of the area its vessels patrol. For example, Triton's vessels will not venture into Libyan territorial waters, where most 'accidents' are known to occur. At the time of writing, Mare Nostrum is continuing, albeit in a reduced and unofficial form, with Italian vessels doing some patrols; the populist Italian right wing and xenophobic parties had carried out an ultimately successful campaign against the government 'abetment of illegal immigration' and against the ensuing alleged invasion of immigrants bringing diseases and eating up key public monies in a time of austerity. On the opposite side of the Italian political spectrum, several NGOs, including Amnesty International and Médecins sans Frontières, have protested against the end of Mare Nostrum, fearing the loss of many further lives: for them, 'closing Mare Nostrum now means saying on behalf of Europe that, despite all the conventions we have signed, all the principles out of which Europe was founded and born, we are closing our eyes' (Davies and Neslen 2014). For commentators, this shift in policy from Mare Nostrum to Triton 'seems a return to the old ideas: use all means to prevent migrants and asylum seekers from coming to Europe, make immigration difficult if not impossible, and eventually criminalize it' (Liberti 2014). From this perspective, and from the perspective of activists and research networks like MIGREUROP, such policy change by Italy and the EU – from humanitarianism back to security while the Libyan and Syrian civil wars are unfolding – represents a further step in the informalization of border management and the retraction or suspension of the asylum right: refugees and asylum seekers are simply left to die, as happened in the infamous case of the 'left-to-die boat', when a boat carrying seventy-three people was left drifting for two weeks within the NATO maritime surveillance area at the time of the organization's Libya campaign in 2011 (see Dijstelbloem 2015).[14]

Critical border scholars, on the other hand, have accused Mare Nostrum of mixing humanitarian with military logics.[15] For Didier Bigo (2015), Mare Nostrum is the 'archetype of this (false) alternative narrative organized around "protection", which is nevertheless embedded into the idea of deterrence and technology' – which seems to be no alternative at all: in other words, border management through technology, in its progressive immaterialization, cannot but contemplate death as a 'male minore' (Weizman 2011), the least of all calculated evils.[16] In this border optics, some bodies are not recognized as grievable (see Butler 2009); therefore they are expendable as 'male minore'. Many of them are European and even Italian former colonial subjects. There are several activists and activist groups, like Fortress Europe, who work precisely to name, individualize, and remember the lives lost in the Mediterranean, a way to make them grievable, to recuperate them to everyday affective taxonomies.[17] No project to officially memorialize them has thus far been realized.

Notes

This chapter is based on and reworks a previous article of mine published in *Memory Studies*, 5(3), July 2012, by SAGE Publications Ltd, http://journals.sagepub.com/doi/full/10.1177/1750698012443888.

1 https://www.detective.io/detective/the-migrants-files/ (last accessed 20 December 2014).

2 For the text of the treaty, see Law no. 7 of 6 February 2009 (*Gazzetta Ufficiale* 2009).

3 Forms of reparations have been provided only in cases of settler colonialism, that is, by national governments in favour of their indigenous populations e.g. in Canada, New Zealand, and the USA (Nobles 2008). Between 2008 and 2009, both Houses of the US Congress issued resolutions apologizing to African-Americans for their suffering under slavery and Jim Crow laws: yet the Senate's resolution clearly specifies that it does not support any reparation claims against the US government.

4 In 2004 the German Minister for Economic Cooperation and Development, Heidemarie Wieczorek-Zeul, apologized for the genocidal suppression of the Herero during their revolt against German colonialism between 1904 and 1908. However, Germany has never paid compensations to the Herero and has only increased development aid to Namibia – aid implying no recognition of wrongdoing and thus no moral obligation as distinct from 'patronising charity' (Correa 2009: 293). The Namibian government itself seems to prefer to receive aid for the entire population instead of reparations for a small ethnic group. Unlike Germany, Belgium has apologized and paid some compensation to one of its former colonies, the Congo, though only for its involvement in the assassination of the former president Patrice Lumumba in the 1960s.

5 Legal arguments against reparations for slavery, colonialism, and neo-colonialism emphasize problems of transgenerational justice, statutes of limitations, and collective responsibility for past actions, that is, the problem of identifying today's descendants/representatives of both victims and perpetrators (Howard-Hassmann, 2008). However, as discussed by Anthony Gifford (2000), there are cases of successful reparation claims being advanced both by the descendants of the victims of colonial crimes, e.g. in New Zealand, and by the nation-state that had to bear the consequences of a past wrong, as in the case of Israel. Another argument against colonial reparations stresses that the law does not mandate retroactive reparations for acts and behaviours that were not illegal at their time of occurrence. However, the notion of 'crimes against humanity' was applied retroactively in the case of the Nuremberg Tribunal, and international lawyers have argued that the Tribunal did not make new law but developed concepts of international criminality that had become accepted over time (Gifford 2000). Moreover, Jeremy Sarkin (2009) insists in relation to the Herero that genocide was already illegal under late nineteenth-century customary international law.

6 However, the final Durban Declaration became the first document with international legal standing to condemn slavery as a crime against humanity (see www.un.org/WCAR/durban.pdf, last accessed 16 May 2018).

7 For the text of Sarkozy's 2007 speech, see www.africaresource.com/index.php?option=com_content&view=article&id=437%3Athe-unofficial-english-translation-of-sarkozys-speech&catid=36%3Aessays-a-discussions&Itemid=346 (last accessed 16 May 2018).

8 For the text of the Treaty, see Law no. 7 of 6 February 2009 (*Gazzetta Ufficiale* 2009).

9 For a critique of the idea of benign Italian Fascism and colonialism, see Ahmida 2005; Del Boca 2005.

10 For example, *Il Corriere della Sera*, among other papers, included a number of interviews with exiled Italian-Libyans (see e.g. Laffranchi 2008).

11   See Multiplicity's *Solid Sea 01: The Ghost Ship*, exhibited at Documenta, Kassel, in 2002, www.radicate.eu/maddalena-bregani/ (last accessed 22 May 2018).

12   http://www.unhcr.org/cgi-bin/texis/vtx/refdaily?pass=463ef21123&id=53ba3e2a8 (last accessed 10 December 2014).

13   See www.unhcr.org/5486e6b56.html (last accessed 10 December 2014).

14   See www.forensic-architecture.org/case/left-die-boat (last accessed 30 November 2014).

15   See http://www.meltingpot.org/Quest-Europa-si-fonda-sui-confini-Intervista-a-Sandro. html#.VI-G5yd1PhC (last accessed 12 December 2014).

16   The British government supported its refusal to back search-and-rescue operations with a similar argument, namely that such operations create an 'unintended "pull factor"' for migrants and that Mare Nostrum encouraged more migrants to attempt the crossing into Europe by making it more secure (Travis 2014).

17   See http://fortressEurope.blogspot.it/ (last accessed 12 December 2014).

References

Agnew, J. (2005). 'Bounding the European Project'. *Geopolitics*, 10: 575–9.

Ahmida, A. A. (2005). 'Italian Fascism – Benign? Collective Amnesia Concerning Colonial Libya'. In *Forgotten Voices*, 35–54. New York: Routledge.

Amnesty International (2010). *Libya/Italy: Bilateral Cooperation Should Not Be at the Price of Human Rights*. Public statement, 27 August, www.amnesty.org/en/library/info/ MDE19/017/2010/en (last accessed 3 June 2011).

Andrijasevic, Rutvica (2010). 'From Exception to Excess: Detention and Deportations across the Mediterranean Space'. In Nicholas De Genova and Nathalie Peutz (eds), *The Deportation Regime: Sovereignty, Space, and the Freedom of Movement*, 147–65. Durham, NC: Duke University Press.

Barkan, E. (2002). *The Guilt of Nations: Restitution and Negotiating Historical Injustices*. New York: Norton.

Barkan, E. (2007). 'Introduction: Reparation: A Moral and Political Dilemma'. In J. Miller and R. Kumar (eds), *Reparations: Interdisciplinary Inquiries*, 1–19. Oxford: Oxford University Press.

Bialasiewicz, Luiza (ed.) (2011). *Europe in the World: EU Geopolitics and the Making of European Space*. Aldershot: Ashgate.

Bialasiewicz, Luiza (2012). 'Off-Shoring and Out-Sourcing the Borders of Europe: Libya and EU Border-Work in the Mediterranean'. *Geopolitics*, 17(4): 843–66.

Bigo, Didier (2015). 'Death in the Mediterranean Sea: The Results of the Three Fields of Action of European Union Border Controls'. In Yolande Jansen, Robin Celikates, and Joost de Bloois (eds), *The Irregularization of Migration in Contemporary Europe*, 55–70. London: Rowman & Littlefield.

Bigo, Didier, and Elspeth Guild (2005). 'Policing at a Distance: Schengen Visa Policies'. In Didier Bigo and Elspeth Guild (eds), *Controlling Frontiers: Free Movement into and within Europe*, 233–63. London: Ashgate.

Boedeltje, F., and H. Van Houtum (2008). 'The Abduction of Europe: A Plea for Less Unionism and More Europe'. *Tijdschrift voor Economische en Sociale Geografie*, 99(3): 361–5.

Brogan, B. (2005). 'It's Time to Celebrate the Empire, Says Brown'. *Daily Mail*, 15 January, www.dailymail.co.uk/news/article-334208/Its-time-celebrate-Empire-says-Brown. html#ixzz1OylFyfk0 (last accessed 7 June 2011).

Brown, Wendy (2010). *Walled States, Waning Sovereignty*. New York: Zone Books.

Butler, Judith (2009). *Frames of War: When is Life Grievable?* London: Verso.

Cervi, M. (2009). 'Ma quella foto la poteva evitare'. *Il Giornale*, 11 June, 1.

Correa, C. (2009). Review of J. Miller and R. Kumar (eds), *Reparations: Interdisciplinary Inquiries*, and R. E. Howard-Hassmann, *Reparations to Africa*, *International Journal of Transitional Justice*, 3: 284–93.

Davies, Lizzy, and Arthur Neslen (2014). 'Italy: End of Ongoing Sea Rescue Mission "Puts Thousands at Risk"'. *The Guardian*, 31 October, https://www.theguardian.com/world/2014/oct/31/italy-sea-mission-thousands-risk (last accessed 22 May 2018).

De Cesari, Chiara (2012). 'The Paradoxes of Colonial Reparation: Foreclosing Memory and the 2008 Italy–Libya Friendship Treaty'. *Memory Studies*, 5(3): 316–26.

De Genova, N. (2010). 'The Deportation Regime: Sovereignty, Space, and the Freedom of Movement'. In Nicholas De Genova and Nathalie Peutz (eds), *The Deportation Regime: Sovereignty, Space, and the Freedom of Movement*, 33–65. Durham, NC: Duke University Press.

De Genova, N. (2012). 'Border, Scene and Obscene'. In Thomas M. Wilson and Hastings Donnan (eds), *A Companion to Border Studies*, 492–504. Oxford: Wiley-Blackwell.

Del Boca, A. (2003). 'The Myths, Suppressions, Denials and Defaults of Italian Colonialism'. In P. Palumbo (ed.), *A Place in the Sun: Africa in Italian Colonial Culture from Post-Unification to the Present*, 17–36. Berkeley: University of California Press.

Del Boca, A. (2005). *Italiani, brava gente?* Vicenza: Neri Pozza.

Del Boca, A. (2009). 'Solo soldi, la memoria non c'entra sui massacri nemmeno una parola'. *La Repubblica*, 3 March, 10.

Di Caro, P. (2008). 'Berlusconi, patto con Gheddafi "Ora meno clandestini e più gas"'. *Il Corriere della Sera*, 31 August, 2.

Dijstelbloem, Huub (2015). 'Mediating the Mediterranean: Surveillance and Countersurveillance at the Southern Borders of Europe'. In Yolande Jansen, Robin Celikates, and Joost de Bloois (eds), *The Irregularization of Migration in Contemporary Europe*, 103–20. London: Rowman & Littlefield.

Donadio, R. (2009). 'Qaddafi Pays a Business Call on Berlusconi'. *New York Times*, 11 June, A6.

European Commission (2005). *Report on the Technical Mission to Libya on Illegal Immigration 27 November – 6 December 2004*. Brussels, www.statewatch.org/news/2005/may/eu-report-libya-ill-imm.pdf *(last accessed 19 January 2012)*.

Gazzetta Ufficiale (2009). 'Ratifica ed esecuzione del Trattato di amicizia, partenariato e cooperazione tra la Repubblica italiana e la Grande Giamahiria araba libica popolare socialista, fatto a Bengasi il 30 agosto 2008'. *Gazzetta Ufficiale*, 40 (18 February), www. parlamento.it/parlam/leggi/09007l.htm (last accessed 16 May 2018).

Gazzini, C. (2009). *Assessing Italy's Grande Gesto to Libya*. Middle East Report Online, 16 March, www.merip.org/mero/mero031609 (last accessed 17 May 2018).

Gifford., A. (2000). 'The Legal Basis of the Claim for Slavery Reparations'. *Human Rights Magazine*, spring, www.americanbar.org/publications/human_rights_magazine_home/irr_hr_spring00humanrights_gifford.html (last accessed 14 November 2011).

Gramaglia, G., and L. Garofalo (2011). *Complici.* Rome: Editori Riuniti.

Guerri, G. B. (2008). 'Un secolo di amore e odio'. *Il Giornale*, 30 August, 6.

Howard-Hassmann, R. (2008). *Reparations to Africa.* Philadelphia: University of Pennsylvania Press.

Human Rights Watch (2009). *Pushed Back, Pushed Around: Italy's Forced Return of Boat Migrants and Asylum Seekers, Libya's Mistreatment of Migrants and Asylum Seekers.* Report, 21 September, www.hrw.org/en/reports/2009/09/21/pushed-back-pushed-around-0 (last accessed 7 June 2011).

Jansen, Yolande, Robin Celikates, and Joost de Bloois (2015a). 'Introduction'. In Yolande Jansen, Robin Celikates, and Joost de Bloois (eds), *The Irregularization of Migration in Contemporary Europe.* London: Rowman & Littlefield.

Jansen, Yolande, Robin Celikates, and Joost de Bloois (eds) (2015b). *The Irregularization of Migration in Contemporary Europe.* London: Rowman & Littlefield.

Klein, N. (2009). 'Minority Death Match: Jews, Blacks, and the "Post-Racial" Presidency'. *Harper's Magazine*, September, www.zcommunications.org/minority-death-match-jews-blacks-and-the-post-racial-presidency-by-naomi-klein (last accessed 14 November 2011).

Klepp, S. (2010). 'Italy and its Libyan Cooperation Program: Pioneer of the European Union's Refugee Policy?' In Jean-Pierre Cassarino (ed.), *Unbalanced Reciprocities: Cooperation on Readmission in the Euro-Mediterranean Area*, 77–93. Washington, DC: Middle East Institute.

Labanca, N. (2005), 'Italian Colonial Internment'. In R. Ben-Ghiat and M. Fuller (eds), *Italian Colonialism*, 27–36. New York: Palgrave Macmillan.

Laffranchi, A. (2008). 'Zard, scappato da Tripoli: di sinistra, ma bravo Silvio'. *Il Corriere della Sera*, 31 August, 3.

Lerner, G. (2009). 'Vacanze romane tra show e farsa'. *La Repubblica*, 13 June, 1.

Liberti, Stefano (2014). 'Whose Europe?' *Le Monde diplomatique*, English edn, December, http://mondediplo.com/2014/12/08migrations (last accessed 20 December 2014).

Mezzadra, S. (2015). 'The Proliferation of Borders and the Right to Escape'. In Yolande Jansen, Robin Celikates, and Joost de Bloois (eds), *The Irregularization of Migration in Contemporary Europe*, 121–36 London: Rowman & Littlefield.

Mezzadra, Sandro, and Brett Neilson (2012). 'Borderscapes of Differential Inclusion: Subjectivity and Struggles on the Threshold of Justice's Excess'. In Étienne Balibar, Sandro Mezzadra, and Ranabir Samaddar (eds), *The Borders of Justice*, 181–203. Philadelphia: Temple University Press.

Mezzadra, Sandro, and Brett Neilson (2013). *Border as Method, or, the Multiplication of Labor.* Durham, NC: Duke University Press.

Nobles, M. (2008). *The Politics of Official Apologies.* Cambridge: Cambridge University Press.

Olick, J. (2007). 'The Politics of Regret: Analytical Frames'. In *The Politics of Regret*, 121–38. New York: Routledge.

Picardi, Marco Thomas (2011). 'What's at Stake for Italy in Libya'. *Limes Online*, 3 March, www.limesonline.com/en/whats-at-stake-for-italy-in-libya (last accessed 17 May 2018).

Romano, S. (2009). 'Le verita' dimenticate'. *Il Corriere della Sera*, 12 June, 1.

Ronzitti, N. (2009). 'The Treaty on Friendship, Partnership and Cooperation between Italy and Libya: New Prospects for Cooperation in the Mediterranean?' *Bulletin of Italian Politics*, 1(1): 125–33.

Salerno, E. (2005). *Genocidio in Libia: le atrocità nascoste dell'avventura coloniale italiana (1911–1931)*. Roma: Manifestolibri.

Sarkin, J. (2009). *Colonial Genocide and Reparations Claims in the 21st Century*. Westport, CT: Praeger Security International.

Scott, James W. (2012). 'European Politics of Borders, Border Symbolism and Cross-Border Cooperation'. In Thomas M. Wilson and Hastings Donnan (eds), *A Companion to Border Studies*, 83–99. Oxford: Wiley-Blackwell.

Scott, James Wesley, and Henk Van Houtum (2009). 'Reflections on EU Territoriality and the "Bordering" of Europe'. *Political Geography*, 28: 271–3.

Shore, Cris (2000). *Building Europe*. London: Routledge.

Shore, Cris (2006). '"In uno plures" (?): EU Cultural Policy and the Governance of Europe'. *Cultural Analysis*, 5: 7–26.

Stoler, A. (2011). Colonial Aphasia: Race and Disabled Histories in France'. *Public Culture*, 23(1): 121–56.

Tan, K. C. (2007). 'Colonialism, Reparations, and Global Justice'. In J. Miller and R. Kumar (eds), *Reparations: Interdisciplinary Inquiries*, 280–306. Oxford: Oxford University Press.

Torpey, J. (2006). *Making Whole What has been Smashed*. Cambridge, MA: Harvard University Press.

Travis, Alan (2014). 'UK Axes Support for Mediterranean Migrant Rescue Operation'. *The Guardian*, 27 October, www.theguardian.com/politics/2014/oct/27/uk-mediterranean-migrant-rescue-plan (last accessed 16 May 2018).

Trouillot, M.-R. (2000). 'Abortive Rituals: Historical Apologies in the Global Era'. *Interventions: International Journal of Postcolonial Studies*, 2(2): 171–86.

Ulrich, S. (2008). 'Das Zeichen der Venus: Ein Vorbild für andere Staaten. Die historische Aussöhnung von Libyen und Italien'. *Süddeutsche Zeitung*, 1 September, 4.

Van Houtum, Henk (2012). 'Remapping Borders'. In Thomas M. Wilson and Hastings Donnan (eds), *A Companion to Border Studies*, 405–18. Oxford: Wiley-Blackwell.

Van Houtum, Henk, and Freerk Boedeltje (2009). 'Europe's Shame: Death at the Borders of the EU'. *Antipode*, 41(2): 226–30.

Von Henneberg, K. C. (2004). 'Monuments, Public Space, and the Memory of Empire in Modern Italy'. *History & Memory*, 16(1): 37–85.

Weizman, Eyal (2011). *The Least of all Possible Evils: Humanitarian Violence from Arendt to Gaza*. London: Verso.

Ontologies of borders:
the difference of Deleuze and Derrida

Tuija Pulkkinen

This chapter is about the concept of border. I will not approach border as if I was going to conceptualize something that we already empirically know about, and nor will I concentrate solely on geographical and political borders. Instead, I will take a step back and consider border in an abstract sense: as a separation of one into two dissimilar entities. This means that I will take the study of border into the area of philosophy and, in particular, into problems of ontology and, further, into problematizing ontology.

The ontological issue of concern here is the philosophical problem of identity and difference, in the sense of one-and-the-same-ness of a thing and distinguishing it from that which is not the same – that is, the problem of individuating entities one from another (see also Demetriou, Chapter 2 above). Individuating is thus ultimately an ontological border issue par excellence. Furthermore, in similar fashion, every classification constitutes an epistemological border issue.

Matter and materiality, which are the main themes of this edited collection, are at the heart of many such ontological discussions. In ontology, matter and materiality are often connected to classical notions of substance or essence, which points to the fact that the question (of matter and materiality) is posed as a question of being. In contrast, instead of looking at 'matter' or 'materiality' as basic ontological issues of substance or essence, I will consider 'processes of materialization'. In other words, along the lines of viewing the border as process (Demetriou and Dimova, Chapter 1 above; Green, Chapter 5 below) my suggestion is to philosophize in terms of becoming and doing rather than in terms of being.

I will consider Gilles Deleuze and Jacques Derrida as two contemporary philosophers who both philosophize border and difference in terms of becoming and doing rather than being. While both problematize approaching the question of identity and difference as a question of being, I argue that they do it in very different ways, and it is this difference that I will explore here. Ultimately, I will argue that the Deleuzian 'becoming' remains closer to traditionally ontological concerns of being than does Derridean thinking in terms of processes of *différance*. Since both

Derrida and Deleuze are very complicated thinkers, I will naturally examine their thought very partially (in both senses of the term), and as an invitation to provoke discussion rather than to conclude it.

In this chapter, I am particularly interested in what borders do, as are most of the authors of this volume. Here, I will focus on the productivity of borders. The most interesting issue that inspires me is that every drawing of a borderline, where previously there was none, produces not only distinction but also new identities of those entities that are differentiated. This is why, as an ontological issue, thinking of what borders do is connected to the issue of individuating. This is also the area of thought which in my view constitutes a difference between Derridean and Deleuzian approaches.

Most classical philosophers have been occupied with the issue of border in the sense of either individuating or classification. For example, Aristotle's system of categories, species, genus and *differentia specifica* is meant to individuate and tackle the questions of what is the same and what is different. Ultimately this is also true of Plato's idea of 'idea' as capturing the essence of a thing. Most philosophers until the time of Leibniz thought of the problem of the same and the different in terms of essences of things: different things have different essences. In contrast, Leibniz provided the definition of identity as identity of indiscernibles, turning attention to qualities instead of essences. In his terms two things that have exactly the same qualities are the same and not different.

Many theological thinkers, or alternatively materialist thinkers, including Spinoza, have philosophized in terms of everything being ultimately ontologically the same: all being is of one and the same substance. Hegel, also a substance thinker, was simultaneously intensely occupied by differences. For him, substance is thought which continuously moves from one thing, and its sameness and identity, into what is not it through negation. This differentiation is the motor that drives the process of thought as the substance-subject.[1]

The modern phenomenological tradition that starts from Husserl deals with the problem of the same and the different through how different things appear, or are given, to transcendentally conceived consciousness. The modern analytical tradition is also occupied by a number of ontological discussions involving issues such as whether there are 'natural kinds' of things. There is no single direction in which the philosophical scholarship would have 'advanced' in this profound speculation, and several strains of thought are simultaneously present.

The works of Jacques Derrida and Gilles Deleuze are part of the long tradition of philosophical texts preoccupied with the quest for differentiating one thing from another in a very abstract sense. However, in this chapter I will not be primarily concerned with Derrida and Deleuze in terms of this philosophical debate *per se*. Instead I will discuss the differences between their philosophical approaches through two particular concrete cases of processes of differentiation, neither of which they themselves have considered in their work.

All classical philosophical considerations are formed with the ambition of being valid at any time and in any place, since philosophy as a discipline has a strong tradition of abstracting and attempting to reach independence from historical contexts. Derrida has called this continuous present the 'omnitemporality' of philosophy, and his own work constitutes a certain challenge to this strong philosophical tradition. The fact that I draw from two historical cases within this chapter points towards Derrida's move in the tradition of philosophy, and is simultaneously a contribution to the idea, in this volume, of looking at processes of materialization rather than at the ontologies of being in effort to understand border. My two examples are drawn from specific concrete spatial-temporal contexts, and they are related to well-studied historical processes and events. One of them is an episode concerning a geopolitical border productive of a nation and in multiple meanings of national identity. The other one is a classification in the realm of scientific knowledge, productive of serious effects on a great number of individuals' lives.

The first example of a process of materialization through a border is situated in the context of Europe after the Napoleonic wars, in 1809, when new geopolitical borders were drawn across the map of Europe. Part of this process at the north-eastern corner of the map was the drawing of a new border which concerned the area now known as Finland. Having been a part of the Kingdom of Sweden for centuries, the area was now incorporated into the Russian Empire. At the time, this was not felt as a huge event in the lives of most people living there: the aristocrats shifted their loyalty from one court to another fairly easily, and the Finnish-speaking peasants did not understand Swedish any better than Russian. The intellectual life of the educated people in the country went on in Latin and their social life in Swedish, as before. Nevertheless, many historians argue that the separation of the area into something distinct from the rest of Sweden, of which it had been a part for 700 years, was productive of a difference that later became the identity of the nation of Finland.[2] Similarly, the new border was also productive of a new identity of Sweden, which, from this time onwards, was more securely on its way towards appearing as a nation instead of the empire it had been.

The production of Finnish identity was an effect of many elements: the Herderian ideas of language and custom as constituting a people, and the political ideas of people having the right to self-government. However, one can argue that had the Swedish-speaking cultural elite of the region not been provided with the space for cultural and political self-reflection by the new border which created the difference, and at a time when so much else contributed to the likelihood of a process of identity construction, it might not have taken place.

The second border case is one of classification within the field of knowledge, and is well known: I am referring to the history of the nineteenth-century science of sexuality, *Sexualwissenschaft*, which introduced categories of different sexualities. The identity of homosexuality as a single thing was produced by drawing a classificatory border between homosexual sexuality and regular sexuality. The identity of heterosexuality was thereby also implied, and with it, as Foucault (1978) has pointed out, the identity of sexuality itself. In addition to this epistemic classificatory border-line, again, other elements also contributed to the reality that the identity 'homosexuality' holds in the Western world, not only in the realm of knowledge but also in culture, politics, and life in general. But again, many argue that had the border (the epistemic distinction) between homosexuality and heterosexuality not been drawn at that time, the homosexuals might not be there, just as Finns might not be there.

Now, from an ontological point of view, the interesting question in both cases is whether there is a difference to begin with without any borderline being drawn, or whether it was the border that was productive of the difference and the identity concerned. The Finns were different from the Swedes to begin with: they spoke a different language, many would say; in the past, some also referred to the notion of race in marking this difference. Others might argue that the Häme people, the Karelian people, and the western Finns were different in many ways, including their speech, before Finnish was made into one language. These different forms of speech could have evolved in different directions, and could have had different histories.[3] Similarly, there are those who insist that on the level of corporeal experience homosexuality has always existed, and that the classification just made that explicit, whereas others maintain that other categorizations could have been produced just as well, and that in that case, perhaps, those distinctions would have directed life in the queer continuity of sexuality into unknown directions.

It is at this juncture of thinking of borders as creating identities such as Finns or homosexuals in distinction to not Finns and not homosexuals that I invoke Derrida and Deleuze as thinkers of identity and difference, and as pursuing different kinds of ontological attachments. I will be very general and sketchy, and textually I will limit myself primarily to Deleuze's book *Difference and Repetition* (1994) and Derrida's article 'Différance' (1982).

Deleuze and Derrida on identity and difference

Deleuze's major topic in *Difference and Repetition* is the philosophical problem of individuating. He draws on Aristotle, Duns Scotus, Leibniz, Kant, and Spinoza, and primarily opposes Hegel in thinking of sameness and difference. Deleuze develops an ontology of 'pure difference' which avoids identities and negation. Instead of the sameness of particular things, there are one multitude and endless becoming in small variations (repetition), and instead of difference in between things (individuated things) there is difference in itself.

Derrida, in his signature article 'Différance', takes issue with the Saussurian structuralist system of signs in which one identity is a negation of another. By replacing the Saussurian difference with *différance* written with an 'a', he emphasizes, among other things, the sense of 'activity', of 'movement' and 'productivity', instead of the static difference that is typical of structuralism. As he says himself: '*Différance* is the "productive" movement of differences, the "history", if that can still be said, of constituted difference, of constituted langue, of (al)ready made *langue*.'[4]

Another point that Derrida makes here (and elsewhere) is that meaning can never be contained in a sign, for it spills over, it takes detours and is deferred: the distinction between one and the same and the different cannot be drawn as a clear line. A more ontological point he makes is about the metaphysics of presence in meaning. His position is against ontology of both substance and subject, and this anti-ontological gesture is something which I see as being always active in Derrida's work.[5]

In these texts, it would seem that both Derrida and Deleuze share the ambition of attempting to find a way to describe difference that is less than a contradiction or negation.[6] Many interpreters, for example Patton and Protevi (2003: 3–4), as well as Descombes (1979), have emphasized the convergence of the two thinkers in developing a non-Hegelian and anti-identitarian philosophical approach. However, I would see a much more profound distinction between the two, and that is in their respective ontological approaches carried through within the discussion on difference.

It is clear, and has been pointed out by many scholars, that Derrida draws more positively from the Hegelian heritage than does Deleuze, and this already establishes a clear distinction between the two. However, the main difference in approach which I see between Deleuze and Derrida lies in how Deleuze constructs and embraces ontological depth and how, in contrast, Derrida resolutely rejects this dimension and entirely avoids framing his issues in terms of ontology.

In the preface to *Difference and Repetition*, Deleuze proposes to study the 'more profound game of difference and repetition' which is, he states, 'the forces that act under the representation of the identical' (1994: ix). The orientation towards something 'more profound' and towards exposure of that which is or acts 'under' is essential in Deleuze's approach. This is not shared by Derrida, who, in contrast, and in a manner reminiscent of Hegel (even if not the same as Hegel), proceeds from concept to concept, or word to word, although not by mere negation, but rather by exposing the limitations of too total a meaning, pointing to the always remaining excess and proceeding through variation by variation – yet never referring outside this process of proceeding in concepts and their traces; Derrida does not refer to any more profound level of difference.

What is the 'difference in itself' for Deleuze, this more profound difference, which is not caught by representations, by conventional drawing of conceptual borderlines? In the chapter 'Difference in Itself' of *Difference and Repetition* Deleuze writes:

> The difference 'between' two things is only empirical, and the corresponding determinations are only extrinsic. However, instead of something distinguished from something else, imagine something which distinguishes itself – and yet that from which it

distinguishes itself does not distinguish itself from it. Lightning, for example, distinguishes itself from the black sky but must also trail it behind, as though it were distinguishing itself from that which does not distinguish itself from it. It is as if the ground rose to the surface, without ceasing to be ground. (Deleuze 1994: 28)

Referring to the ground and the surface is a recurrent way of writing for Deleuze; it is also the manner in which he characterizes significant political events. Of the events of May 1968 he says: 'The people who hate '68, or say it was a mistake, see it as something symbolic or imaginary. But that's precisely what it wasn't, it was pure reality breaking through' (Deleuze 1995: 144–5; see also Patton and Protevi 2003: 7.) 'Pure reality breaking through' involves a double structure of underlying reality and surface, or as Deleuze often expresses it, a double structure of, on the one hand, chaos of intensities, repetitions, and pure differences, and, on the other hand, representations. It is exactly this double structure that creates the ontologizing gesture in Deleuze's thought and binds it strongly to the tradition of ontology of substance in philosophy.

The double structure of representation on the one hand, and what it 'is' at a deeper level on the other, is something Derrida does not endorse in his texts. Derrida precisely avoids the construction of not only a metaphysical level of substance, which is how Deleuze's chaos, or matter, can be viewed, but also of any precise ontology. Derrida's philosophizing is decidedly outside the traditional philosophical ontological question of 'what is that what is'. This is why I argue that in comparison to Derrida, Deleuze acts much more traditionally as a philosopher.

Initially, it looks as if Deleuze would voice a criticism similar to that of Derrida concerning the limits of any conceptual or categorical differentiation: a concept like 'a Finn' or 'a homosexual' appears to be too static. A concept, Deleuze points out, blocks the predicates, which keep on moving in the thing itself (Deleuze 1995: 12). However, while Derrida looks precisely at the historical becoming of the concepts, the traces they involve, and the multiple meanings that make them move, Deleuze often seems to start from the conceptual distinctions as if in a timeless universe of philosophy, science, or mathematics. To counter the fixity of conceptual borders, then, a dimension of ontological depth is needed. This dimension works as the more profound layer of 'pure differences' which comprises actual motion, change, the new, and event, and which only erupts at the surface, without being actually accountable.

On the basis of this Deleuzian approach, so far as I can see, it would be difficult to produce a historical account of the coming into being of a difference, of creation of a border and an identity. Although Deleuze emphasizes becoming instead of being, this becoming remains concealed in the depths of the ontological processes which only erupt for our consideration and analysis later, and are not accountable as such. In contrast, the Derridean considerations of continuous and always partial becoming of a difference, *différance*, on the contrary, draws attention to the processes of the making of the difference. The making of the difference is crucially, for Derrida, never one process, and accounting for it can never constitute one narrative: yet, although it is ultimately not fully explorable, it is crucially not hidden from accounts, but multiply retraceable.

The crucial difference, in terms of accounts, histories, and stories of becomings of borders, is related to these diverse approaches towards ontology. The Deleuzian philosophical approach, which it seems to me is closer to that of the classical philosophical omnitemporality, encourages us to look at concepts and differences such as 'a Finn' or 'a homosexual' within the universe of concepts, in their abstract ontological becoming, and outside specific contexts. Instead, the Derridean approach towards ontology leaves the ontological opportunity to look at those concepts and differences in their time- and place-specific histories of differentiation, and therefore encourages the putting forward of stories about how these differences came about in concrete contexts, which also helps to appreciate their contingency as concepts.

So having asserted that Deleuzian and Derridean approaches suggest distinctly different takes on any instance of a border, of any differentiation or categorization, I will return to the two examples of Finns (nationality) and homosexuals (sexuality) and consider the different accounts that these two approaches to ontology would produce in these cases.

The Deleuzian and Derridean approaches in the two cases

I will begin with Deleuze. Deleuze writes: 'There are internal differences which dramatize the Idea before representing an object' (Deleuze 1995: 26). He refers to the Kantian 'Idea' and to some neo-Kantian interpretations according to which 'there is a step-by-step, internal, dynamic construction of space which must precede the "representation" of the whole as a form of exteriority [which] ... seems to us to consist of intensive quantity rather than schema, and to be related to Ideas rather than to concepts of the understanding' (Deleuze 1995: 26). This underlying level of difference which Deleuze philosophizes has been characterized in many ways: Todd May, for example, uses the medical metaphor of 'palpation', a method through which a sense can emerge without it being directly experienced.[7]

The implication is that in a Deleuzian mode of account, something has happened at the deeper level before the actual border can be drawn, before the category of homosexual, and likewise before the geopolitical border can emerge. The emergence of the classification could be seen as a surfacing of something which had already been accumulating for a long time at a deeper level and had been capable of being sensed, although never caught by a conceptual distinction.

In this sense, one could think that in a Deleuzian account something like homosexuality existed before the classification, and that therefore the classification does not bring anything new to it, but merely brings it to the surface. Similarly, the geopolitical border would have been in the process of becoming before the representation of it in practice.

The trouble with this kind of account of historical events is that it ends up downplaying contingency, action, and event in history. It also easily functions in a simple explanatory mode, as a rationalization of what has happened, as if it had to happen necessarily. Despite Deleuze's explicit emphasis on being interested in nothing but change and the opening up of thought for the future, there is a certain sense of stability involved at the outset in the approach. The efforts, the action, the actual traces of various ideas, are obscured by the self-movement of inexplorable difference. In the cases examined, such ideas are the Herderian idea of nations, or the various thoughts which led to the suggestions of particular distinctions in sexuality. Similarly, actions being obscured include the building of the Finnish-speaking culture through extraordinary efforts by a great number of activists inspired by these thoughts. Instead of on the action of historical activity, the attention is focused on the ontological movement of matter, which provides a strange sense of stability within the motion.

I suspect that this sense of stability is there because Deleuze, despite his genuine concern about becoming and future, and his concern for time, actually functions within what I call 'philosophical omnitemporality', a term that Derrida sometimes uses. Deleuze's gaze is directed at the classifications which are in no place and no time in the same way as are Aristotle's classifications, and in the same way as are the considerations of mathematics and science which are his inspirations. He philosophizes about continuous becoming, and about metamorphosis, but as abstracted from any particular time or place.[8]

In this respect, Derrida is very different. Although also speaking as a philosopher, he clearly distances himself from the philosophical ever-present time, and does so increasingly in his later work. This is manifest in, among other things, the way he never fails to point out that he is speaking and writing in a particular setting, within a particular tradition, a particular situation, and also in a particular language. Although he does not himself engage in giving historical accounts of becoming of differentiations and identities, his approach calls for attention to the plentiful possibility of such stories in particular times and places.

For Derrida, the border issue that he takes up with *différance* is not in order to point out that there is a more profound, or more real, more minute distinction process going on at the depths of ontological matter, which cannot be approached by crude conceptual distinction, such as the ones between Finn and not Finn, a homosexual and a non-homosexual. Much more than this, his *différance* implies that these distinctions are always made at a particular place and in a particular time, in relation to particular other concepts, and that they never succeed in being complete, abstract, and confined to their own meaning and references as they claim to do, but that they are profoundly relative and prone to move on. Derrida avoids further ontological commitments, and there is the incessant motion of concepts, categories, borders, which do not correspond in better or worse way to the real being. They do carry traces from the past (see also Green, Chapter 5 below), they perform detours, they defer the meaning, and they do something, but they do not primarily gather previous sense or experience.

In this sense, I could see the Derridean approach of accounting for what has been happening in the drawing of borders, in the two cases I outlined as drawing attention exactly to the various histories of their concrete becoming, and as keeping in mind that they might not have become at all, had things worked out differently. There is also a sense of the productivity of borders in Derrida's texts: the distinctions he takes up take him further in his texts, leading to subsequent distinctions, to new turns in the productive motion of thought and associations. His own focus is on the production of meaning in language rather than in concretely historical border cases, but the productivity and power of borders to disseminate effects is clearly present.

In contrast to a historian such as Michel Foucault, both Deleuze and Derrida are attached to the philosophical tradition; yet, and for the reasons I have outlined, I maintain that Deleuze is closer to traditional ontology than is Derrida. Derrida's work points to breaking out from the timeless and spaceless considerations of philosophy into something else, in order to renew philosophy. Derrida remains in his 'perhaps' position in terms of his attitude to the omnitemporal tradition of philosophy. In contrast, Foucault's historical work, in its philosophical dimension, goes further in the direction I would see as the critique of ontology that is present in Derrida's work. Foucault's work looks exactly at those processes where differences and identities, which could just as well not have been, are produced and constructed. If Derrida works 'as if' inside the philosophical tradition with a goal to transform it, Foucault actually expresses his philosophical thought in the form of historical accounts. His work as a historian has a philosophical undertone very similar to what Derrida is achieving in his questioning of the ontological approach. The issue of identities and differences and categories turned into accounts of historical becomings which emphasize how things could have gone otherwise, and how the categories might have become different from what they did, places the actions related to such becomings at the forefront of attention.

Conclusion

The two historical cases, the creation of an identity 'Finns' and the creation of the identity 'homosexuality', are issues of border: Finn and not-Finn, homosexual and not homosexual. These border issues can be looked at with different ontological attitudes, which I have tried to expose here as pertaining to two contemporary thinkers who inspired others, both of whom work within the tradition of philosophy, Gilles Deleuze and Jacques Derrida. If the creation of borders, differences, and identities such as those which I have discussed were to be accounted for in the

Deleuzian manner, the account would rely on an underlying ontological process happening before the actual border, difference, and identity became manifest in each case. An account relying on the Derridean ontological – or rather anti-ontological – attitude, on the contrary, would look at the traces, events, and actions that in multiple ways are active in making this border, difference, and identity.

As two different ontological attitudes, these approaches produce different foci of attention, in my view: on the one hand, attention to ontological depth and the motion of underlying substance in the Deleuzian mode, and on the other hand, attention to the action of drawing the lines, and the production of identities of those contingent drawings of line, in the Derridean mode. I would see the Derridean anti-ontological attitude as complementing the Foucauldian move towards genealogical accounts, despite being rather a gesture within the philosophical tradition. In contrast, I would see the Deleuzian ontology as being closer to the philosophical ideal of omnitemporality, and therefore, in combination with historical accounts, rather prone to produce accounts which downplay action and in which the historical drawing of borderlines seem to be attributed to hidden forces, which cannot be fully accounted for as actions. Ontology as a philosophical attitude, I wish to point out, crucially affects the thinking about borders. It is crucial because the one approach makes the creation of differences a matter of historical contingency and therefore open to being deliberately changed, whereas the other approach simply observes apparently random and constant proliferations of difference, in which actions are epiphenomena. And that matters.

Notes

1 More on my reading of Hegelian ontology in Pulkkinen (2010).

2 The historian Matti Klinge has, in a series of books, in many ways expressed the sense of contingency that involves the construction of national coherence that many others have later taken as self-evident. See e.g. Klinge 1975.

3 A good illustration of this is, for example, a group of people, the Kvens, who speak a language very close to Finnish but have been for centuries living in the northern part of Norway. The Kvens have never been seen as part of Finnishness, and neither have the Finnish-speaking populations in northern Sweden.

4 He writes: 'What displaces the a of *différance* in the sense of "activity", of "movement" and "productivity" is this static and statistical structuralism. *Différance* is the "productive" movement of differences, the "history", if that can still be said, of constituted difference, of constituted langue, of (al)ready made *langue*.' Derrida 1968: 85.

5 Derrida emphasizes the motivation of breaking with the opposition between activity and passivity; he recognized that that he was pursuing 'a thought that would frustrate the simple opposition between the active and the passive'. Derrida 1968: 85.

6 See also Patton and Protevi, who note that Derrida himself, in his eulogy for Deleuze, listed this among their points of agreement. They quote Derrida: 'the [thesis] concerning an irreducible difference that is in opposition to dialectical opposition, a difference "more

profound" than a contradiction (Difference and Repetition), a difference in the joyously repeated affirmation ("yes, yes"), a taking into account of the simulacrum' (Patton and Protevi 2003: 3, quoting Derrida 2001: 192–3). See also Descombes (1980).

7 Todd May first provides the metaphor of 'palpation' when discussing difference in Deleuze: 'When doctors seek to understand a lesion they cannot see, they palpate the body. They create a zone of touch where the sense of the lesion can emerge without its being directly experienced … Concepts palpate difference' (May 2005: 20).

8 I discuss the possible effects of this aspect of Deleuzian approach for feminist theory in Pulkkinen (2017).

References

Deleuze, G. (1994). *Difference and Repetition*, trans. Paul Patton. New York: Columbia University Press.

Deleuze, G. (1995). *Negotiations, 1972–1990*, trans. Martin Joughin. New York: Columbia University Press.

Derrida, J. (1968). 'The Original Discussion of "Différance"'. In D. Wood and R. Bernasconi (eds), *Derrida and Différance*, 83–97. Evanston, IL: Northwestern University Press, 1988.

Derrida, J. (1982). 'Différance'. In *Margins of Philosophy*, trans. Alan Bass, 1–27. Chicago: University of Chicago Press.

Derrida, J. (2001). 'I'm Going to Have to Wander All Alone', trans. Leonard Lawlor. In *The Work of Mourning*, trans. Pascale-Anne Brault and Michael Naas, ed. P-A. Brault and M. Naas, 189–96 Chicago: University of Chicago Press.

Descombes, V. (1979). *Modern French Philosophy*, trans. L. Scott-Fox and J. M. Harding. Cambridge: Cambridge University Press.

Foucault, M. (1978). *The History of Sexuality, I: An Introduction*, trans. R. Hurley. New York: Pantheon.

Klinge, M. (1975). *Bernadotten ja Leninin välissä* [Between Bernadotte and Lenin]. Helsinki: WSOY.

May, T. (2005). *Gilles Deleuze: An Introduction*. Cambridge: Cambridge University Press.

Patton, P., and J. Protevi (eds) (2003). *Between Deleuze and Derrida*. London and New York: Continuum.

Pulkkinen, T. (2010). 'Differing Spirits: Reflections on Hegelian Inspiration in Feminist Theory'. In K. Hutchings and T. Pulkkinen (eds), *Hegel's Philosophy and Feminist Thought: Beyond Antigone?*, 19–37. New York: Palgrave Macmillan.

Pulkkinen, T. (2017). 'The Role of Darwin in Elizabeth Grosz's Deleuzian Feminist Theory – Sexual Difference, Ontology, and Intervention'. *Hypatia: A Journal of Feminist Philosophy*, 32(2): 279–95.

Lines, traces, and tidemarks:
further reflections on forms of border

Sarah Green

Conceptually, borders are nowadays more often understood as being processes and acts of the imagination rather than as being objects. Indeed, I myself have participated in that kind of discussion.[1] The debate has been part of a critique of the idea of borders as fixed, relatively self-evident things placed in the landscape by political authorities to mark territory. It has also involved a critique of the idea that borders are lines – an idea that, according to many historical accounts, is the defining characteristic of Westphalian-style borders, the kinds of borders that are built by states, and particularly by nation-states – which includes most contemporary forms of border, with some significant exceptions, such as European Union (EU) borders (Del Sarto 2010; Linklater 1998; Hassner 2002).[2] The key argument is that the idea of border as line is part of a particular political concept of border; it is not something that belongs to borders as a natural characteristic, but is instead historically and ideologically specific. As a result, many border scholars have replaced the idea of line with a panoply of other metaphors to describe a much messier and more complex, fluid, and shifting reality: networks and rhizomes are among the most common of those metaphors.[3]

Given the focus on the discursive construction of the concept of border in this debate, it is unsurprising that the way these fluid or rhizome-like metaphors relate to the material form that borders take has been much less discussed. Of course, that non-materiality is a core characteristic of these debates, which often argue that borders are not things, but activities. Here border is better thought of as a verb, 'to border', rather than as a noun, 'a border' (Van Houtum, Kramsch, and Zierhofer 2005).

An alternative perspective is that borders exist everywhere and nowhere simultaneously and that there is no fixed location for borders, which are discursive rather than material entities (Robinson 2007). That approach has tended to mean that the actual physical entities that are built in the landscape, and which are referred to by most people as 'borders', have been relatively neglected by this conceptual debate. At the same time, those working on the actual architecture of border practices have repeatedly noted not only the visceral power that these objects, techniques, and constructions can exercise, but also how rapidly and sometimes radically these material characteristics are changing (Andersson 2014; Vaughan-Williams 2015; Weizman 2007). My aim in this chapter is to bring that intellectual work on the historically variable, discursive concept of border into relation with the material forms that contemporary borders take in practice, to think through what aspects of the material and immaterial become entangled here.

One of the important departures I will take is to retain the concept of 'line' in thinking about contemporary borders. This is not because I disagree with all the scholarship demonstrating that border thought of as a line is a historically contingent concept. On the contrary, I am retaining the concept because I entirely agree with that analysis (Green 2012), and I want to extend it in order to think through the material implications of imagining borders as lines, as well as considering what kinds of material forms that borders not considered as lines might take.

The geometry of lines

It is important to note from the beginning that, strictly speaking, the physical objects marking the geographical locations of political borders (the walls and fences) are not actually lines, and neither are the borders themselves, for that matter. In mathematical terms at least, lines are a one-dimensional abstraction: they are part of geometry, and they do not have a material (three-dimensional) form. Borders as geometrical lines appear only in images of borders (i.e. on maps). This is worth noting both because it points to the importance of political cartography in the development of the concept of border as line (Cosgrove 1999; Monmonier 1996; Pickles 2004; Jacob and Dahl 2006); and it highlights how easy it is to take an abstract concept (an epistemological entity, like a line) and assume that it is a thing (an ontological entity, like a wall) when discussing borders.

As many have noted, this confusion between cartographic and geographic realities of borders as lines has had some dramatic performative effects at times. The most obvious example is the bizarre straightness of many borders between African states: they have been literally drawn onto a (colonial) map using a ruler, and then made into a geographical reality. Maps showing the divisions between Egypt, Libya, and Sudan, or between Mauritania and Mali, amply demonstrate this territorial effect of the use of a ruler to draw a straight line on a map. As Ingold notes in his phenomenological work on lines as 'wayfaring', the trails left by people as they traverse the landscape are never straight (Ingold 2007). The straightness of the African borders is an indication of how colonial power could ignore any social, political, historical, cultural, or environmental considerations in deciding on the location of a border, and opt instead for what seemed most logical in technical terms: if borders are to be thought of as lines, then in creating new ones they should be drawn as such.

Lines and borders

The difference between lines and borders becomes clear when one considers cases in which borders are one-sided. It is logically impossible, geometrically speaking, for lines to be one-sided (although they have no thickness, they always bisect), but it is perfectly possible for borders to be so. An example is the current separation between the southern and northern parts of Cyprus (Papadakis 2005; Navaro-Yashin 2003). For the northern side (which is called, in the north, the Turkish Republic of Northern Cyprus, or TRNC), the separation constitutes a state border. For the southern side, which does not recognize the north as a state (indeed, internationally, only Turkey recognizes the TRNC), it is an illegal division of the island, so the separation is not a border. After it became possible to legally travel between the two sides in 2003, the northern side set up a checkpoint with border guards and issued visas (Dikomitis 2005). The southern side has police officers controlling the movement of people from the north, but no border checks. The police in the south are controlling the potential movement of people who have arrived in Cyprus via what the southern authorities define as an illegal route: that is, any route where the first port of entry into Cyprus is located in the northern (TRNC or occupied) territories (see also Demetriou, Chapter 2 above).

In sum: if the political authorities on the one side of a wall or barrier do not agree that it represents a border, which would require recognition of the political authority of the other side, then the border will be one-sided. Of course, no borders are supposed to be one-sided, and in contemporary geopolitics, one-sided borders are also always 'unfinished business'. Work always needs to be done to try and either make the border two-sided or remove it. In Cyprus, there is currently still a UN-operated buffer zone, called the Green Line (as it was drawn on a map with a green pen), between the northern and southern parts of the island, which has been there since 1964 and was extended in 1974, after the conflict that led to the current division of the island (Papadakis 2005; Papadakis, Perisitianis, and Welz 2006).

Incidentally, these kinds of one-sided places make clear that the meaning and even material operation of borders are relative: neither people nor governments can define a border entirely by themselves. To have a fully operational contemporary border requires international recognition. That is important, because it points to a simple but often neglected fact: the location and meaning of borders are always established as a relation, as well as a separation, between locations. This is something that I have regularly referred to as 'relative location' in other work (Green 2012; 2013b).

Here, my main point is that it is important to maintain a distinction between the abstract concept of lines and the materiality (and political contingency) of borders. Three-dimensional objects such as walls and fences, which are intended to mark the geographical limits or entry and exit points of many contemporary state territories, are symbols or representations of the geometrical, cartographic, abstract concept of border as a line, rather than being the line as such. When the issue is looked at that way, it does not really matter that it is impossible, or prohibitively expensive, to build a wall or fence around the entire outer limits of most countries. A map of the entire outer limits, combined with a little bit of wall and a policed border-crossing, will do to make the point that a conceptual line, which has cartographic, legal, spatial, and territorial characteristics, relates to some kind of material reality in the landscape that the authority which built those objects wishes to assert. The crossing point or wall is the part that symbolizes the whole.

At the same time, and as the Cypriot example illustrates well, these walls and checkpoints are not only symbols that represent the location of borders. They are also physical objects that have an additional role in materially controlling how the border is maintained, policed, and crossed (which can include transgressive cross-ing, of course). So there is also something metonymic about these objects; they are not only metaphorical. As Caren Kaplan noted in her critique of the concept of the potentially radical or transgressive quality of travel in some postmodern thought, if a person does not have the right passports and visas, let alone the money and physi-cal means to travel, they may not be able to go anywhere at all (Kaplan 1996). In that sense, the material presence of checkpoints, walls, fences, surveillance, and the management of borders matters in a visceral, as well as symbolic, way.

Towards traces and tidemarks

Given this combined metaphoric and metonymic characteristic of the physical objects that mark the locations of borders, I suggest that it might be helpful to think about them as traces. Unlike lines, traces can have material forms, and they also evoke the passage of time in a way that lines do not. In material form, traces can be fragments of the whole entity, or a physical mark of it – the crumbs left from a loaf of bread that has been eaten, footprints in the sand, or a guarded checkpoint which stands for the full extent of the (mostly invisible) separation between one form of modern legal location and another. The point I want to emphasize here is that the metaphor of traces can help us to think about the entangled relation between symbolic, material, and legal forms.

In addition to the way traces can imply material forms in a way that lines do not, traces can also leave much room for doubt, speculation, and interpretation. This is in contrast to lines, which are usually evoked to assert clear divisions between two sides. Indeed, I begin from the premise that a crucial aspect of imagining political borders as lines is part of an effort to create unambiguous cuts: to mark clear, binary, separa-tions between here and not-here. Borders thought of as lines are never intended to mark multiple, fluid, networked, rhizomatic, and constantly shifting differences or relations, but precisely to conceal any such messiness. In that sense, borders as lines are always an effort at simplification: the whole point is to mark a binary separation, backed up by power which officially polices and manages that separation.

The fact that few political borders in the world are anywhere near as clear-cut or straight as the ones drawn up by former colonial powers in Africa demonstrates that political borders are always work in progress. In practice, the location and meaning of borders are highly contingent; they also leave traces of previous efforts at marking a separation between locations; they regularly co-exist with cross-cutting attempts to define places differently; and they are also buffeted by the activities of people going about their daily lives, who may either understand borders differently or deliberately choose to contradict whatever is intended by those who built the border. This is where the metaphor of tidemark comes in. I will be suggesting that tidemark, as an idea, combines line and trace in a way that helps us to think through the ongoing metaphorical, metonymical, and material elements of 'border-ness'.

The original version of this chapter was written for the first meeting of EastBordNet, a network of researchers that was funded by COST working across the Eastern peripheries of Europe on various aspects of political borders.[4] The original paper was intended to begin a conversation about how to rethink borders, how to bring together people's experiences of 'border work' in their everyday lives with the conceptual and political elements of borders. This introduction has brought in many elements of the rethinking that occurred in the subsequent four years, and some changes made to the remainder of the paper similarly adjust my initial thoughts into ones that have developed from the experience. Yet the work is not yet done, so I am leaving the chapter as one that still opens out a conversation, rather than closing one down. The remaining sections, which discuss lines, traces, and tidemarks as concepts a little further, are intended to add some additional detail to the framework I have just outlined.

Critique of border as line: replacing it with transgressive identities

As I implied above, the main complaint against depicting borders as lines is that it confuses a political ideology with an ontological reality. The location and form of political borders are obviously politically determined, and they shift according to the vagaries of political fortunes and conflicts. Three recent, and very different, examples are: the independence of South Sudan in 2011; the Russian annexation of Crimea in 2014; and, most recently, the United Kingdom referendum held on 23 June 2016, in which the majority voted to leave the EU. The first one involved the creation of an independent state out of part of the state of Sudan; the second involved the separation of part of the state of Ukraine and its incorporation into the Federation of Russia; and the third (which is still in discussion as this chapter is being written) involves the separation of a sovereign state from a political, economic, and legal union of sovereign states (the EU).

The creation of an independent state of South Sudan was recognized internationally; the annexation of Crimea is internationally disputed; and nobody quite knows what will happen when the United Kingdom ceases its membership of the

EU, assuming that the plan to leave goes ahead. As several researchers including myself have noted, the EU has developed highly unusual, if not unique, forms of border regime (Del Sarto 2010; Green 2013a). One distinct characteristic is that the EU's border regimes overlap in varying levels of inclusion and exclusion. For example, there are twenty-six states in the Schengen area, within which there is free movement across state boundaries. These Schengen states do not include all the EU member states (e.g. the United Kingdom and Cyprus are outside Schengen) but do include some states that are not members of the EU (e.g. Norway and Switzerland). Two other examples: the euro is the currency of only seventeen of the twenty-eight member states; and the EU Customs Union includes all the EU member states plus four others, including Turkey. And so on. When one looks at the border practices of the EU, it seems obvious that the idea of border as a line has been overlain (rather than replaced, for all the states involved are still sovereign states) by something else.

In this context, it is intriguing to look back at the earlier critiques of the notion of borders as self-evident lines, which were based on studies of the US–Mexican border in the late 1980s and early 1990s. Once people ceased to think of borders as reflecting something self-evident about the relationship between territory and peoples, the possibilities of altering the realities that borders marked became clear. For anthropology, Alvarez summarized this as follows:

> Rather than maintain a focus on the geographically and territorially bounded community and culture, the concepts inherent in the borders genre are alert to the shifting of behaviour and identity and the reconfiguration of the social patterns at the dynamic interstices of cultural practices. ... we need to examine paradox, conflict, contradiction, and contrasts. (Alvarez 1995: 462)

In short, the idea was that border was the location of all kinds of relations and experiences that could challenge the hegemonic story of what kinds of identities border represented. By focusing on movements across, and transgressions of, the US–Mexican border, rather than on what the border contained and separated, a whole slew of hybrids, fluid identities, and mixtures would be revealed.

As interesting as that focus upon uncertainty and transgression was, the perspective offered by Alvarez did not discuss the qualities or characteristics of borders, as such. Many of the approaches within this genre in fact appeared to take for granted what constitutes the concept of 'border': it is the location of the meeting of differences, and therefore border is a site for conflict as well as holding the potential to generate hybrids and other forms of border-transgressing entities.

Researchers who have continued that genre – particularly those in American studies and in cultural studies (e.g. Saldívar 1997) – took the critique of the naturalness of 'border' as key to developing a politics of unsettling the notion of natural identities – particularly raced, gendered, and sexual identities. Note that the identity of borders is not the point here: it is the identity of people that is the point.

This genre of border studies became rapidly involved with post-colonial studies, subaltern studies, and, perhaps particularly, the work of Deleuze and Guattari, especially *Nomadology* and *A Thousand Plateaus* (Deleuze and Guattari 1986; 1988). Their work seemed to carry a promise of escape from the constraints of border through their ideas of nomadism and the Spinoza-inspired idea of singularity – of everything existing on a single fabric of space and time – so that any divisions and subdivisions within the fabric (the constant proliferation of differences), what many people understood as border, were in fact all part of the same entity, in the end all interconnected like a rhizome in a field (see also Pulkkinen, Chapter 4 above).

It was not long before critiques of the more idealistic versions of this perspective began to emerge. As I mentioned earlier, Caren Kaplan questioned the reliance upon the idea of travel, migration, and wandering in this literature, arguing that the idealized notion of being able to travel and wander was borne of a rather old modernist belief that you can transform yourself by travelling (Kaplan 1996). This kind of view does not, Kaplan argued, take into account the political, legal, economic, and social conditions in which travelling, or the inability to travel, radically affects people's lives. She also argued that a failure to distinguish between tourism, enforced travel, documented and undocumented migration, and rather romantic colonial visions of the expatriate made the idea of the singular fluidity of border inadequate to the task of understanding travel, let alone what 'line' might mean in relation to border.

Beside those debates, there were also a number of scholars, including Donnan and Wilson, who pointed out that questioning the naturalness of political borders was a little older than the US–Mexican borderlands studies suggested (Wilson and Donnan 1994). Indeed, a book published in 1973, Cole and Wolf's *The Hidden Frontier*, focuses squarely on border as an entity that is locally generated by historically variable social, political, and economic relations, and is not simply a line drawn by the state (Cole and Wolf 1973). In Cole and Wolf's view, people who live their everyday lives generate border as much as any formal legal or political entity does. Here, the issue still concerned people's identities, but Cole and Wolf pointed out that it was as much local people getting on with their everyday lives that attached identities to borders as it was the states that placed them in the landscape.

In sum, the 1990s debate about borders focused mostly on the transgressive, rhizomatic, fluid, and hybrid identity of people, and as a result, neither the conceptual nor the material character of borders themselves, as entities in the landscape, was really resolved by this debate. What was interesting about borders for this discussion was the way people's identities became entangled with them; what the building of a wall might mean in terms of the concept of border, as such, was somehow beside the point.

Back to spatial borders

Here, I am going to return to the significance of retaining the concept of line in making a start towards trying to understand the actual walls. What that lengthy debate about identities, subjectivities, and rhizomatic relations demonstrated is that the world is highly cluttered: it is full of people moving, interacting, and creating a range of discourses and diverse ways of understanding themselves and their relations and separations with their locations and with each other. It is into that kind of cluttered world that post-Westphalian political authorities attempt to impose clear, simplified cuts: the border as line, the border as wall, a distinction between here and not-here, backed up with law, police enforcement, surveillance, and an ideology that justifies the possession of territory. It is the opposite of a rhizome or network: it is an attempt to stop the endless proliferation of relations and to impose a cut.

Here, Marilyn Strathern's paper 'Cutting the Network' provides an excellent way to think about how this cutting works. In a discussion about Latour's idea of networks and hybrids, Strathern made the point that in order to understand anything as being an entity, it has to be cut out of potentially endless connections:

> Interpretation must hold objects of reflection stable long enough to be of use. That holding stable may be imagined as stopping a flow or cutting into an expanse ... 'Cutting' is used as a metaphor by Derrida himself ... for the way one phenomenon stops the flow of others. Thus the force of 'law' cuts into a limitless expanse of 'justice'. (Strathern 1996: 522)

Strathern's point is that there are various (epistemological, legal) mechanisms that make 'cuts' in the potential endlessness of networks or rhizomes – and it is those cuts which allow an entity to appear as a 'thing'. The examples she uses are patent law, which cuts out all people involved in creating an invention other than those named in the patent; and kinship rules such as exogamy, sister-exchange, or cross-cousin marriage, which limit who can marry whom. The patent effectively creates an invention, and the marriage rules effectively create kin. It is the cutting, not the network, that does this work, that has this creative effect.

I would like to suggest that such cutting is the intention of political authorities who both legally identify the location of borders and build things in the landscape to both symbolize and police such borders: these are attempts at creating a 'thing' (a country, a nation, a state, a territory, a people who belong to that territory, and any number of other things). And like the rules of patent law and the rules of kinship, this form of cutting exists within a recognized system for how to do such things: international protocols, regulations, oversight by the UN, ideologies about what might justify the claim to territory, and so on. The 'line' may be symbolized and physically policed by crossing points, walls and so on; but it also remains an abstraction, a conceptual way of distinguishing here from not-here, mapping that onto the landscape and calling it a thing. In that sense, the concept of line as border is used to cut the network in contemporary border work – meaning the work done, both formal and informal, in creating the spatial and territorially marked realities with which we live (Reeves 2014; Green and Malm 2013; Rumford 2009). For that reason, I think that it is important to retain the concept in thinking about the work that contemporary borders do in practice. It is not, by any means, the only way to do border work, and in a sense, that is the point: it is historically contingent. It is simply a very powerful way that border work is currently done.

This brings me to Tim Ingold's *Lines: A Brief History* (Ingold 2007). Ingold, who takes a strongly phenomenological approach, argues that the whole of life could be seen as the creation, or following, or wandering around, of a series of lines (which are usually not straight in his definition of lines), and that anthropologists should focus on the lines rather than on points. For Ingold, neither networks nor kinship diagrams are about lines, because both focus on the points in between the lines. He prefers the term 'meshwork' to network, to get away from the idea of points with connectors, as opposed to lines interrelated with other lines.

Meshwork, Ingold suggests, more accurately reflects lines as experienced in the world, which are open-ended, curly, intertwined, not necessarily hierarchical. In this discussion, Ingold distinguishes repeatedly between wayfaring and transportation: wayfaring, he suggests, is a form of wandering, whereas transportation is a movement between one point and the next point. His argument is that lines are about the process of travelling and the experience people have while doing it, whereas transportation is about the points – starting point A and destination point B.

This is obviously a starkly different understanding of line from that which I have presented. I began from the geometrical properties of line, and I did so in order to draw out the logic that informs the use of line as a historically specific (post-Westphalian) political metaphor to describe borders. And that was in order to try and understand what kind of work defining borders as lines achieves, both materially and symbolically. I have suggested that the assertion that border constitutes a line can be seen as an official attempt at cutting through the meshwork, rather than constituting the meshwork. And, drawing on Strathern's understanding of network, I have suggested that this cutting is an attempt to carve out a certain reality from the clutter of the world, to simplify and clarify, to remove the knots and tangles, and thus to define what has been cut out of the mess. The act of cutting in the case of border might even be called an effort at performativity: to declare that the difference between here and not-here is a particular kind of thing (e.g. a nation, as Pulkkinen discusses in Chapter 4 above).

In short, my interest in line is as an epistemological and discursive concept that has been deployed in the building of particular kinds of political borders (modern state borders), which I have suggested are efforts at imposing a certain reality onto a cluttered world. In contrast, Ingold's focus is on the cluttering, on the process through which the world becomes enmeshed. Ingold stretched the meaning of line far beyond the logic of geometry to which I confined it; in geometrical terms, most of Ingold's lines are curves and tangles, not lines.

Having linked my use of the term 'line' to its geometric epistemology, I cannot draw upon the term to imply any kind of passage of time, as Ingold does with his much wider metaphorical use of line. So, in order to think about the fact that borders involve not only historically specific conceptualization, but also ongoing 'border work' – all the practices and activities that occur, both officially and unofficially, in generating a particular quality of 'border-ness' at any given time – I am introducing a separate metaphor: the idea of trace.

Trace and border

Many writers speak of traces; indeed, Ingold does so, in suggesting that lines are not all the same, in that some are threads, with direct links between entities, whereas others are traces, with only hints of connections, and yet others are ghosts, apparitions of previously experienced lines (Ingold 2007: 41–50; see also Myrivili, Chapter 7 below). However, as I have outlined, stretching the definition of line so far that it includes curves, tangles, cuts, traces, threads, and other things may help people to understand the sensory experience of line, but does not assist me in understanding the combined conceptual and material work that contemporary borders do. So I am deliberately separating trace from line, making them into two separate concepts.

In particular, I am interested in how the notion of trace includes a sense of time in a way that line does not. There are several scholars who have worked on that. For example, Michael Taussig regularly speaks of traces in terms of what is left from the past in the present, silently nudging our thoughts and understanding. In an article on the history of indigo, the substance used to make a certain shade of dark blue in clothing (the blue-jeans kind of blue), Taussig considers trace in terms of past relationships with diverse parts of the world that is left in that term, 'indigo', and other similar words that emerged during the height of the period of colonial trade. Even though that particular shade of blue is now mostly made from chemicals that no longer have any relationship with indigo (and in that sense, the trace has been erased), Taussig suggests that the trace is always there in the word, even if it is not always consciously present:

> The tongue remembers, but you do not. Life moves on while all around you lie the traces of lost eras, active in the present, hanging on the wall, covering the windows, not to mention the couch on which you sit or the dress you will wear tonight. *Damask.*
> (Taussig 2008: 4)

What Taussig is trying to do here is bring back to consciousness the colonial history of colour – in this case, indigo, a blue that came along the same routes as spices in order to arrive here – from the East (here being, implicitly, the West). The words we use still recall those associations, even though the reliance on the indigo plant for our blues is long gone.

Evocative as that idea might be, it is possible to go further with this notion of trace. Derrida's notion of trace is one of his more obscure concepts, but a couple of aspects are helpful in thinking about contemporary border work. One key point is that trace, for Derrida, refers to something that is always-already absent and may never have actually existed, but that is drawn upon in understanding what does exist in the here and now. In Derrida's words, trace is 'irreducible absence within the presence of the trace' (Derrida 1997: 47). A simple example is the crumbs left from a loaf of bread that has been eaten: the crumbs evoke the whole loaf of bread, but in order for them to act as a trace of the whole loaf, the actual loaf must be absent, and only the crumbs present. In other words, trace evokes something that does not exist in the present, but that helps to make sense of the present – and, in fact, the past and the future as well (Derrida 1997: 65–7). In *Writing and Difference*, Derrida suggests that

> The trace is not a presence but is rather the simulacrum of a presence that dislocates, displaces, and refers beyond itself. The trace has, properly speaking, no place, for effacement belongs to the very structure of the trace … In this way the metaphysical text is understood; it is still readable, and remains read. (Derrida 1978: 403)

And more interestingly for my purposes, Taylor and Winquist directly relate Derrida's notion of trace to notions of border and location:

> trace is conceived of as a radicalized sign: the mark of an event and of a memory that transfigures this event into an 'archive', that is, the *border* of representation itself, its fluid limit. The trace shows the work of time by providing a locus which redefines the 'who' and 'what' questions into a 'where'. (Taylor and Winquist 2003: 404, emphasis added)

This approach emphasizes the irreducibility of historical time in borders, the way time is crucial to experiences of border, and an element that makes clear that border is something that is best thought of as an active entity (and see also Pulkkinen, Chapter 4 above). It also draws out the way the idea of trace could be evoked as a means to understand 'border' as incorporating both time and space simultaneously, as well as evoking a notion of difference (*différance*), without necessarily implying either inequality or separation.

Derrida's notion of trace is interesting for another reason. His notion of *arche-trace*, which refers to traces of the absence of entities that have never existed (crumbs without there ever having been a loaf of bread), echoes quite a lot of scholarship about borders. Borders are replete with the traces of entities that have never existed. One could easily argue that the concept of nation is classically one of those entities. Gourgouris noted that nation has to be always already there: there has to be a sense of its prior existence as an entity, before any legally recognized territory can be created to make 'nation' a legal reality (Gourgouris 1996). In other words, the lack of nation has to be felt before any nation can come into existence. That, Gourgouris suggests, is what the Greek nationalist movements in the nineteenth and early twentieth centuries were all about: claiming the eternal existence of a place that had never yet existed in order to bring it into existence. One could easily see that as a good example of Derrida's notion of trace: sensing the signs of something that has never actually existed, and eventually creating a spatial extension, a territory, to mark or create that entity, to cut it out of the mess and clutter of everything else, and thus bring it (the nation) into existence.

Drawing on Derrida to think about trace in this way points to the historical contingency of creating new realities: the trace provides a sign of something that is not here, that is not visible, but somehow provides tangible evidence, and in the case of borders sometimes material evidence, of the existence of the thing that is absent or invisible. The checkpoint and the wall imply the entire border; and the entire border implies the entity that it contains – the state, the nation, the people, whatever. The checkpoint is a trace in that sense. And in Derrida's view, the trace is always contingent – it never hides an ultimate, timeless, reality; what it signifies is always dependent upon the here and now. The case of the one-sided border in Cyprus is an example of how that works in practice (see also Demetriou, Chapter 2 above).

Yet contemporary political borders are not only attempts at creating lines and the evocation of traces across time. They are also located in space. Here, Doreen Massey's highly evocative understanding of space (Massey 2005), combined with Stuart Elden's more recent study of the history of territory (Elden 2013), have helped me to articulate this combination of line, trace, time, and space, as tidemark, a metaphor that might include all four.

Massey and Elden: making space lively

Unlike Derrida, who describes space as 'dead time' (Derrida 1997: 68), Massey argues that space is entirely lively, constituting a 'simultaneity of stories so far' (Massey 2005: 12). At any one moment, she argues, what constitutes space is the outcome of multiple relations, unpredictable happenings, and everyday activities. In simplistic terms, what is going on in Mumbai at this very moment is different from what is going on in Nicosia at this very moment; they are on different trajectories, and are involved in the world in different ways. There is no reason to think that Mumbai somehow sits on a single time line with Nicosia, moving from less developed to more developed, or from now to tomorrow, in the same way. There may be moments when the two are brought into relation with one another, somehow contribute to each other; but there is no guarantee that even if there is contact between them, they will somehow then become part of the same space or location.

To Massey, then, space cannot be an undifferentiated fabric; nor can it be simply representation, which many argue that it is; nor can it be static, and it most certainly cannot efface time in the sense that Derrida implies. This is because, Massey argues, the mere fact of being spatially positioned means a difference from being positioned elsewhere. Massey also insists that time is historical, and suggests that at any one moment, different and irreversible things are happening. She calls this 'the principle of co-existing heterogeneity. It is not the particular nature of heterogeneities but the fact of them that is intrinsic to space' (Massey 2005: 12).

Massey critiques both the assumption of the naturalness of territorialization and the notion of deterritorialization in this time of globalization – as expressed by Appadurai, for example (Appadurai 1996). She calls the former essentialist, suggesting instead that space should be 'thought of as an emergent product of relations, including those relations which establish boundaries, and where "place" in consequence is necessarily a *meeting* place' (Massey 2005: 68). The imposition of territories over these ongoing relations, Massey argues, is always a political act, part of what she refers to as 'power geometry'.

This approach complements, though is different from, Stuart Elden's detailed study of the emergence of the modern concept of territory (Elden 2013). Drawing on Foucauldian understandings of the history of concepts, Elden argues that contemporary understandings of territory developed out of a combination of epistemological, legal, and political conditions that historically developed in Europe and then spread across the world. The concept combined Western science with politics and understandings of space:

> the notion of space that emerges in the scientific revolution is defined by *extension*. Territory can be understood as the political counterpart to this notion of calculating space, and can therefore be thought of as the *extension of the state's power*. ... Territory comprises techniques for measuring land and controlling terrain. Measure and control – the technical and the legal – need to be thought alongside land and terrain. What is crucial in this designation is the attempt to keep the question of territory open. Understanding territory as a political technology is not to define territory once and for all; rather, it is to indicate the issues at stake in grasping how it was understood in different historical and geographical contexts. (Elden 2013: 322)

The key point for my purposes here is that the emergence of the idea of border as line was something that required both the technical epistemology – the mapping techniques and geometrical knowledge – and the political linking of power with extension – with power over an expanse of land (which was embedded within the Westphalia Treaties), as opposed (say) to power over a people, wherever they happen to be located. In Elden's terms, the idea of territory in this sense, which incorporates the concept of border as line, took many centuries to develop.

Massey, like Elden, emphasizes the historical contingency of the current arrangements: whatever divisions currently exist, and however powerfully backed up they may be, things could be otherwise. The fairly radical experiments occurring within EU bordering practices that I briefly mentioned earlier, in which diverse functions

of borders have been separated out and distributed across states in a variety of partially overlapping spatial regimes (Green 2012), is an example of the potential for
something different to co-exist with the idea of border as line. But it is important
to note that this is co-existence, not replacement of one kind of regime by another.
And it is also important to note that particular understandings of space as extension
(territory) are being brought together here with various types of rights and obligations over that space, and rights and obligations cross-cut the state boundaries. The
euro is used in several EU member states, but not all of them; the Schengen Zone is
both smaller than the extension of all the EU member states, but also goes beyond
them.

What Massey adds to Elden's detailed conceptual history of a single concept
(territory) is the idea of multiplicity: the possibility that a number of different ways
of bringing together space, people, and time could co-exist (Massey 2005: 89).
The EU is currently an example of how that can happen in formal, political, and
legal terms; but many borderland ethnographies since Cole and Wolf's pioneering
studies in the 1970s have shown that this co-existence can happen in a variety of
informal ways as well. This is where the metaphor of tidemark finally comes in.

Conclusion: towards the tidemark

The idea of tidemark aims to combine line and trace with Massey's and Elden's
understanding of space as being power-inflected, but also lively, contingent, and
open to constant redefinition. This is a means to try to bring together the metaphorical and material aspects of contemporary border work. What I have explored is the
way in which the dominant contemporary concept of border, in which the idea of
line plays a crucial part, involves a constant effort at simplification and cutting of a
much more entangled social, political, economic, and spatial reality. The concept
of line as a one-dimensional abstraction rather than a thing can be adequately symbolized or represented in a combination of maps and material objects in the landscape such as border-crossing points and walls, and through the exercise of various
bureaucratic procedures (the requirements of passports, visas, demonstration of
permanent residence, etc.). The idea of all this is to create a spatially bounded,
political, and ideological reality: usually a sovereign state, and often also a nation.

Yet the attempt at generating those realities, as we have seen in the case of
Cyprus and the current complexities of the EU, is often challenged or cross-cut by
other ideas of how to organize the relation between people and space. The meshwork, in Ingold's terms, constantly interferes. So the official attempts to generate
borders and control the meanings they impose upon space always co-exist with a
panoply of other things, both conceptual and material.

The idea of tidemark is a small attempt to metaphorically combine the meshwork, the interweaving of everyday life, with that combination of space, time,
materiality, and the ongoing transformation of things and places that this process

generates. Tidemark partially evokes the sense of trace, without specifying how much of that is a Taussig kind of trace, with visceral connections to histories that have been almost erased from view; and/or a Derrida kind of trace, where border-ness is generated from the always-already existence of differences and otherness that are absent here, and may never have existed, but whose traces (the crumbs and footprints left behind) are crucial to helping to generate a sense of border. Tidemark also combines space and historical time, and envisages both space and time as being lively and contingent. Moreover, in English, the word 'tidemark' refers not only to the mark left in the sand by the water that has receded with the tide, but also to the vertical measuring post that measures the height of the tide: the word describes both the material thing and the epistemology used to measure it, to define it as a mark left by the tide. It is that combination of material and epistemological, within a deeply spatial logic, that I am trying to capture here.

Border-ness in that sense concerns where things have got to so far, in the mul-tiple, unpredictable, power-inflected, imagined, overlapping, and visceral way in which everyday life tends to occur.

Notes

This chapter is a heavily revised version of a paper that was originally presented at the first EastBordNet meeting (COST IS0803, Work Group 1 meeting) in Nicosia, Cyprus, on 14–15 April 2009. I would like to express my deep gratitude to COST for providing the funding to create this network, which generated the cross-disciplinary and transnational research environment needed to develop the concept of border that is presented in this chapter; and to Olga Demetriou, who hosted the meeting.

1 A few examples include Green (2010); Anzaldúa (1987); Balibar (1998); Banerjee (2010); Van Houtum, Kramsch, and Zierhofer (2005).
2 See also Stuart Elden's highly insightful study of the development of the concept of 'territory' in the Western imagination (Elden 2013).
3 E.g. Myrivili (2004); Zartman (2010); Robinson (2007).
4 http://www.cost.eu/COST_Actions/isch/IS0803 (last accessed 9 July 2016).

References

Alvarez, R. R. (1995). 'The Mexican–US Border: The Making of an Anthropology of Borderlands'. *Annual Review of Anthropology*, 24: 447–70.

Andersson, Ruben (2014). *Illegality, Inc.: Clandestine Migration and the Business of Bordering Europe*. Oakland, CA: University of California Press.

Anzaldúa, Gloria (1987). *Borderlands/La Frontera: The New Mestiza*. San Francisco: Aunt Lute.

Appadurai, Arjun (1996). 'Global Ethnoscapes: Notes and Queries for a Transnational Anthropology'. In Arjun Appadurai (ed.), *Modernity at Large: Cultural Dimensions of Globalization*, 48–65. Minneapolis, MN, and London: University of Minnesota Press.

Balibar, Étienne (1998). 'The Borders of Europe'. In Pheng Cheah and Bruce Robbins (eds), *Cosmopolitics: Thinking and Feeling beyond the Nation*, 216–29. Minneapolis and London: University of Minnesota Press.

Banerjee, Paula (2010). *Borders, Histories, Existences: Gender and Beyond*. Los Angeles, CA, and London: SAGE Publications.

Cole, John W., and Eric R. Wolf (1973). *The Hidden Frontier: Ecology and Ethnicity in an Alpine Valley*. New York: Academic Press.

Cosgrove, Denis, E. (ed.) (1999). *Mappings*. London: Reaktion.

Deleuze, Gilles, and Felix Guattari (1986). *Nomadology: The War Machine*. New York: Semiotext(e).

Deleuze, Gilles, and Felix Guattari (1988). *A Thousand Plateaus: Capitalism and Schizophrenia*. London: Athlone Press.

Del Sarto, Raffaella A. (2010). 'Borderlands: The Middle East and North Africa as the EU's Southern Buffer Zone'. In Dimitar Bechev and Kalypso Nicolaidis (eds), *Mediterranean Frontiers: Borders, Conflict and Memory in a Transnational World*, 149–65. London: Tauris.

Derrida, Jacques (1978). *Writing and Difference*, trans. Alan Bass. Chicago: University of Chicago Press.

Derrida, Jacques (1997). *Of Grammatology*, trans. Gayatri Chakravorty Spivak. Baltimore: Johns Hopkins University Press.

Dikomitis, L. (2005). 'Three Readings of a Border'. *Anthropology Today*, 21(5): 7–12.

Elden, Stuart (2013). *The Birth of Territory*. Chicago: University of Chicago Press.

Gourgouris, Stathis (1996). *Dream Nation: Enlightenment, Colonization, and the Institution of Modern Greece*. Stanford, CA: Stanford University Press.

Green, Sarah (2010). 'Performing Border in the Aegean: On Relocating Political, Economic and Social Relations'. *Journal of Cultural Economy*, 3(2): 261–78.

Green, Sarah (2012). 'A Sense of Border'. In Thomas M. Wilson and Hastings Donnan (eds), *A Companion to Border Studies*, 573–92. Oxford: Wiley-Blackwell.

Green, Sarah (2013a). 'Borders and the Relocation of Europe'. *Annual Review of Anthropology*, 42: 345–61.

Green, Sarah (2013b). 'Money Frontiers: The Relative Location of Euros, Turkish Lira and Gold Sovereigns in the Aegean'. In Penny Harvey et al. (eds), *Objects and Materials: A Routledge Companion*, 302–11. Abingdon: Routledge.

Green, Sarah, and Lena Malm (2013). *Borderwork: A Visual Journey through Peripheral Frontier Regions*. Helsinki: Jasilti.

Hassner, Pierre (2002). 'Fixed Borders or Moving Borderlands? A New Type of Border for a New Type of Entity'. In Jan Zielonka (ed.), *Europe Unbound: Enlarging and Reshaping the Boundaries of the European Union*, 38–50. London: Routledge.

Ingold, Tim (2007). *Lines: A Brief History*. London: Routledge.

Jacob, Christian, and Edward H. Dahl (eds) (2006). *The Sovereign Map: Theoretical Approaches in Cartography throughout History*. Chicago and London: University of Chicago Press.

Kaplan, Caren (1996). *Questions of Travel: Postmodern Discourses of Displacement*. Durham, NC, and London: Duke University Press.

Linklater, Andrew (1998). *The Transformation of Political Community: Ethical Foundations of the Post-Westphalian Era*. Oxford: Polity Press.

Massey, Doreen (2005). *For Space.* London: Sage.

Monmonier, Mark S. (1996). *How to Lie with Maps.* Chicago: University of Chicago Press.

Myrivili, Eleni (2004). 'The Liquid Border: Subjectivity at the Limits of the Nation-State in Southeast Europe (Albania, Greece, Macedonia)'. PhD thesis, Columbia University.

Navaro-Yashin, Yael (2003). '"Life is Dead Here": Sensing the Political in "No Man's land"'. *Anthropological Theory,* 3(1): 107–25.

Papadakis, Yiannis (2005). *Echoes from the Dead Zone: Across the Cyprus Divide.* London: I. B. Tauris.

Papadakis, Yiannis, N. Peristianis, and Gisela Welz (eds) (2006). *Divided Cyprus: Modernity, History, and an Island in Conflict.* Bloomington, IN: Indiana University Press.

Pickles, John (2004). *A History of Spaces: Cartographic Reason, Mapping, and the Geo-Coded World.* London: Routledge.

Reeves, Madeleine (2014). *Border Work: Spatial Lives of the State in Rural Central Asia.* Ithaca, NY, and London: Cornell University Press.

Robinson, Richard (2007). *Narratives of the European Border: A History of Nowhere.* Basingstoke: Palgrave Macmillan.

Rumford, Chris (2009). *Citizens and Borderwork in Contemporary Europe.* London: Routledge.

Saldívar, José David (1997). *Border Matters: Remapping American Cultural Studies.* Berkeley, CA; London: University of California Press.

Strathern, Marilyn (1996). 'Cutting the Network'. *Journal of the Royal Anthropological Institute,* 2(3): 517–35.

Taussig, M. (2008). 'Redeeming Indigo'. *Theory Culture and Society,* 25: 1–16.

Taylor, Victor E., and Charles E. Winquist (2003). *Encyclopedia of Postmodernism.* London: Routledge.

Van Houtum, Henk, Olivier Thomas Kramsch, and Wolfgang Zierhofer (eds) (2005). *B/Ordering Space.* Aldershot and Burlington, VT: Ashgate.

Vaughan-Williams, Nick (2015). *Europe's Border Crisis: Biopolitical Security and Beyond.* New York: Oxford University Press.

Weizman, Eyal (2007). *Hollow Land: Israel's Architecture of Occupation.* London: Verso.

Wilson, Thomas M., and Hastings Donnan (eds) (1994). *Border Approaches: Anthropological Perspectives on Frontiers.* Lanham and London: University Press of America.

Zartman, I. William (2010). *Understanding Life in the Borderlands: Boundaries in Depth and in Motion.* Athens: University of Georgia Press.

 **6**

Materializing the border-as-line in Sarajevo

Stef Jansen

A border, Sarah Green has written (2009: 6), 'is not simply a line drawn by the state'. This recurrent point in border studies is echoed in the first chapter of this book (Demetriou and Dimova). Yet we can read this statement in different ways. If, as seems to be the case most frequently, the emphasis is placed on the negative – 'a border is *not* a line drawn by the state' – it urges us to deconstruct notions (a) that borders are drawn by humans over objects (b), that they are best conceived of as lines, and (c) that they coincide with the topographical limits of polity territories. These three deconstructions are congruent with three theoretical developments in anthropology that pose a challenge for our studies of borders.

First, a recent vogue in some sections of anthropology in the United Kingdom, inspired especially by actor-network theory (Latour 2005), argues that we should conceive of a 'flat' social that includes human and non-human 'actants'. Here we find a call to trace how things 'act' to structure practice, how they 'afford' certain forms of engagement, and, sometimes, how they 'exude' affect. When this is applied to the study of borders, the focus is on showing that borders are not drawn by people over things, but are continually produced into more or less stable assemblages by actor-networks of human and non-human actants. In practice, as noted, for example, by Navaro-Yashin (2009: 10), studies in this vein tend to effectively privilege non-human agency. To grasp their opposition to the focus on reification in most border studies – on how people make borders material – I therefore group such approaches under the label 'thingism' (see Jansen 2013).

A second way to read the objection to a notion of the border as 'a line drawn by the state' can be found in the critique of the notion of border-as-line. An influential strand of this criticism has come from what Alvarez (1995) calls the 'a-literalist' approach, where the Mexico–US border has been the inspiration for studies that foreground interstitiality, hybridity, and transgression. This has evolved in tune with, and it has contributed to, anthropological deconstructions of ideas of 'cultures' as discrete, bounded, homogeneous wholes. The notion of border-as-line is then posited as a metaphor for Euroamerican modernity's theoretically and politically pernicious drive towards classification, closure, and exclusion. Highlighting line-drawing as a key logic underlying all kinds of (often forced) separation and disambiguation – for example, in terms of gender, sexuality, nationality, or race – such work tends to shift from empirical studies of polity borders to broader discussions of conceptual and cultural differentiation, particularly in terms of the politics of representation. This criticism of the notion of border-as-line, and the preference for terms such as 'borderlands' or 'border zones', is often part of a rejection of the pretence of self-evident legitimacy that representations of borders-as-lines are seen to involve. This objection therefore revolves around an anti-essentialist critique, which is particularly relevant in the study of nationalism and its border work.

A third reading of the statement that 'a border is not simply a line drawn by the state' can be discerned in studies inspired by Foucault's work on governmentality. Given that sovereignty is graded in a global system, attention is drawn to the functioning of border regimes on supra-state and infra-state scales in an emerging global biopolitical order of mobility with visa and biometrics at its core. Border work, it is shown, is increasingly exercised from locations that are topographically removed from border posts and has become part of diffuse technologies of government. Here authors seek to decentre not only the state but also a concern with territory, focusing instead on the dispersed technologies through which individual and collective bodies are governed (e.g. Hansen and Stepputat 2005).

This chapter proposes an analysis of a particular border in light of those three deconstructions – three formulations of the statement that 'a border is not simply a line drawn by the state' that emphasize the negative ('not') – in order to address the core theme of this book: the mediation of abstraction and materiality in border work. In particular, I draw attention to the question of the intensity of the line-ness of borders over time. I do this by tracing the (re)production of the border that divides Sarajevo (Bosnia and Herzegovina, BiH) as a contingent process in which two asymmetrical projects to mediate between abstraction and materiality clash over the relative line-ness of this border as part of state territorialization.

A border mapped, by flat searches for example

The shape of the Sarajevo agglomeration is conditioned largely by its mountainous surroundings. An elongated inhabited area follows the river Miljacka, with hillside neighbourhoods spreading out from there. The old city centre lies at the far eastern end of the valley, which then narrows into a canyon. The construction of apartment settlements from the second half of the twentieth century onwards has been concentrated at the other side of the city, where the valley broadens. Following the major traffic artery westwards from the centre, one passes a series of planned post-Second World War apartment complexes. Turning south-east at a major crossroads, circumventing a hill, one enters a plain. Its central part is occupied by apartment blocks. Most of these were constructed in the late 1970s and 1980s within the governmental framework of socialist Yugoslav self-management, and, after the 1992–95 war in BiH, many have been reconstructed during the late 1990s and early 2000s. This settlement is called Dobrinja.

During the first decade of the new millennium, the Sarajevo agglomeration expanded further. At the time of my ethnographic research in 2008–10,[1] there were many brand-new flats for sale at the south-eastern end of Dobrinja, with more under construction. In the dire economic situation in BiH, with towering unemployment, many people found it difficult to scrape together enough money to obtain a loan to buy an apartment. At the same time, with the end of the Yugoslav socialist system of tenancy rights, allocated through workplaces, buying a flat had become a priority for many. Renting was widely considered a worst-case scenario. New, spacious flats in the child-friendly outskirts of the agglomeration were thus an attractive option, especially for younger Sarajevo households. The ones at the south-eastern end of Dobrinja were on average cheaper than those in many other outlying parts. Yet few Sarajevans would even consider purchasing one of those flats, except for those who resided in that area already. This could not be explained in terms of any material characteristics of these flats (e.g. type of building, comfort, size, quality of construction, etc.). Nor did this reluctance follow from the materiality of their location, for instance in terms of travel time to the city centre. When travelling by car or taxi from this south-eastern end of the plain there was in fact an alternative, shorter access route to the city centre across a hill. Moreover, many of these flats were within walking distance of the bus and trolleybus terminus that connected Dobrinja to the city centre. Still, given the choice between two almost identical flats a few hundred metres away from that same terminus, very few Sarajevans currently living more to the north would consider moving into the south-eastern buildings, even if they knew they could save money that way. In turn, very few residents of the south-eastern part would consider moving into an identical flat immediately to the north-west. All other parameters being the same, on this plain people's shortlisting of flats for potential purchase would produce a clear line. On aggregate, if we took a map of this area and coloured in all the flats that people would possibly shortlist in one colour and those they would not in another, the coordinates of the line between the two colours would be the same for those on either side of it. That line would run through the middle of a few streets, between buildings, and in one case right through an apartment block.

Many potential buyers would not necessarily be able to point out the precise location of that line on the ground or on a map. Yet, moving between the apartment blocks on this plain, most would, if they so wished, know how to use material indicators to 'tell' (Burton 1978) on which side of it they found themselves at any point. Key to this were markers of ethno-national difference between Serbs and Bosniaks (Lofranco 2007):[2] the script used on shops and billboards, the selection of books for sale in stalls, the relative prominence of pork in butchers' shops, people's names on shops and doorbells, political party propaganda, announcements of war-related commemorative events, graffiti, and so on. The architectural and acoustic presence of an Orthodox church (construction of which started in 1990) and a mosque (built in 2003) on either side of the line could also be read as significant. Still, none of those symbolic indicators allowed completely unambiguous 'telling', nor could they serve to pin down a line on a map or on the ground with exact topographical coordinates. For example, one could find both Cyrillic and Latin script to the south-east, and one could buy pork to the north-west. One could find Orthodox churches further to the north-west and (reconstructed) mosques further to the south-east. A minority of name tags of doorbells too would blur the division, especially to the north-west.

This blurring posed no problem for flat-hunters. For their purposes, they did not need to know exactly where the line lay on the ground or on a map. Any flat located on the south-eastern side of the line would be listed in advertisements as being in 'Istočno Sarajevo' (East Sarajevo).[3] On websites this was a searchable variable. Ultimately, then, it was not the precise topography of the line itself that prevailed in their shortlisting, nor, as we saw, the materiality of the flats in question, but the latter's location in the territorial-administrative set-up of BiH. While they would not start with a map, the line that we could extrapolate from their flat searches would neatly coincide with a line that had already been mapped for them (see Figure 6.1).

Encounters with a border-as-line

This line demarcated 'Sarajevo' from 'Istočno Sarajevo' and, on a larger scale, the 'Federation of BiH' (the Federation) from 'Republika Srpska' (RS), the two 'entities' of BiH.[4] In English it was officially known as the Inter-Entity Boundary Line (IEBL). If they attributed a name to it at all, people living around it sometimes called it *međuentitetska granica* (inter-entity border), sometimes *linija razdvajanja* (line of (dichotomous, splitting) division), sometimes *linija razgraničenja* (line of demarcation/bordering), sometimes *međuentitetska linija* (inter-entity line), and sometimes simply *linija* ('line'). On this plain at the south-east of the Sarajevo agglomeration it cut through the far end of Dobrinja, where, during my research, I lived a few metres to the north-west of this border, on Federation territory. From the bedroom window, I looked out on some rough greenery, a cluster of outlying 1980s Dobrinja buildings and an Orthodox church. Beyond that I saw a new settlement with more construction under way. I knew that the IEBL ran through this overgrown green area, through the middle of some streets between the reconstructed 1980s apartment blocks, and right through one of them. But for a long time, I didn't know its exact topography. Some local residents didn't either, whereas some who lived very near to it could pin it down pretty precisely. Until recently, none of the most widely used city maps of Sarajevo had depicted this border.[5] Moreover, they had contained swaths of open land which were now occupied by the new buildings of Istočno Sarajevo. On the main roads around Dobrinja, there

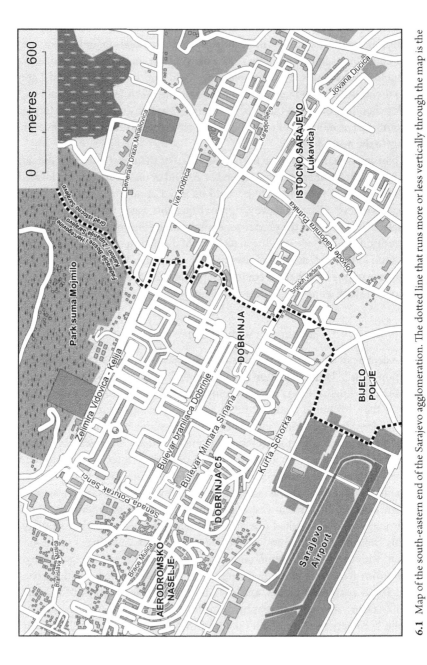

6.1 Map of the south-eastern end of the Sarajevo agglomeration. The dotted line that runs more or less vertically through the map is the Inter-Entity Boundary Line (IEBL)

were signs welcoming people to 'Republika Srpska', 'City of Istočno Sarajevo', and, more recently, in the other direction, to 'Kanton Sarajevo' (the Federation consists of ten cantons; there was no sign welcoming one to the Federation). Yet there were no such signs in the residential centre of Dobrinja. Nor was there a fence, a barbed wire, or a barrier. There were no checkpoints and no uniformed border officers. There were no border posts.

Still, as the flat search example shows, this was a very significant border. The mediation between abstraction and materiality here could also be observed in more mundane bodily movement. As I have discussed elsewhere (Jansen 2013), in their everyday practice, many people living on either side of the line were mostly facing away from it. They did not cross this border at all, or did so only occasion-ally.[6] Others did so more frequently. In actual movements across the line we can discern a clear asymmetric pattern. On aggregate, those who lived in Istočno Sarajevo crossed it much more frequently than those living on the other side. Their destination was usually somewhere in or around the city centre, where they went to work, engaged in consumption and leisure, made family visits, or attended to specific administrative issues (e.g. in embassies). Inhabitants of the 'Federal' part of Dobrinja crossed the border only occasionally, if they did so at all. Some did so to save on certain shopping expenses, and some for transit to other places.

When people on either side reflected on their movements across the IEBL in informal conversations or in interviews, they often signalled that they experienced an acute sense that they were in fact crossing a line in those instances. Bodily move-ment across the line, or the thought of doing so, evoked some fear but, above all, a sense of unease. To explain this, people often brought up the ethno-national identitarian markers mentioned above, indicating a heightened feeling (felt or imputed) of 'Bosniakness' or 'Serbian-ness' that was considered incompatible with the surroundings on the opposite side. Crossing, then, did not necessarily subvert this border's demarcating work. Indeed, the asymmetrical pattern in frequency of crossing did not correlate at all with resistance or aversion to the felt intensity of its line-ness. As we shall see, people in Istočno Sarajevo generally displayed the strong-est commitment to this polity border and were most likely to frame their concerns in ethno-national identitarian terms. Yet it was they who were most likely to cross it. In practice, then, affect was often subordinated to pragmatic concerns. Just as in many other urban agglomerations, there were incentives for regular centripetal bodily movement towards the city centre. For those residing in Istočno Sarajevo, this implied crossing the line. For others, it did not. In this sense and to this degree, crossing or not crossing was a by-product of other pursuits.

This brings us to a broader issue. Bodily movement around the IEBL gains much of its structure from practices of government. Material interventions in the land-scape by government institutions are indicative here. There were clear differences in street name plates (the names themselves, the shape of the plates, colour, and script), official notices, plaques on the entrances of public institutions, police cars and uniforms, and so on. With these official markers, there was no blurring. Again, none of them marked the exact location of the line, but they all flagged government practices on particular territories demarcated by it. Clearly, they could be read as (partly ethno-national) markers of 'identity', setting out symbolic stakes. Yet I suggest that their significance to our analysis of the border lies more in the way in which they constituted sovereignty claims, flagging patterns in the government of populations on particular territories. They testified to the fact that people living on the south-eastern side of the line were subject to government by the various, nested institutions of RS and those on the north-western side to those of the Federation. All of them were also subject to government by BiH state institutions, but these had such a limited mandate that their 'state effect' was extremely weak (Mitchell 1999; Jansen 2015). Instead, it was in entity or cantonal organs that we could discern the most effective work of state spatialization according to the principles of verticality and encompassment (Ferguson and Gupta 2002). Public transport was organized separately, away from the line, and the IEBL also demarcated where inhabitants were subject to surveillance, tax, or judicial procedure and where their lives were plugged into mechanisms of public provision. In terms of government, then, the logistics of everyday life continuously made people on either side of the IEBL into two different 'populations' (Foucault 1991; Foucault 2007: 67ff.). And with very few exceptions, this entailed an 'embrace' of citizens on particular *territories* (Torpey 1998).

Despite its weak material presence on the spot, this line was therefore very significant. The politics of sovereignty over territory structured people's practices to a large extent and, independently of their knowledge of its exact location, these practices, in turn, largely materialized the border as a line. Above all, this was a polity border. This is clear even in the asymmetrical patterns in crossing: for example, employment opportunities were subject to formal and informal ethno-national and entity quotas operated by BiH state institutions and foreign organizations, and price differences reflected diverging taxation systems. My description paid special attention to flat searches because in them we can catch a future-oriented glimpse of possibility in relation to space – of connections that could be made or not be made (Massey 2005: 106; see also Green, Chapter 5 above). Most people were reluctant to purchase a flat on the other side of the line – that is, they refrained from making connections – partly because they could not be certain how this polity border would develop in the future: no-one could guarantee that it would not become an even more significant polity border (an inter-state border, for example). As for the few who might consider options on either side of it, their decision process would never be totally oblivious to it. The line was there to be reckoned with, and its future was there to be speculated about.

Importantly, this temporal dimension of the making of space was equally important with regard to the past. To grasp the relevance and the intensity of this border over time, we have to account for the ways in which this particular set of streets and buildings had become a border in the first place, that is, how certain connections had been made and others had been destroyed and rendered difficult or impossible to establish in the future. This is what I turn to in the next section.

Drawing lines over time

The legitimacy of the IEBL as a border was deeply contested. Yet no-one denied that it was the product of recent political practices. Not even those who were most committed to its line-ness claimed that it was 'natural' or 'historical' – these favourite labels in conflicts over territorial sovereignty. Nor was it inherited and scaled up from pre-existing local borders on a smaller scale (see e.g. Sahlins 1989). Instead, most residents remembered all too well how it had been drawn by human beings as part of competing state-making projects. The IEBL existed as the effect of violent polity-making practices that had produced it in the absence of any territorial, natural, dichotomous, ahistorical, necessary difference that could be symbolically 'expressed' in a polity border on those particular coordinates. Nowhere on its over 1,000 km stretch was this more obvious than in Dobrinja. This border, and the entities it established, were non-natural, 'multiple, non-dichotomous, formed in trajectories and historically contingent' (Green 2009: 6). Rather than interpreting it as 'symbolizing' a timeless truth of national difference, then, I propose a Benjaminian 'allegorical reading', 'plucking an image or object out of history's stream and examining it "at a standstill", as a dialectical image in which past and present exist simultaneously' (Stead 2003: 57). Benjamin focuses on the figure of the ruin, which he sees as a sign of 'brokenness and transience' because it bears 'physical traces of time on its surface' (Stead 2003: 56). In what follows, the 'ruination' of connections will be central to my reconstruction of the historically specific, contingent materialization of the Dobrinja border as a line.

First drawing: war

It was in early 1992 that this border first appeared in the lives of people in Dobrinja. This was a particularly truthful genesis: its creation occurred through the kind of constitutive violence that accompanies many territorializing state-making projects but that in much of our everyday life remains hidden from contemporary experience. At the time, the Yugoslav Socialist Republic of BiH was marked by a political stalemate in the governing coalition between the parties that had won the first multi-party elections after the Second World War: the Bosniak nationalist Stranka Demokratske Akcije (SDA), the Croatian nationalist Hrvatska Demokratska Zajednica (HDZ), and the Serbian nationalist Srpska Demokratska Stranka (SDS). In late 1991 SDS had organized a plebiscite in the territories it controlled to stay within the remainder of Yugoslavia, now dominated by the Milošević government of the Republic of Serbia. In January 1992, it proclaimed the Serb Republic of Bosnia and Herzegovina and thus established de facto polity borders within BiH, many of which would remain in place when it was renamed RS. Less than two months later, with war raging in Croatia, and with violent incidents ever more frequent across the country, the Sarajevo-based BiH government (now formally abandoned by SDS) organized a referendum on independence from what was left of the Yugoslav federation. In line with calls by SDS, a majority of Bosnian Serbs did not take part in the poll, but 62.68 per cent of the total electorate (almost the entire turn-out) voted yes. The government proclaimed independence, and the Republic of BiH (RBiH) was soon widely recognized internationally (most European Union states and the USA recognized it on 6 April 1992). Yet it could not establish a minimally effective presence over its entire territory. SDS declared independence of its own 'Serbian' state – RS – and HDZ soon left the government too to consolidate and expand its 'Croatian' territories. In Sarajevo, after a period of intermittent violence and barricades by various armed formations, the then de facto increasingly Serbian 'Yugoslav People's Army', which later morphed into the Army of RS (Vojska Republike Srpske, VRS), took control of some peripheral parts of Dobrinja and laid siege to the city. Most of Dobrinja (and of Sarajevo) remained under control of logistically inferior pro-BiH police and (para)military forces, later to become the Army of the Republic of BiH (ARBiH). With the exception of the airport, which was taken over by the United Nations early on, and a narrow and dangerous throughway towards the city centre, all sides were under control of VRS and its allies (Jansen 2014).

During the first weeks of the war, military violence thus linked up a series of dots into a siege line and/or frontline. This was referred to as *linija*, a military term for the first line of defence (*prva linija*). Dobrinja's apartment blocks – both its main ARBiH-controlled part and its peripheral VRS-held areas – suffered extreme devastation, and the composition of the population changed sharply owing to massive displacement. In ARBiH-held Dobrinja, there was an influx of Bosniaks expelled from east BiH and from the suburb's outskirts by VRS, while many more people of various national backgrounds (not one national grouping had numbered an absolute majority here before the war) escaped from the settlement. Even with its large refugee intake, the overall population of Sarajevo shrank dramatically during the war: over 10,000 were killed, and hundreds of thousands of people of all nationalities sought safety elsewhere. Sarajevo citizens identified as Serbs were in a specific situation, in ARBiH-held Dobrinja as elsewhere. The city was besieged in their name and under flags that appealed to their nationality. They were called upon by the SDS leadership and its armed forces to close national ranks and to move out to outlying areas under VRS control. Many did so – often before the closure of the siege – with varying degrees of enthusiasm for the 'Serbian cause'. Those who stayed were at risk from snipers and shelling by the besieging VRS forces, like all their co-citizens, and many suffered additional discrimination owing to their suspected status as fifth columnists. This included violence by Bosniak warlords close to the RBiH government, which was increasingly controlled by SDA. At least

10,000 Serbs stayed in Sarajevo throughout the siege (International Crisis Group 1998: 3), with some occupying positions of relative influence in ARBiH and in the RBiH government, but the vast majority moved out, often to peripheral areas of Sarajevo under control of VRS.

In 1993, SDS announced grand plans for a 'Serbian Sarajevo' as a counterpoint to what it called 'Muslim Sarajevo'. It established municipal assemblies parallel to the municipalities in the city, consisting of Serbian members only (but not all of them) and organized separate institutions of government and provision, including utilities, policing, health care, education, and so on. Aiming to prevent Serbian Sarajevo from becoming a satellite of the city it had separated from, SDS projected its own capital city as a centre for government, higher education, and industry. In the Assembly of RS, its leader Radovan Karadžić stated that 'Sarajevo will be divided and become two cities ... Everything that is Serb we will retain' (27 August 1993, quoted in Donia 2006: 324). Four months later, he argued that

> SDS policy is to hold on to Sarajevo. ... We must create a critical mass of intelligentsia here. We will be in contact with a huge world, the aggressive world of Islam. Our capital, our education, our culture, our economy will be in contact here on the Miljacka [river] with this entire world, the exponents of which will be the Bosnian Muslims. We don't dare lose this battle, never or in any way ... I have already talked to Milošević about this. Serbian Sarajevo will be supported by all twelve million Serbs. (30–31 December 1993, quoted in Donia 2006: 324)

Yet, at that time, the actual VRS-controlled areas in this region did not really look like a city at all. In addition to a small set of 1980s apartment blocks at the far end of Dobrinja, they consisted of some parts of Sarajevo closer to the city centre, some further outlying suburbs, and a scattered collection of distant villages and small mountain towns. Only very few people who identified as non-Serbs remained in this 'City of Serbian Sarajevo'. In addition to its pre-war Serbian population (minus those who had moved abroad), it housed thousands of Serbs who had fled territories now controlled by ARBiH (Armakolas 2007).

The border was thus co-produced by military violence and by the regularities in two-way displacement shaped by competing state-making projects. Among the displaced in either direction, crossing the *linija* and leaving it behind one's back was understood to promise a degree of safety. And the more such movements were massive and systematic, the more the line hardened. It also became increasingly fortified. At its south-eastern end, the *linija* in Dobrinja ran through a set of streets between apartment blocks. Most inhabitants had fled those buildings in either direction early on, and others were evacuated as the blocks were occupied by VRS on one side and ARBiH on the other. Throughout the war, this line remained more or less on the same topographical coordinates. Yet in military and political strategy it was in principle considered temporary, a potential starting point for territorial gains or losses. It was where the clash between two asymmetric state-making projects was fought out: to return to Massey, this struggle, evolving over time, concerned which possible connections *should* be made and which existing ones *should* be ruined or rendered impossible in the future. One project, led by SDS, sought to draw a line that would demarcate 'Serbian' territories from 'Muslim' ones. The other, led by SDA, rejected any border within RBiH but aimed to upgrade the existing border around the entire territory of what had been the Yugoslav Republic of BiH into a state border.

Second drawing: Dayton

The 1995 Dayton Peace Agreement simultaneously recognized both these two constitutive political acts to a degree. On the one hand, it reaffirmed the sovereignty of BiH as an independent state within a global state system as per the outcome of the 1992 referendum. This was in tune with the principle of the Badinter Commission (1991) that European Union states would recognize independent polities established through an upgrading of existing borders between federal units of Yugoslavia. On the other hand, the Agreement consolidated the division of BiH into two 'entities': the Federation and RS. On the whole, the war-time *linija* became the IEBL, with a security zone on either side, dotted with checkpoints manned by United Nations blue helmets and other patrols. Large stretches of it were characterized by devastation, minefields, and lack of human habitation. Yet in some areas the Dayton negotiators drew a *new* line rather than regularizing the military 'situation on the ground'. In the Sarajevo agglomeration, many suburbs held by VRS were to be 'reintegrated' into the capital city (and, thus, into the Federation). In the RS Assembly session, held a few weeks after the Dayton negotiations, some politicians argued in favour of encouraging Serbs in those territories to stay put; but most argued against. The president of the SDS Assembly, Momčilo Krajišnik, for example, stated that:

> The mission of this republic and its first strategic goal is for us to divide from the Muslims and Croats, and no one has the right to create a strategy whereby Serbian Sarajevo remains in a common state ... No one is allowed now to create a new solution to stay together, nor do the folks in Sarajevo want it, namely the people, nor does the leadership in Sarajevo. ... At the end of it all, the best solution is that people leave Sarajevo and locations are found to accommodate them. (17 December 1995, quoted in Donia 2006: 338)

In winter 1996, most Serbs left the suburbs that were to be reintegrated into the city, where many had themselves arrived as displaced persons during the war. After the already substantial exodus of Serbs into territory held by VRS before and during the war this further entrenched the homogenization of the population in ethno-national terms. The evacuation involved propaganda, the withdrawal of services and infrastructure, and, eventually, the use of force against those who wished to stay. Yet many Serbs did not require SDS encouragement to move across the redrawn border into the territory of RS as consolidated in the Dayton Agreement. Under the circumstances, they were afraid or unwilling to 'live under the Muslims'. After initial demonstrations against reintegration, including strong criticism of the SDS politician Krajišnik, who was blamed for 'selling Sarajevo to the Muslims', an estimated 60,000 people left (Sell 2000). Hiring trucks, they took everything they could carry, sometimes including the corpses of family members dug up from their wartime graves. Many of the houses and flats were stripped bare and set alight before 'Federal' police entered these suburbs. Some of those who fled were allocated accommodation owned by expelled Bosniaks in north-east BiH. Yet a large number of them remained closer to Sarajevo, in the parts of Serbian Sarajevo that remained under RS control. As during the war, the central coordinate in the reasonings that underlay this population movement consisted of a line drawn in the interaction of state-making projects.

Third drawing: arbitration

To come to an agreement on the topography of the IEBL the negotiators on the US Air Force base in Dayton, Ohio (USA), had employed sophisticated technology provided by their hosts, including a flight simulator. Yet, as a result of the particular scale on which the mapping equipment operated, the IEBL was not precisely topographically fixed everywhere: in Dobrinja its exact coordinates were initially left undecided. In 2001, a judge from Ireland appointed by the Office of the High Representative (the supreme agency of the foreign intervention in the post-war BiH semi-protectorate) determined them in a process known as 'arbitration'. On the basis of legal representations by various authorities and consultations with current and former residents, Judge Diarmuid Sheridan refrained from allocating the whole Dobrinja apartment complex to one of the entities. Nor did he give preference to any geological features or legalize what had been the *linija* up to then: the area between devastated apartment blocks that had been the siege line and remained, for some time after the war, mined, barricaded, and policed. Instead, the arbiter allocated some buildings and streets that had until then been de facto RS-controlled to Sarajevo (and thus to the Federation), but left some others in Serbian Sarajevo (and thus in RS). The line was thus redrawn a little towards the south-east, but it still ran through the middle of streets and between identical buildings of the same apartment complex. In one case, for reasons that remain unclear, Sheridan drew it through such a building.

Initially, arbitration met with dissatisfaction on both sides of the IEBL, but, again, not in a symmetric manner. As we saw, the mission of the besieging VRS had been to divide BiH: the objective here was a strong border (ideally an interstate border) within the territory of the former Yugoslav Republic of BiH and a weak border (or no border at all) between RS and neighbouring Serbia. Many inhabitants of Serbian Sarajevo, including those in the outlying parts of Dobrinja that Sheridan allocated to RS, had lived in more central parts of Sarajevo before the war, and many had spent the war in suburbs held by the besieging VRS until these had been reintegrated into the city in 1996. They saw the 2001 arbitration as one more 'anti-Serbian' measure, and when it was implemented, a few hundred people put up barricades, built an improvised wall, and stoned blue helmet patrols. Yet this protest soon died out. After all, for most of them, the very existence of the IEBL was itself a positive phenomenon: a material consolidation of RS's sovereignty, which they considered a guarantee of their safety and of Serbian national interests. To them, the precise topography was wrong and some would have preferred it if it had demarcated states rather than 'entities', but they saw it as the best available option in the given geopolitical circumstances. It was not drawn at the ideal place, it was not enough of a line, but at least it was a line.

People on the other side of the border, who had spent the war in besieged territory under control of ARBiH, considered the allocation of a set of buildings at the outer edge of Dobrinja an irrational break-up of an organic whole on several scales. They were dissatisfied that it separated out a small part of this apartment complex; that it thereby separated out a small part of the city of Sarajevo; and, more generally, that the IEBL as a whole separated out just under half of the territory of the state of BiH into the entity of RS. Like most people in Sarajevo and like most Bosnians committed to BiH statehood – Bosniaks and others – they perceived the meandering IEBL that embodied these separations also as a deeply unfair geopolitical reward for a bloody military Serbian nationalist campaign against BiH sovereignty which had held them under siege for over three and a half years. The problem with the IEBL, for them, was not so much its unjust location, but the fact that it was too much of a line, or that it was a line in the first place.

Still drawing

The border, like the entities it demarcated, was thus produced as an ad hoc compromise between two incompatible sovereignty claims over territory. So was Istočno Sarajevo (the new name for Serbian Sarajevo after a 2004 decision of the Constitutional Court of BiH), which saw vast construction projects – including the new apartment blocks at the south-eastern end of Dobrinja – and soon housed tens of thousands of people.[7] The topography of the IEBL has not changed since, but the drawing process continues as competing forces seek to thicken this line or thin it, that is, to intensify it or de-intensify its effectiveness in terms of sovereignty over territory.

By the time of my research in 2008–10, those who had fought to establish an undivided BiH did not refrain from seeking to delegitimize RS. Yet because of the very limited mandate of the 'central' BiH state institutions, there was not much they could do in practice. As Kostovicova (2004) has analysed in detail, successive RS governments have tried to keep BiH encompassment to a minimum. Sometimes this involved calls for independence, and much rhetoric continued to invoke fully-fledged statehood for RS. This rarely breached the IEBL and did not involve much concrete action on the borderline itself. The focus was on territorial integrity: on consolidating RS itself within its existing borders. It was thus not only through inflammatory rhetoric of statehood but also through non-spectacular technologies of government that the line-ness of the border remained at the centre of contestation. This logic ran through most parliamentary stalemates in BiH long after the war. If delegates from Sarajevo-based parties sought to diminish the line-ness of the IEBL, RS delegates called for measures to increase its intensity, aiming to consolidate a discrete population to be governed on a discrete territory. The first continually sought to thin the line, and the second continually sought to thicken it. Maps produced in RS, such as those used in television weather or traffic reports, tended to either show the IEBL clearly or depicted the territory of RS only. Their Federation colleagues always depicted the entire territory of BiH, with or without the IEBL. RS politicians rarely went as far as seeking actual demarcation on the ground, but they did emphasize, for example, the need for precise cadastral mapping. When, in 2012, a crisis erupted around the issuing of citizen identification numbers (Jansen 2015), they insisted that the territorial units for registration should be shaped according to the post-war municipal borders, that is, according to the IEBL. When a census was finally held in 2013, RS insisted that 'entity citizenship' be recorded. It was included as an optional question. Sarajevo-based parliamentarians, of course, objected in all cases. In 2010, provoked by the statement by the SDA politician Bakir Izetbegović that 150,000 Serbs lived in Sarajevo (implying that he was including Istočno Sarajevo), Milorad Dodik, then Prime Minister of Republika Srpska, even proposed to rename 'Istočno Sarajevo' by removing the mention of Sarajevo altogether (*Nezavisne Novine* 2010). The RS war-time claim to Sarajevo had thus made way for a commitment to a line that should be as much of a line as possible.[8]

'Not' and 'simply'

This chapter has approached the Dobrinja border as a 'dialectical image in which past and present exist simultaneously'. It has shown that it is the contingent product of recent state-making projects and that its relative line-ness is crucial to war and post-war contestation. This process included human beings drawing lines on maps as well as many other practices, such as warfare, collective population movement, government, routine bodily movement, and so on. How then, does this add up with regard to the three deconstructions with which I opened this chapter? What light does it shed on the thingist privileging of non-human actants, the a-literalist aversion to conceive of borders as lines, and the shift away from territory in some studies in the governmentality paradigm? I now deal with these three formulations of the statement that 'the border is not simply a line drawn by the state' in turn.

First, what can a thingist approach contribute to the study of this border? Since I have explored this question in detail elsewhere (Jansen 2013), I only briefly summarize my argument here in relation to the material provided above. I have shown that any genealogy of this border must place human border work at the core. Clearly, it needs to account for how these human practices congealed around things (shells, barricades, buildings, a flight simulator, etc.), yet we find that *ultimately* none of these particular things were necessary conditions in the making of this border. Human practices thus trumped any agency of things. For example, the logic of the post-war Serbian exodus from previously VRS-held areas in 1996, which considerably contributed to the consolidation of the IEBL as a line, did not heed the materiality of flats or landscapes. It was structured by human practices of line-drawing: had the Dayton negotiators drawn the line elsewhere, patterns of population movement would have shaped up differently. Likewise, the materiality of a Dobrinja apartment building did not affect the way in which an arbitrating judge drew the border in 2001: his line simply cut through it. Hence, to provide an adequate description of the production of this border on these particular topographical coordinates, and to allow critical reflection on the crucial political issue of accountability in this process, I had to conceive of it first and foremost as contingent human practice over things. In that way, I kept my own account accountable too. Rejecting any postulations of a thingist ontology, however, I did find a focus on things to be a valuable methodological choice to prevent an overemphasis on semiotics and particularly on ethno-national symbolism. This allowed me, for example, to uncover a pattern of centripetal governmental and suburban logistics in post-war asymmetrical routine bodily movement and, in the case of flat searches, a built-in exposure to the possibility of future (dis)connections that tends to 'thicken' the border in ethno-national terms through residence patterns.

Second, what of the a-literalist approach to borders? The critique of the border-as-line, I found, is a useful warning against any assumptions that the line-ness of borders is given. As such it remains a crucial riposte against nationalist naturalizing treatments of culture and territory. Yet this should not lead us to refrain from taking seriously what the introduction to this book calls 'ideological' projects to *achieve* line-ness and to try to account for particular historical formations where such projects are materialized to a large degree. 'Borderlands' may indeed be sites of indeterminacy and subversion, but the ethnographic record contains much evidence to warn us against any automatic assumptions that this should be the case (Donnan and Wilson 1999). Donnan (2005), for example, shows how people may invest in the maintenance and fixity of borders, fiercely resisting any hints of hybridity, and Berdahl (1999) and Pelkmans (2006) found little fluidity or blurring even after the dismantling of the fortifications of previously almost impermeable borders. In Dobrinja, as we have seen, there was little material bordering infrastructure at the precise location of the limits of sovereignty claims, nor was it represented on many maps at the time of my research. Yet this did not give rise to any hybridity. The whole point of the drawing of this particular border had been to concentrate a nationally defined population (Serbs) on a particular territory. I would argue that the tendency in a-literalist studies to privilege the crossing of borders has an unintended, paradoxical consequence: it ends up further emphasizing the importance of their line-ness without acknowledging it properly. Indeed, one may ask if celebrations of such transgression, in which authors often locate emancipatory potential, do not reinforce rather than weaken conceptions of borders-as-lines. The case of the Dobrinja border shows us that routine (non-)crossing – much of which was driven by the logistics of government and suburban life – is not necessarily subversive of the line-ness of borders at all. It also tempers the implied assumption in the 'borderlands' genre that the notion of a line automatically implies a pretence of naturalness or self-evidence. In contrast, speaking of a line allows handsomely for pointing out that it is being drawn. And that returns us to the question of who drew the Dobrinja border, which requires us to focus on the politics of sovereignty over territory.

Regarding this third deconstruction, my analysis paid much attention to government without letting go of a focus on territory. As Reeves (2011) has shown, there is a tendency in some work in the governmentality paradigm to treat the sovereignty–territory axis as a remnant of obsolete forms of politics and political analysis. Yet the political rationality of governmentality has not done away with or necessarily reduced the relevance of territorial claims in the name of statehood, although it has reconfigured the framework within which they can be furthered (e.g. Chalfin 2010; Heyman 1994). Cowan (2007) has demonstrated that sovereignty has long been a matter of degree, articulated within a global state system. Even if border work occurs in a multi-layered globalizing order, even if it is exercised away from border posts, even if it focuses on governing bodies and populations, it may still be aimed to an important extent at the establishment of a clear delimitation of one territory from others. Line-ness, then, remains an important objective in many ways. For example, the use of biometrics for the policing of mobility in a globalizing mobility regime (Salter 2006; Wilson 2006) does not seek to govern just any bodily movement but specifically that *across* such territorial delimitations. Rather than setting up an (evolutionist) opposition between concerns with government and concerns with territory, Foucault's refusal to take the latter as an unproblematic given may lead us precisely to investigate 'how territorial integrity get[s] *done*' (Reeves 2011: 906). This is what I have attempted in this chapter.

In conclusion, considering the statement that 'a border is not simply a line drawn by the state', I suggest that it is more productive to focus on the word 'simply' than on the word 'not'. This chapter has analysed the *degree* to which a particular border can be conceived of as a line drawn by the state, that is, as the ongoing product of projects of linear demarcation of territory by human beings who make sovereignty claims.[9] Clearly this is not a 'simple' process, and it certainly does not imply representations of borders as natural lines and/or as necessarily impermeable, static, complete ones. Instead it raises questions of *relative* materialization as part of territorial state-making. Surely, we can analyse the way borders are 'drawn by the state' as contingent rather than necessary, as political rather than natural?

Competing projects of territorial integrity, I have shown, structured the practices of people who lived around the Dobrinja border, and these practices, in turn, reproduced it as a border. Yet I also demonstrated the need for sensitivity to qualitative differences between specific projects of territorial state-making projects: the logic of competition here did not primarily pitch two states (or would-be states) against each other in a contest about *where* to draw the line. Instead, the sovereignty claims at play were asymmetric: the competing state-making projects rested on opposed conceptions of the degree to which there should be a border in the first place. In other words, what was at stake was a clash of two mediations between abstraction and materiality, and at the core of contestation was the *relative line-ness* of the border and, in that way, the question of *which* state(s) should be territorialized. Much political energy was invested, and much blood was spilled, in efforts not only to establish precise territorial coordinates for particular borders-as-lines, but also, more importantly, to ensure or prevent that they became more line-like in the first place. Reconstructing the short but brutal history of the Dobrinja border, this chapter has sought to demonstrate the value of tracing such contestations of the intensity of the line-ness of borders. For when conceived of and engaged with as lines, borders can be materialized *more* or *less* into lines, depending on how abstraction and materiality are mediated in any particular case. They can be more effective or less effective in terms of structuring the reach of practices of government on different scales, 'ruining' certain connections across space, preventing the making of other ones, and strengthening other ones still. As such, the relative line-ness of borders reflects the degree of success of the projects of territorial integrity that invest in them.

Notes

1 My thanks go to the people who agreed to participate in this research; to Jelena Ostojić, Melina Sadiković, and Mirjana Ostojić for research assistance; to the Leverhulme Trust and the British Academy for financial support; and to the editors and participants at EastBordNet events for constructive criticism.

2 Since 1993, 'Bosniak' has overtaken 'Bosnian Muslim' as a self-identifying and official label for Bosnians with Islamic socio-religious heritage.

3 Or another territorial-administrative category, also containing the term 'east', on a smaller scale.

4 In addition, there was a small district in the far north of BiH.

5 A widely available, undated printed map produced in Serbia by Intersistem Kartografija (scale: 1:20,000) depicted the Sarajevo agglomeration as it was around 1990. A 'fifth, updated edition' of another printed map on the same scale, produced in Slovenia by the Geodetic Institute in 2008, provided a modest update of most of Sarajevo's outskirts. An on-line map developed for the city council by the Sarajevo firm Atlantbh (www.naviga tor.ba) was updated somewhat further. But none of the three depicted the border (and none showed any of recently built Istočno Sarajevo). It was only on some larger-scale

maps used in BiH or abroad, covering larger territories, that the IEBL was present. Later, it appeared on on-line zoomable maps such as the one in Figure 6.1.

6 Since the vast majority of Bosnians with various national backgrounds are indistinguishable from each other in terms of looks, speech, or clothing, much crossing was done anonymously and was therefore not noticeable to anyone at all. The foreign-imposed introduction of uniform non-national BiH licence plates in 1998 also facilitated the possibility of unnoticed crossing of the IEBL by car.

7 Figures depend on the territory included and are unreliable since no post-1991 census had been held in BiH by the time of my research.

8 Istočno Sarajevo never became the Serbian capital projected by SDS. This was partly due to a shift in power to politicians whose strongholds lay in north-west BiH. In 1998 RS government institutions were officially installed in Banja Luka, the largest town in the entity.

9 I thereby also resist the metaphorical sprawl of border terminology. For reasons of analytical rigour I favour confining the terminology of 'borders' exclusively to spatial demarcations between polities, i.e. to the projected topographical limits of the reach of territorial claims to sovereignty, and not to other patterns of separation and classification (e.g. of a conceptual, identitarian, disciplinary, or other nature) whose primary terrain is not on the intersection of territory and polity.

References

Alvarez, R. R. (1995). 'The Mexican–US border: The Making of an Anthropology of Borderlands'. *Annual Review of Anthropology*, 24: 447–70.

Armakolas, I. (2007). 'Sarajevo No More? Identity and the Sense of Place among Bosnian Serb Sarajevans in Republika Srpska'. In X. Bougarel, E. Helms, and G. Duijzings (eds), *The New Bosnian Mosaic: Memories, Identities and Moral Claims in a Post-War Society*, 79–100. Aldershot: Ashgate.

Berdahl, D. (1999). *Where the World Ended: Re-Unification and Identity in the German Borderland*. Berkeley: University of California Press.

Burton, F. (1978). *The Politics of Legitimacy: Struggles in a Belfast Community*. London: Routledge.

Chalfin, B. (2010). *Neoliberal Frontiers: An Ethnography of Sovereignty in West Africa*. Chicago: University of Chicago Press.

Cowan, J. K. (2007). 'The Supervised State'. *Identities: Global Studies in Culture and Power*, 14(5): 545–78.

Donia, R. J. (2006). *Sarajevo: A Biography*. London: Hurst.

Donnan, H. (2005). 'Material Identities: Fixing Identity in the Irish Borderlands'. *Identities: Global Studies in Culture and Power*, 12(1): 69–106.

Donnan, H., and T. M. Wilson (1999). *Borders: Frontiers of Identity, Nation and State*. Oxford: Berg.

Ferguson, J., and A. Gupta (2002). 'Spatialising States: Toward an Ethnography of Neoliberal Governmentality'. *American Ethnologist*, 29(4): 981–1002.

Foucault, M. (1991). 'Governmentality'. In G. Burchell, C. Gordon, and P. Miller (eds), *The Foucault Effect: Studies in Governmentality*, 73–86. London: Harvester Wheatsheaf.

Foucault, M. (2007). *Security, Territory, Population: Lectures at the Collège de France 1977–1978*, trans. G. Burchell. New York: Picador.

Green, Sarah (2009). 'Lines, Traces and Tidemarks: Reflections on Forms of Borderli-ness'. Paper presented at COST IS0803 Work Group 1 Meeting, Nicosia, 14–15 April 2009.

Hansen, T. B., and F. Stepputat (eds) (2005). *Sovereign Bodies: Citizens, Migrants, and States in the Post-Colonial World*. Princeton, NJ: Princeton University Press.

Heyman, J. McC. (1994). 'The Mexico–US Border in Anthropology: A Critique and Reformulation'. *Journal of Political Ecology*, 1: 43–65.

International Crisis Group (1998). *Minority Return or Mass Relocation?* Sarajevo: International Crisis Group.

Jansen, S. (2013). 'People and Things in the Ethnography of Borders: Materialising the Division of Sarajevo'. *Social Anthropology*, 21(1): 23–37.

Jansen, S. (2014). 'Hope for/against the State: Gridding in a Besieged Sarajevo Suburb'. *Ethnos*, 79(2): 238–60.

Jansen, S. (2015). *Yearnings in the Meantime: 'Normal Lives' and the State in a Sarajevo Apartment Complex*. Oxford: Berghahn.

Kostovicova, D. (2004). 'Republika Srpska and its Boundaries in Bosnian Serb Geographical Narratives in the Post-Dayton Period'. *Space & Polity*, 8(3): 267–87.

Latour, B. (2005). *Reassembling the Social: An Introduction to Actor-Network-Theory*. Oxford: Oxford University Press.

Lofranco, Z. T. (2007). 'L'altra Sarajevo'. *Archivo di Etnografia*, 2: 93–106.

Massey, D. (2005). *For Space*. London: Sage.

Mitchell, T. (1999). 'Society, Economy, and the State Effect'. In G. Steinmetz (ed.), *State/Culture: State Formation after the Cultural Turn*, 76–97. Ithaca, NY: Cornell University Press.

Navaro-Yashin, Y. (2009). 'Affective Spaces, Melancholic Objects: Ruination and the Production of Anthropological Knowledge'. *Journal of the Royal Anthropological Institute*, 15(1): 1–18.

Nezavisne Novine (2010). 'Dodik: mijenjati ime Istočnom Sarajevu zbog spekulacija'. 13 January.

Pelkmans, M. (2006). *Defending the Border: Identity, Religion and Modernity in the Republic of Georgia*. Ithaca, NY: Cornell University Press.

Reeves, M. (2011). 'Fixing the Border: On the Affective Life of the State in Southern Kyrgyzstan'. *Environment and Planning D: Society and Space*, 29(5): 905–23.

Sahlins, P. (1989). *Boundaries: The Making of France and Spain in the Pyrenees*. Berkeley: California University Press.

Salter, M. B. (2006). 'The Global Visa Regime and the Political Technologies of the International Self: Borders, Bodies and Biopolitics'. *Alternatives*, 31: 167–89.

Sell, L. (2000). 'The Serb Flight from Sarajevo: Dayton's First Failure'. *East European Politics & Societies*, 14(1): 179–202.

Stead, N. (2003). 'The Value of Ruins: Allegories of Destruction in Benjamin and Speer'. *Form/Work*, 6: 51–64.

Torpey, J. (1998). 'Coming and Going: On the State Monopolization of the Legitimate "Means of Movement"'. *Sociological Theory*, 16: 239–59.

Wilson, D. (2006). 'Biometrics, Borders and the Ideal Suspect'. In S. Pickering and L. Weber (eds), *Borders, Mobility and Technologies of Control*, 87–110. Dordrecht: Springer.

 **7**

Borders as ghosts

Eleni Myrivili

Two chapters in this volume precede and inform, or, I should rather say, 'haunt' this piece of writing. One is Sarah Green's discussion of the 'border-ness' of borders, that is, their distinctive quality. Green argues that what is distinct about borders is their quality of creating, embodying, and demonstrating 'difference', on both the level of space and that of time (Green, Chapter 5 above). She reads this notion of difference first through the Derridean 'trace' and then through Massey's discussion of difference as intrinsic to location. The second haunting is by Tuija Pulkkinen's analysis of difference in Deleuze and Derrida. Here the notion of difference (and repetition) opens up to us through an insightful and nuanced elaboration (Pulkkinen, Chapter 4 above).

I have been thinking of 'the border as ghost' for some time now. First it was a sensation, and it was what attracted me to borders and their study in the first place: borders have an uncanny, mysterious, and performative quality. Trying to grasp this sensation, I started thinking through the metaphor of 'border as ghost', and thus came across the Derridean concept of 'spectre'. The spectre is very close to the 'trace'. Both 'trace' and 'ghost' introduce and describe a particular kind of experience in regard to space and, mostly, to time: 'that which remains for the first time', 'the radical Other which returns as non-presence'.

In order to access the present as such, Derrida claims that there must be a rapport with something else (Derrida 1994). The trace, the very condition of non-presence of the presence, is the experience of a return to something else: to another past, present, and future, to another kind of temporality, to something other than being, to others in general ... This Other, the trace, he tells us, is a minimum of repeatability, which is there at every event, enabling it. It is a hiatus, an interruption of presence and being, and inassimilable to representation. For Derrida, the trace is an infinite mediation disrupting all claims to presence and all questions regarding ontology (what is), a negation that is the very condition of being.

The spectre, the ghost, is also something that is non-present, non-localizable, non-being. It, like the trace, intrudes and disrupts all self-presence, closure, and, mostly, our sense of temporality (any solidity of the past, present, and future). But, unlike the trace, the ghost may appear or disappear, and its voice addresses us, its gaze compels us … We don't know when it will visit us or how to adequately respond to the spectre, even though its Otherness compels us to do so. There is theatricality, a threatening quality and mystery to the ghost. It, unlike the trace, is not a negation; it has agency, authority.

Now, the relation of these two terms to performance is that they both question and also speak of that which is beyond, or the limit, of presence and representation. These two notions, trace and ghost, and the philosophical pursuits they instigated, have contributed a lot to the critical theory produced around the notion of performance, parts of which have been spear-heading what in the 1980s and 1990s was recognized as a paradigm shift, the so-called 'non-representational turn' (Thrift 2007). This is the framework within which I find it productive to rethink borders. These are the conceptual connections that the liquid borders that cross the Prespa Lake, where Albania, Greece, and Macedonia meet and divide, call forth.

The real, the border, and the ghost

The end of the cold war and the turn of the century constituted a significant time of transformation for the national borders of south-eastern Europe. In the microcosm of the Prespa Lake, whose waters are traversed by three national borders, these changes were both very significant for some of the Prespa border people and of little importance for others, depending on their particular positioning vis-à-vis those borders. The role and the character of the three borders did change. The Albanian border, the newly established national border of the Republic of Macedonia, and the Greek one re-arranged the ways in which they formed and organized subjects, objects, and types of movements around them.

More specifically, the end of the cold war in this part of the world meant the fall of the Hoxha regime in Albania. In 1989 parliamentary democracy was established and the constitution was renewed. In 1990 Albanian people were allowed to travel abroad, after five decades of living in an 'in vitro' social experiment in which Albania was progressively cutting its ties to the rest of the world, ending up in a virtual bell-jar of total socio-political, cultural, and economic isolation. In the early 1990s the Albanian border moved from being hard and opaque to being softer and more porous (Pearson 2006: 617–66; Draper 2010; Green 2005). In 1991 the Republic of Macedonia, after more than four decades of being one of the six Yugoslavian Socialist Republics, declared its independence and re-established itself as a nation-state. Within the context of the bloody Yugoslav wars that were raging around it, Macedonia succeeded in transitioning to independent nationhood peacefully. It managed to agree with Yugoslavia on a few minor changes to their common border, resolving problems demarcating the limits of the two countries. Here the borders were changing as part of a nation-building project (de Munck and Risteski 2013; Roudometof 2002). As for the Greek border, in the 1990s it too was changing. It was becoming an external European Union (EU) border, progressively shaped and hardened by the 1985 Schengen Agreement,[1] the 1993 Maastricht Treaty, and its three EU pillars. These contained policies respectively on (1) customs, citizenship, and asylum, (2) a common European security and defence, and (3) trafficking, smuggling, and other judicial issues including immigration. They entered into force with the 1997 Amsterdam Treaty policies regarding external EU borders (see also Papagianni 2006).

From the ground, on the Greek side of the Prespa border region, some of these changes mark people's experience of the border significantly. On the Greek side, Albanian immigrants bring cheap labour to the villages around the Prespa Lake that depend largely on agriculture, animal husbandry, fishing, and tourism.[2] On the other hand, the nationalistic discourse about the name 'Macedonia' (surfacing also around the agreement signed in June 2018) and its long history of conflicting and overlapping referents creates new types of desires and fears in relation to boundaries, and these ones in particular (see also Dimova, Chapter 8 below; Cowan 2008; Myrivili 2004). The end of the cold war was just another episode in the life of these national borders, which, since their establishment in the early twentieth century, have never been inanimate or stable. Like all other borders, they are historically specific, different from every other, but also, as 'borders', on some level the same. This brings us back to the question of the borders as such: as 'ontological' entities or as entities possessing a particular quality, experienced on the phenomenological level of perception. How do we talk about borders, what they are, what makes them what they are, and how might 'that' be analysed?

Even though I will proceed to argue that these borders exist only as the events of their apparition, materializing suddenly when they are transgressed and radically different as experiences through time, I would also insist that there is an inalienable quality that engenders the national borders, which is the excessive violence that subtends and animates them. That violence may be outside representation (as such, as the limit of representation), or it could be argued that this violence which subtends the border is to a large extent a representation, a reiteration of the inaugural acts of violence (wars of independence, military coups, revolutions, occupations, annexations, colonizations, and all nation-state-building policies that aim to eradicate difference, including genocide, ethnic cleansing, population exchanges, deportations, etc.) that engender or have engendered the nation-state. This violence, which is productive, institutes the border as such.

The liquid border of Prespa, this particular materialization of state power, has formed and is constantly in the process of forming around itself particular subjectivities: ethnic minorities, immigrants, displaced populations, army and police, and so on. These border subjects are both formations of the territorial power of the nation-state, and exemplary sites of its articulation.[3] With their negotiations and representations, their haunting by past violence, their excesses and their secrecy, they carve out the border as a material sphere essential to the legitimacy of nation-state authority. The border is essential because it provides the nation-state with a 'state of exception' (Benjamin 1969: 257; Agamben 2005). This 'state of exception' is the space of distance between the nation and the subject, the no man's land where nation and subject meet and institute each other anew (Myrivili 2004: 268–71). It is a space pregnant with the possibility of engendering difference, and in a sense, to some extent, also outside discourse and representation.

Michalis

In the summer of 1996 a young fisherman named Michalis took me out onto Prespa Lake in his fishing boat. He was going to check his fishing nets, and I went along for the ride.

'Michali,' I screamed over the noise of the engine, 'let's go to the border.' He signalled 'yes' with his head and turned the boat towards the centre of the lake. After a few minutes of racing through the waters he stopped and turned the engine off.

'What happened?' I asked.

'Here it is! The Border!' he said, with a little smile.

'Where?' I asked.

'We're right on it,' he said and smiled.

'How can you tell?'

'I grew up on this lake, I know every inch,' he answered.

'I mean, what are the signs?'

He then turned and pointed at a crevice on a mountain slope, and then with his other hand he pointed at a grey rock formation across the lake on the other side and said: 'If you draw an imaginary straight line connecting the two points over the water, with your mind's eye, you'll see the border.'

Michalis stood there, for a few seconds, all stretched out as if hanging from a tight rope that passed right through him. He was embodying the nation's limit, translating for me with his body the Greek–Albanian legal border.

'And what if we crossed over the border, into Albanian waters? What would happen then?' I asked.

'We would eventually be spotted by the Albanian border patrol guards, who would shoot once up in the air.'

'And what if we turned around quickly and went back into Greek waters?'

'Then they would shoot at us. If they were any good, they could even kill us. The shot in the air is a signal that we have crossed illegally, that we've committed a crime. We'd have to stop and surrender ourselves to the guards. We'd get arrested and escorted to the nearest Albanian police station.'

He paused.

'This is nothing! Just a few years ago during the Hoxha regime, the Albanian land borders, all the way to the water, had electricity running through barbed wires and armed guards every few hundred metres all around the lake. There were no warning shots then. The guards just shot to kill anyone that crossed the border. We still crossed.' We stayed silent for a moment.

'And what about the other side, the Macedonian side?'

'There too, if you don't stop, they will shoot you. And they have much tougher police and much better patrolling than the Albanians. Only the Greek policemen are afraid to shoot on trespassers because of the EU. They are wary of international incidents. So they shoot in the air and then they have to chase the trespassers. You see, all the illegal immigrants, the Albanians that sneak into the country through these mountains since 1991, they all know that the Greek soldiers are not going to shoot at them, so they run, they run as fast as they can ...'

He smiled, shook his head, and turned the engine on. He then turned the boat around and headed back towards the village.

Secrecy

Apart from some floating buoys on the waters and a few cement pyramids (land demarcations) scattered among rocks and trees on mountain slopes surrounding Lake Prespa, the only other material evidence of the borders in Prespa is the pervasive but elusive presence of police and army forces. There are no checkpoints in the Prespa region, no large edifices of surveillance announcing the limits of the nation-state. The borders here in Prespa are like ghosts: neither present nor absent.

The policing of these boundaries seems to be done mostly in secret. Only if you cross the boundary is the policing apparatus of the border revealed. It is the transgressing of the border that reveals this otherwise invisible boundary as a clear manifestation of state power: the police or the army. Criticizing the mixture of legislative and executive power of the police institution in democracies, Benjamin says, 'its power is formless, like its nowhere tangible, all pervasive, ghostly presence in the life of civilized states' (Benjamin 1986: 287).

In his essay 'Critique of Violence', Benjamin describes the 'unnatural combination' of law-making and law-preserving violence accorded to the institution of the police by the modern nation-state as a 'kind of spectral mixture' (1966a: 286). In the institution of police, he says, there is a suspension of the separation between law-preserving violence (violence as means to legal ends) and law-making violence (violence that establishes new law), as the police have the right of executive decree (i.e. without legislative approval or recourse to judicial power). Therefore, the police intervene 'for security reasons' in 'countless cases where no clear legal situation exists ... accompanying the citizen as a brutal encumbrance through a life regulated by ordinances ...' (Benjamin 1986: 287). Benjamin elaborates the spectrality of the police by juxtaposing it to the law. The institution of law, he says, has essence (presence, being) because it 'acknowledges in the "decision" determined by place and time a metaphysical category that gives it a claim to critical evaluation'[4] (Benjamin 1986: 287). But 'a consideration of the police institution encounters nothing essential at all', and though it may 'everywhere appear the same', it is in democracies that 'their spirit' is most devastating, as they, the police, exemplify the 'greatest conceivable degeneration of violence' (Benjamin 1986: 287). Thus the police haunt the rule of law. How can an institution meant to maintain the rule of law exemplify 'the greatest conceivable degeneration of violence'? How can an institution meant to uphold the rule of law exemplify the dissolution, the suspension of that which is fundamental to it, the separation of legislative, executive, judicial powers? Agamben in *State of Exception* (2005) meticulously analyses the trajectory which has caused exceptional legislation by executive decree to become a regular practice in modern European democracies. In Western democracies, Agamben claims, people are increasingly subject to extra-judicial state violence as the rule of law is routinely displaced by the state of exception, or state of emergency, revealing the deep, secret nexus of law and unsanctioned violence in our democracies. The border, either localized or dislocated, as territorial limit or as unmoored spatiality travelling with the bodies of border-subjects through national territories, describes a social space characterized by a particular juridico-political structure. It is a materialization of the state of exception, instrumental to the institution of the nation-state and the legitimation of its power (Myrivili 2004: 271–5). As Benjamin asserts, borders are 'primal phenomena of lawmaking violence'; their existence reiterates and reaffirms the law's instituting violence (Benjamin 1986: 295). At the Prespa borderland, there is one outpost per border, a small guard-post camouflaged in some way. Usually, there is a guard in it, who is hidden, waiting for something to happen in his vicinity, in order to mobilize the 'border-policing-machine'. Then, indeed, out of nowhere, they appear, with their cars, jeeps or boats, with great efficiency, immediately on the scene, in full view, and in full regalia they terrify and take you away.

The scene brings to mind Michael Taussig's fascination with 'secrecy' which 'lies at the very core of power'. Taussig's work on secrecy builds on Elias Canetti's 'zoomorphic fantasy of hunter and prey, where infinite patience and camouflage is abruptly transposed into speed of attack, the flash of exposure ... followed by the slow and deliberate absorption of the Other' (Taussig 1999: 57, Canetti 1984: 290–6).

Consider that, apart from the police, there are even more spectral creatures lurking around these borders: the secret police. I do not know the extent of the power of the secret police, or how much of a state-within-the-state is established in the region. I did have several unpleasant encounters with some of these people during the years that I lived there in the late 1990s: visits at my house late at night by men dressed in casual clothing full of questions about why I was there and what my work was all about, or full car and body searches from what seemed to be under-cover policemen, who stopped me on the road without any explanations. There was no way of knowing what they were or who they were. Not really. It is possible that these men were not related to any legitimate or official centre of state power. I mean that the origin of their power was and is beyond knowing. Who are they? Is there no way of finding out? Who can identify them? Their identification, as members of the secret police, may ultimately depend (as we have been told by many secret agent movies) on some specific member of the police apparatus who knows them as such. Like free-floating signifiers, like simulacra, the secret policemen and their power have no referent. Or rather, there may be some kind of a referent here: the gun or the possibility of a gun. Is the gun a signifier of violence or the referent? Is it a metonymy? Or is the gun a ghost? The men who searched me were carrying guns, but beyond the guns there was something else that made the questions of 'what' or 'who' they were redundant. That was 'where' they were. They did not need to provide any reasons or use any pretence for searching me. We were at the borders: anything goes in this exceptional zone; anything can be a matter of national security. The Prespa region, with all its deceiving beauty and calmness, is and has been a 'high-security' zone from the moment these borders where drawn after the Balkan wars and the First World War. The performative utterance 'security' has always had the power to conjure up the ghost of violence (the memory of past violence together with the threat of future violence) and thus compel us (see Waever 1995, Bigo 1998, Bigo 2002, Bialasiewicz et al. 2007, and Huysmans 2006).

Spectres

The spectre is not similar to a spirit in that it always involves a threat, writes Derrida in one of his lattter works, *Specters of Marx* (1994). The threat of the spectre, or as Derrida calls it 'the spectrality effect', is the deep disturbance of all boundaries set in space or time (1994: 39–40). Ghosts thus most dependably embody Derrida's work of deconstructing the metaphysical desire of presence and origins.

The Derridean spectre is bound up with the experience of language. For Derrida all language, all meaning, is the phantom effect of a trace, which is neither present nor absent, but is the condition of possibility of difference, of the opposition of presence and absence. As Sarah Green (2009) asserts, border is difference, and if we are to try to think of absolute difference, then in Derrida we encounter the concept of the trace (see also Green, Chapter 5 above). In Derrida's *Specters of Marx*, difference, *différance*, the trace, becomes spectrality itself: the revenant at the origin (see also Pulkkinen, Chapter 4 above). But as mentioned above, there is a difference.

Before elaborating on the spectre of communism that is haunting Europe and other such ghosts, Derrida starts his book by talking about a very famous Danish ghost. He describes how Hamlet is compelled by the absent presence of the ghost of his father. Derrida describes this relation between ghost and human as the 'visor effect', which, he says, is what establishes our submission to the law and conditions all other types of obedience. He says that when something 'looks at us and sees us not see it when it is there', when 'someone other, of absolute, unmasterable disproportion looks at us', when we 'feel ourselves seen by a look which it will always be impossible to cross', which is the 'visor effect' that we inherit from the law (Derrida 1994: 7). And 'since we don't see the one who sees us, and who makes the law, who delivers the injunction' we essentially blindly submit 'to the secret of his origin ... [T]his is the first obedience to injunction and it will condition all the others' (Derrida 1994: 7).

Think of the secret police, or any police for that matter, demanding that we step out of the car and that we spread our legs and arms. Think of the customs officer who disappears behind a door with your passport. Think of Michalis embodying the border whose crossing constitutes a security violation that calls forth police or army violence. The ghost consists of 'autonomising a representation and in forgetting its genesis as well as its real grounding' (Derrida 1994: 171).

This secret of the origin is a large part of the technology of state power. We respond to the manifestations of state power as if to an apparition of something Other, unknown, unknowable. That is the ghost. The ghost captures a relation of contradiction and repulsion between appearance and identity, disrupting our sense of temporality and grounding. The ghost appears, but is not localizable. It is historical, but it presents the impossibility of capturing, conceptualizing the past. It doesn't belong to a place or time, it is no longer 'that being' that it looks or sounds like, it is no being at all. Like the ghost, the manifestations of state power are 'hauntological' in that they forcefully intimate a spectrally deferred non-origin.

Animal

Again: how is the border a ghost? The border is a ghost because, as an institution of the nation-state, the border or limit is both the beginning and the return of the nation-state as violence, both singular and a repetition all at the same time. Consider the nation-state border making a sudden, spectacular appearance at the otherwise calm Prespa border region: the moment of its transgression. At that moment, the border reveals itself as the highest form of army or police violence: a (sanctioned) threat over the perpetrator's life. Benjamin calls this type of violence 'predatory' violence (violence not as means but as ends), which always has an inherently 'lawmaking' character (Benjamin 1986: 283). He claims that where a decision over life and death is taken, '[i]ts purpose is not to punish the infringement of law but to establish new law' (Benjamin 1986: 286). Even within the law, within the confines of 'law-preserving', that is, state-sanctioned violence, 'in the exercise of violence over life and death more than in any other legal act, law reaffirms itself' (Benjamin 1986: 286).

It is in this most singular of acts, the taking of a life, when 'the origins of law jut manifestly and fearsomely into existence' (Benjamin 1986: 286), that the nation-state repeats and reaffirms itself anew. The spectral image of the border as a violently erupting predator reveals the most primal nature of the modern nation-state, the ultimate event of inaugural violence that establishes and subtends the law. This particular technology of violence, the memory and threat of the nation-state's power over life, configures the social landscape of the whole border region. It dictates the ways in which the subjects (and objects) of Prespa attune themselves to the border.

It is like a smell, a tonality. The people in Prespa, the ones who stay for a little while as well as those who live there, are disciplined in their movement around the lake by those invisible presences. While fishing, shepherding or hunting, hiking, swimming, or driving they have to organize their movement and their sense of space through this limit of the nation-state's territorial sovereignty. They have to stand vis-à-vis the nation-state. Through this territorial type of knowledge and practice different types of subject positions develop.

What does it mean to internalize such a threatening invisible wall as the Prespa liquid border, as Michalis has? What kind of subjectivity is this? Is it based on disciplinarity? Do borders function as transparent edifices, powerful 'architectural' mechanisms distributing bodies? Are they invisible political institutions organizing disciplinary gazes and proliferating, amplifying power relations? I mean, are the borders like 'the tall outline of a central tower' of Bentham's prison schema, an empty tower, which through its presence ensures the fictitious relations out of which subjection is mechanically born (Foucault 1979: 201–2)? Are they producing the 'visor effect' that Derrida talks about in his ghosts, the unseen gaze of unmasterable disproportion that sees us not see it, that is the law, the voice, the discourse that we blindly obey? What kind of power relations gave birth to the Prespa subjects, subjects formed by their interactions with and their positioning vis-à-vis those national boundaries? How are these power relations, the ones produced and played out at border sites, different from those organized around the usual disciplinary institutions of the urban or less urban centres?

Michalis's embodiment of the national boundary, as a limit that hides a violent threat, seems to suggest a different analytic lens: disciplinarity does not seem to form the organizing principle of psychic structuration. According to Foucault's evolutionary trajectory, punition is progressively distanced from the visible practice of physical violence. Discipline takes the place of violence. As a result, the exteriority of power that is pressed onto the subject passes over to the other side, to 'its surface of application' (Foucault 1979: 202). Thus power is internalized as the subject comes into being by assuming 'the responsibility of the constraints of power' (Foucault 1979: 202). This is the famous double twist of *assujetissement*: the becoming of the subject (agency) through the process of subjection (subordination to power) (Foucault 1979; Althusser 2001). And it is through the discursive matrices of disciplinary institutions that the social subjects are formed, exactly through the process of their subjection, the regulation and management of their bodies. As Allen Feldman points out in the case of Northern Ireland, here in Prespa there is little historical evidence for Foucault's sanitized application of the ocular aggression of disciplinary institutions (Feldman 1997: 29–30).

The creation of subjectivity around these borders seems less discursively bound, less related to disciplinary practices, since the bodies orient themselves in space in relation to a power that exposes itself concretely as physical violence. Precisely because of the presence of that absurd edifice, of the haunting quality of the nation-state's limit, at the same time quite definite and absent, dangerous and dull, the regime of Prespa is very particular. The story of Michalis's embodiment of the Greek–Albanian border brings to mind the kind of zoomorphic subjectivity that Henri Lefebvre talks about in *The Production of Space* (1991). The inaugural act of the subject according to Lefebvre is not the sign (the reproduction of semiotic or symbolic structures), but the body's spatial practice, which is presemiotic, precultural, almost prehuman. For Lefebvre bodies orient themselves in space like spiders that produce space, that 'secrete' space, as they appropriate it.

This zoomorphic imagining points in the direction of a base materialism that goes beyond the subject of discourse, knowledge, and representation. Rather than going back to originary or reflexive narratives and dialectics, beings, appearances, and representations, I would prefer to think of the border through what Bataille (1994) calls a 'base materialism', which necessarily violates any self-enclosed identity or objectivity. In this Bataillian economy, the focus is not on reproduction or representation of identities and structures, but instead on their violation by their materiality, by their baseness. So ideas – which, like stars, 'shine only in the night of nature' (Bataille 1994) – gather creatural life not in order to reveal it, nor to open it to human language, but rather to give it back to its closedness and muteness.

I am thus referring to a Bataillian materialism where a practised space produces and is produced by acting subjects that belong to a very different kind of economy. The Bataillian 'general' economy burns its limits and passes beyond political economy, which traditional economy and all Marxist thought are powerless to do according to the internal logic of value. It is also the sphere of non-knowledge. It contradicts all of the axioms of economy properly so called. It is an economy that, in becoming general, blows apart the limits of 'closed economy', of socio-economics predicated on utility, production, and rational consumption, and develops an alternative theory that takes into account the human tendency to lose, destroy, and waste.

Prespa is organized through territorially specific acts of orientation in relation to the nation-state's ability to materialize as the possibility of violence. Whether through Michalis's body stretching out into the border, or through the repression, secrecy, and endless violent reconfigurations of people's lives due to the border, or through the displacements, marginality, and stigmatization that characterize all these lives, these are the practices that make up and maintain the national border.[5] These border practices are to a large extent acts of expenditure: the creation of subjects that spend themselves for the borders.

Moving

And if this institution of nation-state power, the border, is the spectre of violence and the baseness of its materiality, what does this tell us about the rest of state power?

It would be wrong to assume that the border regions create a reified spatiality, a spatiality detached from the nation-state that sanctions arbitrary uses of force and the erratic exercise of authority. It cannot be understood as the fetishized space par excellence which stands in for all those other remote worlds of violence: the faraway countries, the faraway wars, those dark, borderless, dangerous Other Places where violence lurks, having somehow escaped the peace and of the order of the nation-state. The border brings all these worlds home. Its practices penetrate deep into the centre of law and order of the modern nation-state (see also Dimova, Chapter 8 below).

Taussig calls the power of the nation-state a 'nervous system', as the arbitrariness of power swiftly changes places with the legitimacy of authority, as reason and violence keep dancing around, the discursive and the non-representational, the exception and the rule. The modern nation-state can easily switch between ordered system and unstable agent of terror, as that is the nature of its power. The border, broken up and unmoored, travels among us, in perpetual movement throughout the territories, 'now you see it now you don't', nervously twitching and switching, revealing itself, as per Benjamin's dictum, every time that we experience the '"state of emergency" in which we live in not as the exception but the rule' (Taussig 1992:11–35; Benjamin 1969: 257).

Notes

1 The 'Schengen Agreement' – i.e. the gradual abolition of the internal borders between countries and an extended control of the external borders – was originally signed on 14 June 1985 by five European countries: France, Germany, Belgium, Luxemburg, and the Netherlands. Today the Schengen zone consists of twenty-six European countries. Article 17 reads: 'With regard to the movement of persons, the Parties shall endeavour to abolish checks at common borders and transfer them to their external borders. To that end they shall endeavour first to harmonize, where necessary, the laws, regulations and administrative provisions concerning the prohibitions and restrictions on which the checks are based and to take complementary measures to safeguard internal security and prevent illegal immigration by nationals of States that are not members of the European Communities' (1985 Schengen Agreement).

2 On Albanian migration and the Greek–Albanian border region see Baldwin-Edwards (2004) and De Rapper (2005). For the passage through the border and into Greece see King, Iosifides, and Myrivili (1998). For the construction of Albanian identity in Greece and of the Greek–Albanian border through the media see Papailias (20003). For further examination of Albanian immigrant employment see Lyberaki and Maroukis (2005). For an investigation of the Albanian–Greek border see Seremetakis (1996).

3 For further analysis of border subjects and the border subjects of Prespa see Myrivili (2004).

4 Derrida in the famous Cardozo School of Law symposium of 1989 deconstructed the notion of justice presented by Benjamin, while introducing the workings of the spectre. He there claimed that there is no moment during which a decision could be called present or just, as the ordeal of the undecidable is never past, but keeps coming back as a

'phantom' that 'deconstructs from the inside every assurance of presence, and thus every criteriology that would assure us of the justice of the decision' (Derrida 1992: 24–5).

5   This point is elaborated in Myrivili (2004).

References

Agamben, Giorgio (2005). *State of Exception*. Chicago: University of Chicago Press.

Althusser, Louis (2001). *Lenin and Philosophy and Other Essays*. New York: Monthly Review Press.

Baldwin-Edwards, Martin (2004). 'Albanian Emigration and the Greek Labour Market: Economic Symbiosis and Social Ambiguity'. *South-East Europe Review for Labour and Social Affairs*, 1: 51–65.

Bataille, Georges (1994). 'Base Materialism and Gnosticism'. In *Visions of Excess*. 5th edn, pp. 45–53. Minneapolis: University of Minnesota Press.

Benjamin, Walter (1969). *Illuminations*. New York: Schocken Books.

Benjamin, Walter (1986). *Reflections*. New York: Schocken Books.

Bialasiewicz, L., et al. (2007). 'Performing Security: The Imaginative Geographies of Current US Strategy'. *Political Geography*, 26: 405–22.

Bigo, Didier (1998). 'Frontiers and Security in the European Union: The Illusion of Migration Control'. In M. Anderson and E. Bort (eds), *The Frontiers of Europe*, 148–64. London and Washington: Pinter.

Bigo, Didier (2002). 'Security and Immigration: Toward a Critique of the Governmentality of Unease'. *Alternatives*, 27: 63–92.

Canetti, Elias (1984). *Crowds and Power*. New York: Farrar, Straus and Giroux.

Cowan, Jane (ed.) (2000). *Macedonia: The Politics of Identity and Difference*. London and Sterling, VA: Pluto Press.

de Munck, Victor C., and Ljupcho Risteski, Ljupcho (2013). *Macedonia: The Political, Social, Economic and Cultural Foundations of a Balkan State*. London: I. B. Tauris.

De Rapper, Gilles (2005). 'Better than Muslims, not as Good as Greeks: Emigration as Experienced and Imagined by the Albanian Christians of Lunxheri'. In Russell King, Nicola Mai, and Stephanie Schwandner-Sievers (eds), *The New Albanian Migration*, 173–94. Brighton: Sussex University Press.

Derrida, Jacques (1992). 'Force of Law: The "Mystical Foundation of Authority"'. In Drucilla Cornell et al. (eds), *The Deconstruction and the Possibility of Justice*, 3–67. New York: Routledge.

Derrida, Jacques (1994). *Specters of Marx*. London: Routledge.

Draper, Stark (2010). 'The Conceptualization of the Albanian Nation'. *Ethnic and Racial Studies*, 20(1), 123–44.

Feldman, Allen (1997). 'Violence and Vision: The Prosthetics and Aesthetics of Terror'. *Public Culture*, 10(1): 24–60.

Foucault, Michel (1979). *Discipline and Punish*. New York: Vintage Books.

Green, Sarah (2005). *Notes from the Balkans: Locating Marginality and Ambiguity on the Greek–Albanian Border*. Princeton, NJ: Princeton University Press.

Green, Sarah (2009). 'Lines, Traces and Tidemarks: Reflections of Forms of Borderli-ness'. Paper presented at COST IS0803 Work Group 1 Meeting, Nicosia, 14–15 April 2009.

Huysmans, Jef (2006). *The Politics of Insecurity: Fear, Migration and Asylum in the EU*. New International Relations Series. London: Routledge.

King, R., T. Iosifides, and L. Myrivili (1998). 'A Migrant's Story: From Albania to Athens'. *Journal of Ethnic and Migration Studies*, 24(1): 159–75.

Lefebvre, Henri (1991). *The Production of Space*. Oxford and Cambridge, MA: Blackwell.

Lyberaki, Antigoni, and Thanos Maroukis (2005). 'Albanian Immigrants in Athens: New Survey Evidence on Employment and Integration'. *Southeast European and Black Sea Studies*, 5(1): 21–48.

Myrivili, Eleni (2004). 'Liquid Border: Subjectivity at the Limits of the Nation-State in Southeast Europe'. PhD thesis, Columbia University.

Papagianni, Georgia (2006). *Institutional and Policy Dynamics of EU Migration Law*. Leiden: Koninklijke Brill NV Publishers.

Papailias, Penelope (2003). '"Money of Kurbet is Money of Blood": The Making of a "Hero" of Migration at the Greek–Albanian Border'. *Journal of Ethnic and Migration Studies*, 29(6) 1059–78.

Pearson, Owen (2006). *Albania in the Twentieth Century: A History*, vol. 3: *Albania as Dictatorship and Democracy, 1945–99*. London: I. B. Tauris.

Roudometof, Victor (2002). *Collective Memory, National Identity, and Ethnic Conflict: Greece, Bulgaria, and the Macedonian Question*. Westport, CT: Greenwood Publishing Group.

Seremetakis, Nadia (1996). 'In Search of the Barbarians: Borders in Pain'. *American Anthropologist*, 98: 489–91, September.

Taussig, Michael (1992). *The Nervous System*. London and New York: Routledge.

Taussig, Michael (1999). *Defacement*. Stanford, CA: Stanford University Press.

Thrift, Nigel (2007). *Non-Representational Theory: Space, Politics, Affect*. London: Routledge.

Waever, Ole (1995). 'Securitization and Desecuritization'. In D. Ronnie Lipschutz (ed.), *On Security*, 46–87. New York: Columbia University Press.

8

Materialities of displacement: borders in contemporary Macedonia

Rozita Dimova

The 246 km long border between the Republic of Macedonia (hereinafter Macedonia) and Greece sets off at Lake Prespa, crosses the fertile Pelagonia valley, runs across the steep mountainous wedges of the Nidze and Kozuf mountains, cuts short the valley of the river Vardar, and ends north of the Dojran Lake in eastern Macedonia (see Figure 8.1). The two countries are connected by three border crossings: Medzitlija-Niki near the towns of Bitola-Florina, Bogorodica-Evzoni near Gevgelija-Polikastro, and Nov Dojran-Dojrani. These crossings experience flows of movement of differing intensity and exchange across them throughout the year. As the most popular, the Bogorodica-Evzoni crossing is connected by the main highway passing through the entire length of the Former Yugoslav territory, connecting the Greek border to Ljubljana and then further to Italy and Austria (see Dimova 2011). The architecture of the border crossings does not give a hint of the violent history of this area in the nineteenth and twentieth centuries, and nor does it reveal anything of the political conflict in which Greece and Macedonia have been embroiled since 1991 (see also Green, Chapter 5 above, and Myrivili, Chapter 7 above). Its current outlook complies with the generic appearance of a contemporary nation-state border crossing stripped of excessive ethno-national iconography.

By adopting the distinction offered by Green (Chapter 5 above, the border under scrutiny can be seen as a line materialized as fences, wires, and walls built to mark the state delineation between Greece and the Republic of Macedonia. But the material traces of the borders between the two countries around the borderlines reveal what Green calls 'the entangled relation between symbolic, material, and legal forms' (Chapter 5 above).

The traces left by the complicated history of this region and its borders (a history that cannot be fully told in the following pages) are scattered beyond the linear appearance of the state borders. Drawn in this version at the Bucharest Treaty in 1913 – the treaty that ended the second Balkan war – this border divided the region of Macedonia between Greece, Bulgaria, and Serbia (for more see Cowan 2008; Mazower 2000). Physically and topologically, this border has remained more or

8.1 Map of the Republic of Macedonia

less in the same place. Politically, however, several states have changed their existence around the border: in the period between 1913 and 1943 the border divided Serbia (the Kingdom of Yugoslavia since 1921) and Greece. With the establishment of the Yugoslav Socialist Federation (1943–45), it became a state border between Yugoslavia and Greece, and with the dissolution of Yugoslavia in 1991, it turned into a state border between the Republic of Macedonia and Greece.

Traces of these conflicts, as this chapter will show, appear in the areas around the borders. Moreover, the conflicts are indexed by material structures not situated at the borders, but are washed off in a tidal wave at the centre of Skopje. Alternatively, we can even look at the border effect that ripples outwards from the heart of the country, so that it is almost imperceptible by the time it reaches the border. The main point in this gradation is to distinguish between the linear, material, and tidal entanglement of the borders and how this gradation affects the borders' materiality (see also Demetriou and Dimova, Chapter 1 above).

Temporal circuits of the border

The temporal shifts of and changes around the border reference the violent history of this region, although very few material traces are visible at the actual border crossings. The first Balkan war, fought from October 1912 until April 1913 between the Ottoman army and the Balkan alliance consisting of Serbian, Greek, and Bulgarian states and kingdoms, placed the border and the region of Macedonia at the centre of the battles. The claims over the region of Macedonia were the main reason for the second Balkan war in 1913, when the former allies turned against each other – Serbia and Greece on one side and Bulgaria on the other. With the beginning of the First World War (which, as many historians argue, was a logical consequence of the second Balkan war that made Serbia a strong regional force through its victory in 1913 and its alliance with Russia), this border coincided almost literally with the Salonica front (*Solunski Front*), where Serbia, supported by the Entente allies France and Britain as well as Greece (although officially Greece remained neutral during the First World War), fought Bulgaria and its allies Austro-Hungary and Germany. Each side suffered tremendous losses in this war. The only material traces of the battles of this period are the Serbian, French, and British cemeteries in Bitola, Dojran, Kajmakcalan, Policastro and Thessaloniki (see Figures 8.2, 8.3, 8.4, and 8.5).

There is also a scarcity of material markers from the Second World War or from the period during the Greek civil war between 1946 and 1949, despite the fact that the border towns of Bitola (on the Macedonian side) and Florina (on the Greek side) are of great importance to Macedonian nationalism. Florina was at the centre of strong Slavic (Macedonian and Bulgarian) presences and influences, especially in the late nineteenth century, when it became an intellectual centre of Slavic agitation for independence from the Ottoman Empire. The Slavic presence remained strong

8.2 The Serbian military cemetery, Zeitnlik, Thessaloniki

8.3 The French military cemetery, Bitola

8.4 The British military cemetery, Policastro

8.5 The British military cemetery, Dojrani

throughout the first half of the twentieth century. For part of the Greek civil war, Florina was under communist control. The Macedonian National Liberation Front (NOF) had a significant presence in the area: by 1946, seven Macedonian (Slavic) partisan units were operating in the Florina area, and the NOF had a regional committee based in Florina. When the communists withdrew from Florina in 1949, thousands of people were evacuated or fled to Yugoslavia and the Eastern Bloc.

These were people who joined the communists during the Greek civil war and who, as refugees, were forced to migrate to other countries, primarily socialist bloc countries such as Hungary, Romania, Poland, and Bulgaria, but also the USA, Canada, and Australia (see Rossos 1991; Mojsov 1954; Kitanoski and Donevski 2003). The *decata Begalci* (child refugees) who left Greece while their parents fought in the war were also dispersed throughout the former socialist bloc or sent overseas to Canada and Australia (Voss 2003, 2005). Because of the political schism between Stalin and Tito in 1948, Yugoslavia did not accept a large number of political refugees after the defeat of leftist forces at the end of the Greek civil war in 1949, forcing the refugees and their children to seek asylum in many places far from home. Nevertheless, through their efforts to maintain contact with one another, hold family reunions, and be politically active, these refugees have come to play an important role in the contemporary political landscape, serving to link the Republic of Macedonia with the larger region that includes Greek Macedonia. They have used their diasporic networks to form important nationalist alliances, fostering what Anderson (1991) calls 'long-distance nationalism'; which Danforth has explored in depth in his research on refugees in Australia and Canada (Danforth 1997: 79–109). Despite the fact that these Slavic speakers from Greece are now dispersed throughout the world, their existence and political activism have been a major problem for the Greek government, particularly in the domain of property restitution. For some time now, this question of property has been officially brought before the European Court of Human Rights in Strasbourg. The large exodus of Slav Macedonians and the child refugees involved in this relocation have been one of the cornerstone national myths of contemporary Macedonia, playing a significant role in the contemporary conflict with Greece around the name. The national trope of the child refugees from the Greek civil war, dispersed around the world and abandoned by Tito and Yugoslavia, is seen as an open wound that cannot be healed. The government's initiative to build a memorial of the child refugees on the Medzitlija-Niki border crossing, however, and to acknowledge the suffering of these people and mark the exact place where most of the child refugees escaped Greece, has not been realized as yet.

The name conflict between Macedonia and Greece, which began in 1991, with the independence of Macedonia, also left barely noticeable traces on the border itself. The crux of this dispute lies in the political schism between Greece and Macedonia. The official Greek position has been that there is only one 'Macedonia' – Greek Macedonia. No region in the Balkans except for the Greek province of Macedonia can be associated or identified with the ancient kingdom of Macedonia, and no people, except Greeks, are entitled to call themselves Macedonians, either as a cultural-ethnic or as a geographic-regional denomination. Politicians and mainstream scholars in Greece have argued that the Hellenic character of ancient Macedonia should not be called into question. They have also argued that, by usurping the name of Macedonia, the newly independent state to their north was automatically making irredentist claims for the annexation of Greek Macedonia.

The dispute has triggered a forceful surge of nationalism in the Republic of Macedonia too. In the 1990s and early 2000s, however, the main point of national reference in the country was the presence of the Albanian minority and the tensions occurring with its claims of secession to form Western Macedonia and Great Albania.

Contemporary materialization of the border in central Skopje

While there were efforts to bring in antiquity as a legitimate reference in the historical record in the 1990s too, it was only after the 2008 NATO summit in Bucharest that the government led by the right-wing nationalist VMRO-DPMNE party marked the conflict with a new material outlook and erected new borders between the two countries. These borders were in fact in central Skopje. It can be argued that it is from there that they ripple out to the periphery. But one could also argue that the conflict between the two countries, manifested at the border, where the Greek border control stamps a special piece of paper instead of the official passports issued by the Ministry of Foreign Affairs of the Republic of Macedonia because Macedonia is not officially recognized by Greece, washes off on the shores of the capital Skopje and becomes tangible in the new buildings and monuments from the project 'Skopje 2014'. In any case, the cutting that takes place in central Skopje with the new materiality – the recently erected buildings and monuments that I discuss in the following pages – causes the ripple effect and the tidal swelling that I suggest should be seen as a tidemark, 'that ... as an idea, combines line and trace in a way that helps us to think through the ongoing metaphorical, metonymical, and material elements of "'border-ness"' (see Green, Chapter 5 above).

VMRO-DPMNE's reign relies on a deep ideological attempt to revive and re-create a new political subject: the 'real human'. This revival has taken place in the domain of aesthetics and materiality, which is best illustrated in the project 'Skopje 2014', with new aesthetic components, as part of the ongoing 'revival'. This was a political undertaking that originated with VMRO-DPMNE's political victory in the 2006 elections and the defeat of the social democrats. This initiative gradually turned into a well-crafted political and ideological platform that acquired full-blown power during the 2008 early elections, when the main electoral programme of VMRO-DPMNE was entitled 'Prerodba vo 100 cekori' ('Revival in 100 Steps').

The revival outlined a series of economic, political, and cultural promises aiming to improve the overall life of the nation. The doctrine states the revival to be the end of the fifteen years of transition that started in 1991 with the independence of the Republic. The consecutive rule of the Social Democratic Alliance (SDSM) since the 1991 independence of Macedonia – with the exception of the period between 1998 and 2002, when VMRO-DPMNE and the Democratic Alternative won the 1998 elections – was viewed by the right-wing nationalists in VMRO-DPMNE as a continuation of the socialist legacy, not only detrimental to the economic well-being of the citizens, but especially disadvantageous for the preservation of Macedonian national identity. The revival introduced in 2006–07 thus aimed at correcting the lingering socialist 'anomalies' by introducing (and producing) radically different views of the society and its members. According to this doctrine, the basic unit of the society should be a 'real human' different from the socialist universal subject of artificial uniformity.

At the 2008 NATO summit in Bucharest, Greece vetoed Macedonia's membership of NATO while Croatia and Albania became full members. The year 2008 thus inaugurated an unprecedented phase of the conflict between Macedonia and Greece epitomized through a construction frenzy centred on the project 'Skopje 2014'. While, as mentioned earlier, the actual border crossings are almost entirely stripped of any presence or aesthetic manifestation referring to the conflict,[1] in this chapter I argue that the venues and monuments from 'Skopje 2014' become not only effective borders mapping the surge of nationalism, but also novel financial and political activities practised by the government led by VMRO-DPMNE and its leader, Nikola Gruevski.

The massive embellishment of the Macedonian capital was officially and pompously announced in 2010 with a video simulation of 'Skopje 2014', which initially envisaged the construction of some forty monuments, sculptures, façades, and new buildings. Fast forward to 2015 and the number of buildings and monuments had tripled. The price tag of Skopje's new look had meanwhile also become known, far surpassing the initially announced figure of €80 million to reach around €560 million, as the association of investigative journalists BIRN shows.[2] Its eight-month investigation draws on data gathered through the Access to Public Information Act, the official web page of the Public Procurement Bureau, the 'Skopje 2014' audit, and a joint report by the government, the Municipality Center in Skopje, and the Ministry of Culture, presented after the 2013 local elections.

Only through recent reports and analyses of the 'Skopje 2014' project, an undertaking conducted by the mayor of the Municipality Center in Skopje, who comes from the oppositional SDSM party, were some striking data revealed pointing to legally dubious contracts, lack of transparency in the bids, and other issues relating to the commissioned artists and architects. The opposition party openly accused the government of using 'Skopje 2014' for money-laundering purposes to assist politicians from the governing bloc to profit and to establish clientelistic networks that have since then helped VMRO-DPMNE remain in power. Additional support for the project comes from the flourishing construction industry, where the government is the biggest investor. It also comes from supporters of the governing party working towards the goals of strengthening the national identity and embellishing central Skopje. While 'Skopje 2014' contributed to the boom in the overall economy in 2011, which registered an amazing 5.3 per cent, recent analysis of this period reveals that the real profiteers from this project are only a handful of construction companies closely related to the governing party. The oppositional media reported that one of these companies had a rise in its yearly profit of 1,700 per cent, and the other of 250 per cent.

Elsewhere I have discussed in detail the monuments and buildings of the project 'Skopje 2014' (see Dimova 2013, 2015). The neoclassical buildings housing state institutions on the banks of the Vardar river undoubtedly allude to the classical past. The monument *Warrior on a Horse*, placed on the central square in Skopje, is a crowning example of this effort. Arriving only nine days after the early elections of 5 June 2011, when VMRO-DPMNE won for a third successive time, the statue, which bears a striking resemblance to Alexander the Great, was brought into Skopje in several pieces. Cast in the Ferdinando Marinelli foundry, the most prominent artistic foundry in Florence, *Warrior on a Horse* was designed by the artist Valentina Stefanovska. The media speculated that the cost of the monument reached a figure of €5.3 million (€650,000 was paid to the artist). An additional €4.1 million was allegedly spent on the base, which consists of a grandiose fountain surrounded by eight warriors from the ancient Macedonian army, each three metres high, and eight lions, four seated facing the square and four standing facing the fountain, from whose mouths water jets spring into the basin. The total height of the monument and the fountain is 27 metres. The bronze *Warrior on a Horse* alone is 14.5 metres high and weighs 30 tonnes. The official inaugural festivities took place on 8 September 2011, on the twentieth anniversary of Macedonia's independence (see Figure 8.6).

Corresponding with the intention of the government to make a direct connection to the classical past was also the construction of the Portal Macedonia, built in Pella Square in central Skopje and also designed by Valentina Stefanovska. Rising to 21 metres in height, this construction cost around €4 million and celebrates the twenty years of Macedonian independence. Its façade is embellished with 193 square metres of reliefs carved in marble, depicting scenes from the history of Macedonia. It also contains interior rooms, one of which functions as a state-owned souvenir shop, as well as elevators and stairs providing public access to the roof for panoramic viewing (see Figure 8.7).

The government, especially the Ministry of Culture and the mayor of Skopje, have insisted on the positive aspects of this project in rebranding the former (ugly) socialist face of the Macedonian capital. The reconstruction of the former socialist façades or the erection of the buildings and monuments that tower over and dominate the socialist architecture of central Skopje therefore should be viewed

8.6 The *Warrior on a Horse* monument in central Skopje

also as a bordering device in delineating the reign of the nationalist party from the earlier socialist past.

In addition to the conflict with Greece and the evident claim to antiquity, the buildings and monuments from 'Skopje 2014' also intend to draw a sharp material and temporal border with the socialist legacy in Macedonia. This is, I insist, a critical aspect of the construction activities in central Skopje. The new architecture has attempted to effectively erase the presence of the socialist façades built since 1945, and especially after the 1963 earthquake, in Skopje in the wake of which the city was reconstructed as a text-book example of modernist architecture.

8.7 Portal Macedonia

It is arguable that VMRO-DPMNE intends to 'return the fallen dignity of our great nation and glorious past', as an art historian employed in the Ministry of Culture told me. 'Correcting the mistakes' committed by the previous reign of the social democrats, who received the blame for accepting the acronym FYROM (Former Yugoslav Republic of Macedonia) in 1991, seems to be part of the mission of the current government, which 'makes no compromise regarding the constitutional name of our country'.[3]

The project 'Skopje 2014' came under stern criticism from many intellectuals, politicians, and the public in Macedonia, regardless of their age, ethnicity, or social background. The most vocal reactions have been against the funding of these projects amid severe economic crisis and a recorded unemployment figure of 28 per cent. Architects, especially those who valued the modernistic outlook of Skopje achieved after the 1963 earthquake, have criticized the neo-Baroque and neoclassical transformation of central Skopje.[4] The 'eclecticism' and 'unoriginality' of 'Skopje 2014'[5] for many underlines only the intentions of the ruling VMRO-DPMNE to create a version of history that deliberately erases the memory of socialism and the place Skopje occupied on the global architectural scene after 1963. The city's master plan designed by the famous Japanese architect Kenzo Tange in 1964 introduced the metabolic style and futuristic layout of the city. Many of the newly erected buildings were inspired by Ottoman architecture. For example, the medieval fortress of Kale inspired the residential complex 'Gradski Zid' ('City Wall') and the central post office, and the old Ottoman house inspired the architect Petar Mulickovski in 1972 to build the headquarters of the Communist Party, a building that underwent a total makeover in 2014.

In addition to erecting borders in relation to Greece and socialism, the new construction in central Skopje also effectively erases the visibility of the Ottoman architecture and also the presence of Islam in the city. The buildings along the river Vardar cover up the minarets and the mosques concentrated on the left side of the river, which once revealed the religious diversity in Skopje and the presence of Islam as the dominant religion of the Albanian minority, which comprises 25 per cent of the overall population in Macedonia.

Conclusion

The actual border between Greece and Macedonia, stripped of signifying hints of the turbulent history of the twentieth century and the ongoing ideological struggle between the two countries around the name 'Macedonia', nonetheless leaves traces and tidemarks that reveal alternative realities. Drawing on Green, I propose to think about traces 'as signs of something that has never actually existed, and eventually creating a spatial extension, a territory, to mark or create that entity, to cut it out of the mess and clutter of everything else, and thus bring it (the nation) into existence' (Green, Chapter 5 above). In this way traces reveal the historical contingency of creating new realities: 'the trace provides a sign of something that is not here, that is not visible, but somehow provides tangible evidence, and in the case of borders sometimes material evidence, of the existence of the thing that is absent or invisible' (Green, Chapter 5 above).

The seemingly 'neutral' border, devoid of architectural and material indications related to its historical or ideological contexts, confronts us with a dilemma of how to reconsider this invisibility or absence of past and contemporary events at the border itself. The inevitable answer, however, is located in the excessive materialization of traces and new constructions in the capital of the Republic of Macedonia.

The importance of the urban space of the capital Skopje, where 30 per cent of the total population in Macedonia is concentrated, is one of the factors that propelled the constructions described above. In their proper historical context, the dramatic styles of Baroque and Classicism also appeared as urban styles used as a means of impressing visitors and expressing triumphant power and control. They became associated with excess and abundance of details, which sharply contrasted with the clear and 'sober rationality' of the Renaissance (Beverley 1988; Egginton 2010; Lambert 2004). As dynamic art that reflected the growth of absolutist monarchies, these styles had as their primary aim to manifest power. Through the use of exaggerated decorations, colossal sculptures, huge furniture, and so on, where a sense of movement, energy, and tension are dominant impressions, the Baroque and Classicist styles gave special attention to animation and grandeur achieved through scale and the dramatic use of light and shadow.

I have argued that the aesthetic remodelling of central Skopje is both a trace of the conflict with Greece that results in a tidemark, and a ripple effect swelling towards the actual borders and the edges (peripheries) of the country. The visual traces left by the new buildings in central Skopje effectively establish the borders of the country that delineate Macedonia from the denial of its name but also from its socialist past and the presence of Islam. I have also suggested that one could argue for many similarities between the Baroque history and the changes occurring in Skopje and all over Macedonia since the political changes and the implementation of the 'revival' in 2006, owing to the material traces left by the Baroque effect of the new buildings and their dramatic decorations. As was the case with the Catholic Church several centuries ago, in contemporary Macedonia the governing power also needs to interpellate as many subjects as possible (by rendering them 'real humans'), and, in order to have a successful campaign, it needs to offer an aesthetically and emotionally pleasing and moving experience. Indeed, in drawing aesthetic borders owing to the conflict with Greece, and building boundaries with the previous socialist regime, the current regime uses aesthetics as its main vehicle in a way that is similar to what the Catholic Church did in the sixteenth and seventeenth centuries to counter the Reformation by using art and architecture as its main propaganda tools.

The politics of the last decades of the twentieth century and the first decades of the twenty-first century have affected the Macedonian nation-building project, which has been carried out by using projects such as 'Skopje 2014' to engineer 'suitable' subjects by reconstructing the central cityscape. The new buildings are intended to be reminiscent of 'the past that existed prior to socialism', as an employee at the Ministry of Culture in Skopje observed.[6]

Arguably, the new aesthetics in Skopje were introduced partly to appeal to the masses and to glorify the current rule of the governing party by adopting a new rhetorical, theatrical, and sculptural fashion, expressive of the 'triumph' of the state (and the church as well). But it is also an attempt to insert a variety of aesthetic and historical styles that would link Macedonia to the West. An employee in the Ministry of Culture has affirmed that Skopje has become a 'real European city now'.[7] Here again we see the power of a trace to provide a sign of something that is not visible, but somehow provides tangible evidence. We also see the attempt to create space in central Skopje as power-inflected, but also lively, contingent, and open to constant redefinition (Green, Chapter 5 above).

The erased the traces from the socialist or Ottoman past are an inseparable part of the national 'revival' enterprise. Propelled by the conflict with Greece over the name 'Macedonia', and the permanent conflict with the Albanian (primarily Muslim) minority, the remodelling of Skopje deserves a closer political and symbolic scrutiny through the metaphor of border as a line, a trace, and a tidemark, because it reveals the radical aestheticization of contemporary politics in Macedonia.

By focusing on the architectural interventions in Skopje this chapter has revealed the wider context of the activities of the state, particularly in the context of its transnational relations, and in its attempts to use architecture and monuments to assert a certain kind of truth about the country, as well as its right to exist in a par-ticular form. I have argued that the creation and definition of the idea of Macedonia have been shaped to a great extent in relation to the challenges against the name 'Macedonia' by Greece. These recent events in Macedonia reveal that places do not define themselves alone, but are always defined in relation to other places. Given the furore raised by the Greek government over its neighbour's choice of name, the evidence of the recent nationalistic project is a particularly explicit one.

What I can state with certainty is that the political disputes discussed above have played a key role in the process of rebranding the country – a process in which aesthetics have been critical not only as tools for creating new borders through symbols, signs, and content required during rebranding, but also as the very terrain where the rebranding takes place. In this sense, I build on Rancière's (2005) argument that politics, as a struggle of an unrecognized party for equal recognition in the established order, relies fully on aesthetics, because this struggle takes place over the image of society – over what it is permissible to say or to show. By coin-ing the term 'the ethical regime of art', Rancière (2005) alludes to the relevance of artistic images for the utility of the society. Faced with strong international pressure to make compromises and find a solution to the name dispute with Greece, and also facing heavy international scrutiny regarding the implementation of the Ohrid Framework Agreement on minority rights especially towards its Albanian minority, the state has utilized the art of crafting its borders and image through an artistic expression in a similar vein to Rancière's ethical regimes of art.

Notes

1   The only exceptions are the inscription on the Virgina Star Rosetta decorating the border underpass in the Medzitlija-Niki crossing near Bitola stating that Macedonia was born

Greek, and the monument of the 'Ancient Warrior' on the Greek side of the border crossing.

2   The website http://skopje2014.prizma.birn.eu.com/en (last accessed 12 May 2017) features details of the costs and distribution of finances used for the 'Skopje 2014' project. A click on each building or monument featured on the interactive map reveals more detailed information on who commissioned the building or monument, who built it, and the final costs.

3   Interview with a government official, October 2013.

4   The official labels of the architectural and aesthetic style of 'Skopje 2014' have been used inconsistently by government officials as well as architects and artists in charge of the project, varying between 'classical', 'neoclassical', 'Baroque', and 'neo-Baroque'. Such inconsistency has also been used in the public sphere among ordinary people.

5   Interview with an architect critical of 'Skopje 2014', November 2013.

6   Interview, autumn 2013.

7   Interview, autumn 2013.

References

Anderson, Benedict (1991). *Imagined Communities*. London: Verso.

Beverley, John (1988). 'Going Baroque?' *Boundary*, 2(15–16): 27–39.

Cowan, Jane (2008). 'Fixing National Subjects in the 1920s Southern Balkans: Also an International Practice'. *American Ethnologist*, 35: 1–20.

Danforth, Loring (1997). *The Macedonian Conflict: Ethnic Nationalism in a Transnational World*. Princeton: Princeton University Press.

Dimova, Rozita (2011). 'Border Synergies in the Southern Balkans'. In Wilfried Heller (ed.),: *Identitäten und Imaginationen in Grenzräumen: Ostmittel- und Südosteuropa im Spannungsfeld von Regionalismus, Zentralismus, europäischem Integrationsprozess und Globalisierung*, 209–26. Region – Nation – Europa, 64. Berlin: Lit-Verlag.

Dimova, Rozita (2013). *Ethno-Baroque: Materiality, Loss and Conflict in Neoliberal Macedonia*. Oxford and New York: Berghahn.

Dimova, Rozita (2015). 'Between Borderlines, Betwixt Citizenship: Gender, Agency and the Crisis in the Macedonia/Greece Border Region'. *Women's Studies International Forum*, 49: 66–72, https://doi.org/10.1016/j.wsif.2014.07.003.

Egginton, William (2010). *The Theater of Truth: The Ideology of (Neo)Baroque Aesthetics*. Palo Alto, CA: Stanford University Press.

Kitanoski, Miso, and Gjorgji Donevski (2003). *Deca begalci od egejska Makedonija vo Jugoslavija* [The Child Refugees from Aegean Macedonia to Yugoslavia]. Skopje: Združenie na decata begalci od Egejskiot del na Makedonija.

Lambert, Gregg (2004). *The Return of the Baroque in Modern Culture*. London: Continuum.

Mazower, Mark (2000). *The Balkans*. London: Weidenfeld & Nicolson.

Mojsov, Lazar (1954). *Okolu prašanjeto na makedonskoto nacionalno malcinstvo vo Grcija: eden pogled vrz opsežnata dokumentacija* [About the Question of the Macedonian National Minority in Greece: A Glance over the Vast Documentation]. Skopje: Misla.

Rancière, Jacques (2005). *The Politics of Aesthetics: The Distribution of the Sensible*. London: Continuum.

Rossos, Andrew (1991). '(The) Macedonians of Aegean Macedonia: A British Officer's Report, 1944'. *The Slavonic and East European Review*, 69(2): 283–309.

Voss, Christian (2003). 'The Situation of the Slavic-Speaking Minority in Greek Macedonia: Ethnic Revival, Cross-Border Cohesion, or Language Death?' In S. Trubeta and C. Voss (eds), *Minorities in Greece: Historical Issues and New Perspectives. Jahrbücher für Geschichte und Kultur Südosteuropas*, 5 (2003): 173–87.

Voss, Christian (2005). 'Linguistic Divergence and (Re)convergence in the Macedonian Standard/Dialect Continuum'. In R. Detrez and P. Plas (eds), *Developing Cultural Identity in the Balkans: Convergence vs. Divergence*, 45–58. Multiple Europes, 34. Brussels: Peter Lang.

Index

affect 10, 12, 20, 31, 84, 89
  affective positionings 32n8
  affective taxonomies 50
agency 6, 8–11, 14, 84, 98, 104, 111
Albania 104, 122–3
  Albanian border 104, 106, 112, 113n2
  Albanians 10, 104–5, 107, 113n2, 122, 127, 129
Althusser 1, 8, 111
anthropologists 75
anthropology 72, 84
architecture 1, 13, 67, 116, 124–9 *passim*
Arda river 17
art 1, 126–9 *passim*
asymmetry
  bodily movement 98
  pattern 89–90
  projects 85
  state-making 93, 100

Badiou, Alain 6, 12
Benjamin, Walter 1, 6–7, 91, 106–8, 110, 113, 113n4
boats 4, 7, 16, 36–8, 43–4, 49–50, 106–8
body 7, 40, 48, 66n7, 106, 108, 112
border
  materialization through 17, 20, 36, 48, 58, 90–1, 98–100, 105, 108, 122
  productivity of 57, 59, 64, 65n4
  Bosnia and Herzegovina (BiH) 85–7, 90–2, 94–7, 100nn4–5, 101nn6–8
boundary commission 17–18

capitalism 1–2
cars 86, 101n6, 108, 110

categories 16, 57–8, 62, 64, 100n3, 107
categorization 29, 59, 62
cemeteries 6, 36, 119–20
  military 6, 119–20
checkpoint 69, 70, 78, 89, 94, 107
citizens 8, 9, 11, 30–1, 90, 92, 97, 107, 123
citizenship 3, 8, 22, 97, 105
classification 56–9, 62–3, 85, 101n9
colonialism 3, 8, 37, 39, 41–8 *passim*, 51nn3–5, 51n8
community 2, 12, 14, 38, 72
consumerism 1, 4, 8
consumption 1, 6, 89, 112
contingency 62–3, 65, 65n2, 69, 78–9, 127
corporeality 13, 45
  corporeal aspects 16
  corporeal experience 19, 59
  corporeal shifts 7
Council of Europe 26
crossing 10–11, 18–29 *passim*, 32n9, 36–7, 49, 52n16, 70, 74, 80, 89–90, 93, 98–9, 101n6, 110, 116, 118, 121, 123, 129n1
Cyprus 3, 10, 12, 18–20, 23–4, 27–31, 32n9, 33n13, 69, 72, 78, 80

Deleuze, Gilles 1, 13, 56–7, 59–64, 65n6, 66n7, 73, 103
deportation 8, 30, 105
Derrida, Jacques 13, 56–64, 65nn4–6, 74, 77–9, 81, 103, 109–11, 113n4
dialectics 10, 112
différance 56, 59, 61, 63, 65n4, 77, 109

difference 2–3, 5, 7, 10–12, 16–18, 22, 56–63, 65, 65n4, 65n6, 66n7, 69, 75, 77, 79, 86, 91, 103, 105–6, 109
   pure 59, 61
displacement 5, 116–31 *passim*
distinction 1, 5, 9, 44, 49, 57, 59–64, 69, 74, 116
distinguishing 6, 12, 56, 60–1, 73–5, 118
division 5, 8, 19–20, 68–70, 73, 79, 87, 94
documents 2, 3, 8, 10, 26, 51n6
duality 12, 16

economy 26, 43, 93, 112, 124
Edirne, Turkey 17, 25
emancipation 6
enmeshment 5, 10–11, 13–14, 21–2, 75
environment 10, 26, 68
ethnic conflict 18, 20, 23
European Union (EU) 3, 23–31, 33n13, 36–8, 43–4, 48–50, 67, 71–2, 79–80, 105, 107
'Event' 6
events 41, 48, 58, 61, 63, 77, 103, 110
everyday 12, 48, 50, 71, 73, 78, 80–1, 89–91
Evros river 17, 22–4, 26–7

far right 23, 26
financial crisis 25–6
First World War 14, 109, 118
fishing 105–6, 111
Fortress Europe 18, 36–7, 50
Foucault, Michel 8, 32n2, 59, 64, 85, 90, 99, 111
Frontex 17, 28, 36, 44, 49

ghosts 4, 13, 76, 103–4, 107–11 *passim*
Golden Dawn 23, 26, 32n11
governance 2
government 6, 8, 26–31, 41–4, 50, 51nn3–4, 52n16, 58, 69, 85, 89–93, 96–100, 101n8, 121–4, 126, 129, 130nn3–4
governmentality 7–10, 16–17, 23, 27, 32n2, 85
Greece 3, 10–12, 17–18, 22–5, 29, 32n3, 104, 113n2, 116, 118, 121–3, 125, 127–9
guards 4, 8, 10, 19, 25–6, 69, 106–8
guns 42, 109
   gunshots 106–7

history 6–7, 23, 39–42, 45, 48, 58, 60, 63, 65n4, 76, 78–80, 91, 100, 105, 116, 118, 124, 127–8
home 19–20, 28–9, 121
house 11, 19–20, 30–1, 86, 95, 108, 127
human 1, 9, 84, 91, 94, 97–9, 109, 112, 122–3
   non-human actants 9, 84, 97
human rights 25–7, 37, 39, 41, 44, 46, 48

identity 24, 38, 56–9, 61, 64–5, 72–3, 90, 110, 112, 113n2, 123–4
ideology 1–3, 5–6, 10–11, 40, 45, 71, 74
imbrex 21
imbrication 3, 11, 13, 17–18, 20–3, 26, 31–2
individuating 56–7, 59
infrastructure 3–4, 8, 13, 16, 23, 25–6, 32, 94, 98
Inter-Entity Boundary Line (IEBL) 3, 87–91, 94–8, 100n5, 101n6

Kastanies 17, 32n3

Lacan, Jacques 5–6, 19
lake 3, 4, 10, 104–15, 116
landscape 8, 10, 13, 20, 67–8, 70, 73–5, 80, 89, 98, 111, 121
Latour, Bruno 1, 9, 15, 22, 34, 74, 84, 102
law 3, 8–9, 11, 13, 17–18, 23–4, 27, 29, 30–5, 37–8, 44, 46–8, 51, 74, 107–11, 113–14
Lesvos 24–6
line 2–9 *passim*, 13, 16, 17, 18, 19, 20, 26–9, 32, 37, 56, 60, 65, 67–102, 106, 114, 116, 122, 129,
   line-ness of 4, 85, 97–100
   drawing of borderline 57–8, 60, 64–5, 98
   intensity of 85, 89–90, 100

Macedonia 4, 7, 11, 14, 83, 104–5, 107, 114–15, 116–18, 121–31
map 2, 16, 55, 58, 68–70, 74, 79–80, 82–3, 85–8, 95, 97–8, 100, 117, 130
Maritza river 17
Marx, Karl 109, 114
Marxist 1, 23, 112
materialization 5, 56, 58, 91, 99, 105, 108, 122, 127
media 40, 45, 48, 113, 124
mediation 1, 2, 4, 6, 8–14, 20, 29, 85, 89, 100, 103
Meriç river 17

migration 3–4, 8, 12, 14, 18–19, 23–9, 31, 33, 36–40, 43–4, 47, 49, 52–4, 73, 81, 113–15
monuments 4, 11, 55, 122–5, 130
  Portal Macedonia 124, 126
  Warrior on a Horse 124–5
multiplicity 10, 38, 52, 80

Nancy, Jean-Luc 12
nationalism 1, 4, 85, 118, 121–3, 130
Nicosia 4, 7, 18, 19, 22, 27, 30–1, 78, 81, 102, 114
night 108, 112

omnitemporality 58, 62–3, 65
ontology 2, 9, 15, 22, 36, 56–7, 59–65, 64–6, 68, 71, 98, 103, 105

passports 4, 8, 11, 70, 80, 110, 122
philosophy 2, 6, 14, 56, 58, 61, 64, 66, 114
police 13, 26–37 *passim*, 44, 69, 74, 89, 92, 95, 105–10
power 1–4, 7–10, 13–14, 26, 41, 46, 64, 68, 70–1, 75, 79–81, 101, 105, 107–14, 122, 124, 128–9
Prespa, Lake 3, 4, 7, 22, 104–13, 116
production 8, 37–8, 58, 64–5, 85, 98, 102, 112
  of border 5, 104–5
  of difference 58–60, 65n4
  of identity 58
  productive 5, 58–9

refugees 12, 19–20, 22–4, 26–7, 29–37, 43–4, 49–50, 54, 92, 121, 130
resistance 5–6, 89
ripple effect 4, 118, 122, 128
rivers 10, 17, 23–5, 27, 85, 93, 116, 124, 127
roads 20, 87, 108
roof 17, 21, 31, 124

sameness 57, 59
Sarajevo 3, 4, 7, 84–9, 92–7, 100–2
Second World War 41, 85, 91, 118
shores 38, 45, 55, 122
similarity 7
Skopje 4, 7, 11, 118, 122–30
  'Skopje 2014' 11, 122–8, 130

socialism 127, 128
  architecture 124
space 1–8 *passim*, 13, 15–18, 22, 32, 34–5, 45–6, 52–3, 55, 58, 62, 64, 73, 77–81, 83, 90, 100, 102–3, 106, 108–9, 111–13, 115, 128–9
spiders 112
state 1–10, 12–13, 15–18, 22, 25–8, 30–5, 38, 43, 45, 48, 51–3, 60, 67–80 *passim*, 83–5, 90–118 *passim*, 122–4, 128–9
statue 2, 4, 39, 124
subjectivity 1, 6, 8–9, 12, 14, 20, 23, 54, 83, 111–12, 115
substance 24, 56–7, 60–1, 65

Taussig, Michael 76, 81, 83, 108, 113, 115
terrain 17–18, 22, 24, 27, 31–2, 79, 101, 129
territory 2, 14, 17, 34, 67, 72, 74, 78–82, 85–101 *passim*, 116, 127
'thingism' 84
Thrace 7, 18, 24
topography 87, 95–6
trace 1, 3–5, 7, 9, 12–13, 27, 47, 60–81 *passim*, 83–4, 91, 102–4, 109, 114–22 *passim*, 127–9
treaties 17, 27
  Amsterdam 105
  Bucharest 116
  Italy–Libya friendship 3, 36–55
  Lausanne 17, 32, 35
  Maastricht 105
Turkey 3, 14, 17–19, 23–6, 28, 30, 32–5, 69, 72

United Nations High Commission for Refugees (UNHCR) 36

violence 7, 9, 14, 22, 26, 47, 55, 91–3, 105, 107–14
visibility 10, 40, 127
void 6–7, 47

war 1, 7, 18–19, 22–7, 41–2, 44, 49, 50, 53, 58, 60, 62, 65, 82, 85–7, 89, 91–8, 101, 104–5, 109, 113, 116, 118, 121

Yugoslavia 91, 94, 104, 118, 121, 130